Introduction to Scholarship in Modern Languages and Literatures

Edited by
Joseph Gibaldi

The Modern Language Association
of America
New York
1981

Copyright © 1981 by
The Modern Language Association of America

Library of Congress Cataloging in
Publication Data
Main entry under title:
Introduction to Scholarship in
    Modern Languages and
    Literatures.

    Includes bibliographical references.
    Contents: Introduction / by Joel
Conarroe—Linguistics / by Winfred
P. Lehmann—Textual scholarship /
by Thomas Tanselle—[etc.]

    1. Philology, Modern—Research—
Addresses, essays, lectures. I.
Gibaldi, Joseph, 1942-
PB35.I57   402   81-1254
ISBN 0-87352-092-0   AACR2
ISBN 0-87352-093-9 (pbk.)

Published by
The Modern Language Association of America
62 Fifth Avenue
New York, New York 10011

First printing, 1981, 4,000 copies
Second printing, 1983, 3,000 copies

Contents

Preface

Joseph Gibaldi

The present volume boasts a distinguished publication history, one that dates back three decades and includes two previous similar collections. In 1952 the Modern Language Association's Committee on Research Activities presented a report entitled "The Aims, Methods, and Materials of Research in Modern Languages and Literatures," which first appeared in *PMLA* (67 [Oct. 1952], 3–37) and was later reprinted in pamphlet form. The four sections of this initial collection, all of which were written by persons who were then members of the Committee on Research Activities, were "Linguistic Science" by Albert H. Marckwardt, "Editing and Textual Criticism" by Lawton P. G. Peckham, "Literary History" by René Wellek, and "Literary Criticism" by James Thorpe.

The success and wide use of the collection prompted George Winchester Stone, Jr., then Executive Secretary of the MLA, to suggest in 1962 that the Committee consider updating the report with an entirely new set of essays on the same subjects. Four members of the Association were invited to contribute essays. The essays and authors of this publication included "Linguistics" by William G. Moulton, "Textual Criticism" by Fredson Bowers, "Literary History" by Robert E. Spiller, and "Literary Criticism" by Northrop Frye.

The second collection proved as widely accepted as the first. A second edition was published in 1970. By the end of that decade, however, the Committee on Research Activities decided that the time was right once again for a new collection of essays by a new group of authors, a collection that would reflect the state of linguistic and literary scholarship as the last two decades of the twentieth century were beginning. The Committee accordingly assigned appropriate topics, this time, to *six* distinguished scholars—Winfred P. Lehmann ("Linguistics"), G. Thomas Tanselle ("Textual Scholarship"), Barbara Kiefer Lewalski ("Historical Scholarship"), Lawrence Lipking ("Literary Criticism"), Paul Hernadi ("Literary Theory"), Wayne C. Booth ("The

Scholar in Society")—and invited them to submit drafts of essays for the new publication. Each draft received a number of readings, from specialists and nonspecialists alike, and was revised in accordance with readers' suggestions before it was accepted as part of the final manuscript.

Like its predecessors, the present publication is aimed primarily at a student audience. Indeed, what James Thorpe wrote of the second collection holds true for this, its successor:

> This collection of essays is about becoming and being a scholar. It is tendered to any members of the scholarly community who would like to read a review of some current ideas on the aims and methods of scholarship. But it is primarily addressed to students, into whose hands the future of American scholarship will in due course fall. We hope that they will find these essays a useful introduction and a sound orientation.

Those familiar with the Thorpe volume will detect, however, at once that the aims and methods of scholarship set forth in that work are very much different from those described in the essays that follow. The present state of scholarship in modern languages and literatures is, as the reader will discover, at once far more complex and wide-ranging and far more lacking in unity of purpose than was evident in the decades prior to 1970. Probably nothing indicates the changes more vividly than our decision to add two additional topics to the four that were treated in the first two collections. These new essays—"Literary Theory" and "The Scholar in Society"—show two very widely differing directions in which scholarship in language and literature has been proceeding. On the one hand is the movement toward the more speculative and the more abstruse; on the other is the growing interest in the complex relationship between scholarship and the "real" world, beyond the walls of academia, that warily supports and often mocks or vilifies scholars and that increasingly demands of them varying forms of professional accountability. (Sometimes these divergent trends are embodied among the active concerns of a single scholar—like Wayne Booth himself, for example.) The alterations we have made in the titles of two other essays—"Textual Scholarship" and "Historical Scholarship" rather than "Textual Criticism" and "Literary History"—similarly reflect significant qualitative and quantitative changes in those disciplines. Finally, even the essays that repeat titles used in earlier collections (i.e., "Linguistics" and "Literary Criticism") describe fields of study that are no less multifarious, complicated, and seemingly lacking in unity than the others.

Yet the disunity that seems to mark the present state of scholarship in modern languages and literatures is unquestionably matched by an exhilarating intellectual vitality that continues to attract bright young minds and by a persistently inquisitive spirit that impels modern scholars into areas of thought previously little explored in the study of language and literature. Furthermore, as the essays also demonstrate, there remains a very real, though often not acknowledged or not perceived, interdependence between literary and linguistic scholars and their diverse fields of study. It is this interdependence that lends the volume its own unity and coherence. After an introduction by Joel Conarroe, Executive Director of the Modern Language Association, the collection proper begins with the word and the sentence ("Linguistics") and proceeds to text ("Textual Scholarship"), to context ("Historical Scholarship"), and to both the practice and theory of literary interpretation ("Literary Criticism" and "Literary Theory"). The final essay, offering in its own intensely personal way a synoptic view of the entire collection, presents theoretical and practical interpretations of another kind of "text" (the scholar) in a different kind of context (society).

Although each of the six essays will of necessity incline somewhat toward the special interests of its author, a genuine effort has been made in each instance to be objective, inclusive, and wide-ranging, including especially an attempt to describe each field of study from an international point of view. Lest specialists unfairly find fault with the limited nature of the bibliographical listings appended to the essays, it should be pointed out that considerations of space and of the intended student audience prevented us from allowing contributors to compile the kind of extensive and comprehensive bibliographies that some would have preferred to include. Instead, each essayist has been asked simply to supply a brief, selected bibliography specifically for the nonspecialist student reader. In each case, though, we have permitted the contributor to present a listing based on the bibliographical situation of the field treated in the essay. Thus the format varies from essay to essay, from a bibliographical essay, on the one hand, to a list of works cited, on the other.

The preparation of a publication such as this requires the support and assistance of a large number of persons, including members of the sponsoring Committee on Research Activities, the MLA headquarters staff, and the Association at large. Among the many who have lent this project valuable support as well as invaluable scholarly, editorial, and administrative expertise are the following: Walter S. Achtert, John Algeo, Richard D. Altick, Gerald L. Bruns, Don L. Cook, James C. Cowan, David J. DeLaura, Robert J. Di Pietro, William B. Edgerton, Richard C. Exner, Judy Goulding, S. K. Heninger, Walter H. Hinderer, Sarah N. Lawall, A. Walton Litz, Gita May, John Neubauer, Donald H. Reiman, Egon Schwarz, Charles T. Scott, Walter H. Sokel, Stuart M. Tave, Madeleine B. Therrien, Mario J. Valdés, and Helen H. Vendler.

The dimension and complexity of our assignment make it difficult for us to hope to repeat the success of the two predecessors of this collection. We must remain content, therefore, to hope that the volume will serve reasonably faithfully as a kind of mirror, reflecting the activities and endeavors of scholars in modern languages and literatures, and as a kind of lamp, guiding readers to what seem the more promising paths for future linguistic and literary study.

Introduction

Joel Conarroe

"The ordinary growth of a mind," Ralph Waldo Emerson observed, "especially till the old age of man, depends on aliment procured from without." No aliment, or nourishment, whatever its source, is ever redundant to a literary scholar. As with a novelist or poet, virtually any experience is grist for the mill, be it of a communal nature or the sort gained in solitude. Whether listening to Schubert, poring through a bibliography, feeding the children, or reading Cervantes, a scholar constantly receives and synthesizes information and impressions. Whatever happens, hour by hour, affects his or her sense of reality, and the work that is ultimately produced tangibly reflects the sort of nourishment taken in. This activity involves the "strange process," again quoting Emerson, "by which experience is converted into thought, as a mulberry leaf is converted into satin."

No humanist, it seems, can ever have too much experience, ever know too much about gothic architecture, the Spanish Civil War, macroeconomics, or Miro's aesthetic theories. Effective research and writing involve exposure to an immense body of thought, and anyone who has ever been in the thrall of a work in progress knows that there are no shortcuts either to wisdom or to understanding. Moreover, humanists discover that the more information they acquire the more thoroughly uninformed they know themselves to be, Alps upon Alps rising before their astonished eyes. Students of language and literature in particular are constantly reminded of how little they understand, which means, paradoxically, that an increase in knowledge is always accompanied by a heightened sense of intellectual unworthiness. This awareness, though, like eyestrain, goes with the territory, and the scholar learns to live with it. The compensations, the sources of delight, more than make amends.

Among those things certain to gratify any research scholar are a challenging problem, access to a good library, and a quiet place to work, far from telephones, committee meetings, and the ubiquitous contemporary beat. Also of inestimable worth is a block of time sufficient to permit uninterrupted brooding, unhurried browsing in peripheral topics, and frequent revisions. There should be, ideally, a wide margin for error. Deadlines are the scholar's bane; research, like satin, cannot be hurried. It is unfortunate that the achievement of young humanists in our academic institutions is invariably evaluated after only a very few years; premature scrutiny often forces projects to precipitous conclusions and makes not only for work that is tentative but for habits of research that are incompatible with sound scholarship.

Our own deadlines, fortunately, did not prevent the scholars represented in this volume from completing essays that appear to be unhurried, properly seasoned. These six papers, dealing with several approaches to research in literature and language, are not intended to provide *ex cathedra* pronouncements about academic discourse, but rather to introduce (or reintroduce) readers to certain terms and attitudes characteristic of different kinds of humanistic research. The topics are presented in discrete essays, but as I suggest above and as the papers themselves make clear, a scholar never stands completely alone. Anyone engaged in research soon discovers that everything is related to everything else. And although students of literature or language may dwell mostly in their own chosen provinces—of linguistics, say, or criticism—they are frequently, by choice and necessity, visitors in the enclaves of their peers, and receive visits in return. Few things are as consequential as the assistance, moral support, and criticism one receives from colleagues, be they down the hall or across an ocean. A scholar, by definition, is a citizen of the world of ideas.

The individuals invited to contribute to this volume have, through humane articles and books, shown themselves to be exemplary citizens. Winfred P. Lehmann, Ashbel Smith Professor of Linguistics and Germanic Studies at the University of Texas in Austin, discusses, in the opening essay, some ways in which various theories put forward by linguists help us gain an understanding of language. Then G. Thomas Tanselle, Vice-President of the John Simon Guggenheim Memorial Foundation, approaches the frequently misunderstood question of the production, by scholarly editors, of accurate texts. In the third paper Barbara Kiefer Lewalski, Alumni-Alumnae University Professor at Brown University, analyzes the interrelationship among literary texts and the historical continuities in which these works participate.

The essays that round out the collection address current ideas on criticism, theory, and the scholar in society. Lawrence Lipking, Professor of English at Northwestern University, describes the development of literary criticism in recent decades, touching on biographical speculation, reader response, textual indeterminacy, and responses to formalism. Paul Hernadi, Professor of English and Comparative Literature at the University of Iowa, approaching an increasingly controversial subject, discusses various ramifications of the "prodigious" growth in both America and Europe of theories of literature. Finally, the scholar's role in society ("Every scholar, good or bad, becomes a scholar by associating") is examined by Wayne C. Booth, Pullman Professor of English at the University of Chicago and 1982 President of the Modern Language Association.

"The skill developed from constant practice in the direct experience of literature," Northrop Frye has suggested, "is a special skill, like playing the piano, not the expression of a general attitude to life, like singing in the shower." These quite dissimilar essays, products of the sort of sustained practice that permits authoritative performance, help document the distance between professional and amateur. The contributors, however, avoid the sort of distancing pedantry that too often makes the word "critic" a synonym for "educated shrew." In their range, moreover, they offer an implicit rebuke to the narrow specialist who recognizes only one chosen field and never its interrelationship with other disciplines. And finally, to bring the Emerson reference full circle, the essays provide the sort of aliment by which our own minds can be nourished, our skills developed. As Emerson's friend at Walden Pond suggested, though, it takes two to speak the truth: one to speak, and another to hear.

Linguistics

Winfred P. Lehmann

I. Introduction

Linguistics has as principal aim the understanding of language. In this effort it follows various paths. The primary concern of current linguistics is the formulation and testing of theories, in accordance with the view that an understanding of any phenomenon, including language, is to be sought and improved by means of a theory. Half a century ago the emphasis fell on assembling and describing data, as from the native languages of the Americas, Africa, and other little-known areas. Half a century earlier, indeed from about 1820, history was held to provide the key to the understanding of language, especially its earliest ascertainable forms. Though these periods produced numerous gifted linguists, the characteristic activity of each may be illustrated by one scholar. Jacob Grimm (1785–1863) exemplifies the period in which historical linguistics predominated, for by formulating the relationships between the consonants of Germanic and other Indo-European languages he gave the impetus to investigations pursued throughout the nineteenth century and beyond it.[1] Leonard Bloomfield (1887–1949), with his attention to little-known languages like Tagalog and Menomini as well as to general linguistic theory, typifies the second period. A break with Bloomfieldian theory was triggered by Noam Chomsky (1928–), the central figure in generative transformational grammar. Because much of the energy of recent linguistics has been expended in confrontation between Bloomfieldian and Chomskian theory, as well as departures from these theories, any concern for linguistics today involves primary attention to theory.

Since linguistics is an empirical science, linguistic theories are based on data. Rather than concentrate explicitly on theory, then, many linguists devote themselves to assembling and explaining data. The data may be from languages of the present or the past, from languages of civilization or languages of preliterate groups, from literary or nonliterary texts. Starting from such varied data, linguists differ in the studies they carry out. Yet, whether or not they state as much, their efforts to understand language are carried out— their data are assembled and accounted for—in terms of a theory.

Linguistic theories differ in accordance with not only the presuppositions of their proponents but also the proponents' views on the scope of their field, inasmuch as the shape of a theory is determined to some extent by the phenomena it is to account for. Some consider understanding the central data of language the sole task of a linguist, the understanding of sentences like this:

Jack and Jill went up the hill.

For others, full understanding can only be achieved by accounting at the same time for additional sentences in a text, especially sentences with ellipses, such as:

Jill came tumbling after (Jack).

Still others take account of the events surrounding the use of sentences. For even others, linguistic theory must be concerned as well with the perception of language and with the functioning of the mind in representing and interpreting concepts. The varying scope assumed has given rise to differing activities among individual linguists.

The activities of a linguist may be determined by further considerations, such as scientific modesty. In this way Leonard Bloomfield directed his own activities, and consequently those of his followers, primarily to form; he justified this restriction on the grounds that the study of meaning is properly the aim of all scientific and humanistic study, not merely of the scientific study of language. Other linguists restrict their activities to a particular segment of the overall field. Considering the field of linguistics far too broad to master, many linguists today confine their attention to the sounds of language, others to the sentences, others to particular approaches. Such scholars identify themselves as phonologists or as syntacticians and the like. Some specialists, such as epigraphists or even lexicographers and experimental phoneticians, are so restricted to one approach to language that they are scarcely identified with linguistics any longer.

Another kind of restriction may be applied by linguists who seek to enrich the field by clarifying cruxes remaining in thoroughly studied areas such as classical Greek or Latin, or the Romance languages. Such scholars may choose to carry out their studies within a theoretical framework developed by predecessors, with no explicit attention to rejecting or even modifying that theory. Such linguists are often referred to as traditionalists, but little effort is made to identify the tradition. Many of the linguists who devote themselves to the study of languages preserved only in written texts carry out their work in this way. These scholars must acquire skills other than those used purely in attention to language, like the interpretation of writing systems, of bygone cultural characteristics, of the treatment of texts handed down from the past. Scholarship carried out with the help of such skills is generally referred to as philology and, when concerned with historical linguistic study, as comparative philology. Older handbooks, and conservative scholars, may still maintain the term in this sense, referring to linguists also as comparative philologists.

In contrast with the attention to literary texts in the nineteenth century, current linguists are likely to study linguistic problems arising among the various social strata in the complex societies of today, or problems faced by bilingual persons and by children in learning languages, or the procedures assumed for the interpretation of utterances. Such interests lead to cooperation with scholars in other disciplines and to techniques such as sociology, statistical methods, psychology, and logic. As a result, students of language and literature may find many linguistic writings forbidding and of little practical benefit. Attempts to relate linguistic findings with the concerns of such scholars are pursued under the heading "applied linguistics." This is a broad area and a difficult one to define. It includes pedagogical activities, work with the handicapped, efforts to remodel languages and writing systems, and so on. Linguistics is only one of the disciplines involved, for these matters also depend on social views, political systems, and individual attitudes to language.

Whatever their data and whatever their theory, linguists must deal with issues that are fundamental in any study of language. Many of these issues have long been debated, as by the ancient Greeks and Indians. They were reviewed most incisively perhaps by Ferdinand de Saussure (1857–1913) in a series of lectures given in Geneva, Switzerland, between 1906 and 1911. Published posthumously in the *Cours de linguistique générale*, this review of linguistic theory is often held to be the beginning of contemporary linguistics, or even of linguistics as a separate discipline. The central issues will be sketched before we examine current approaches to linguistics.

II. Fundamental Concepts of Linguistics

Ideas presented by Saussure as fundamental to linguistics have been reexamined and often restated by subsequent linguists in different terminology. Their background and their relationship with intellectual currents of his day have also been discussed. Because of space limitations we can only discuss the ideas briefly, leaving other matters for further reading.

Langue and *parole*—Competence and Performance
For Saussure and for linguists generally "the subject matter of linguistics comprises all manifestations of human speech . . . not only correct speech and flowery language, but other forms of expression as well."[2] That is, linguistics does not limit itself to treating an accepted standard, such as the Queen's English, or to analysis of the language of literature. These are treated as variants, or registers, of a given language and emphasized or neglected no more than the colloquial or technical or even substandard varieties. All such variants are to be identified and treated in linguistic study, with the aim of understanding language as a phenomenon.

Saussure notes that linguistic study is twofold. On the one hand it must deal with language, "which is purely social and independent of the individual."

On the other hand, it must deal with "the individual side"—that is, speech. For these two concerns, Saussure used the terms *langue* and *parole*; together they constitute the general phenomenon, *langage*. French makes available three terms for these concerns of linguistic study, whereas many languages, among them English, do not. Through the influence of Chomsky, the two kinds of study are identified today by the theories developed from them. The study of *langue* leads to a theory of competence; the study of *parole* to a theory of performance. The word "theory" is often omitted, so that handbooks speak only of competence and performance.

Concern with competence is viewed as the central aim of linguistic theory. Competence deals primarily with the "conventions that have been adopted by a social body," without attention to individual peculiarities or even inadequacies (Saussure, *Course*, p. 10). Such study, in Saussure's view, is purely psychological, directed at the mental structures underlying the utterances of speakers. Competence, then, is social, shared knowledge of the principles governing the organization and interpretation of utterances in a speech community.

Yet the linguist cannot neglect performance, for utterances apply and disclose competence. In the words of Saussure, *parole* is "both the instrument and the product" of *langue* (*Course*, p. 19). The study of competence and the study of performance are then interdependent. As in all disciplines, specialists may devote themselves to one facet. Phoneticians and students of style are especially concerned with performance, as are sociolinguists. General linguists and some psycholinguists direct their attention primarily to competence.

Signifiant and *signifié*—Language as a Semiotic System

In using language, speakers aim to communicate, whether on an artistic, practical, formal, or intimate level. Communication is carried out through the use of signs, which are combinations of concepts and sound-images. Such signs are arbitrary: there is no inherent relationship between the sound-image or shape of the word and the concept it signifies. The existence of different words for the same concept supports this view. We have, for example, English *tree*, German *Baum*, French *arbre*, and so on. The study of language is a subclass of the study of signs, or semiotics. Language is viewed as a link between sound and thought (Saussure, *Course*, pp. 67 and 112).

Saussure was concerned to achieve a clear treatment of semiotics, including appropriate terminology. For him a sign has two aspects: its form, or signifying element (*signifiant*), and its value, or signified element (*signifié*). Both are best visualized within systems. One example of a simple sign system is that of stoplights, which often consist solely of the signifying elements, or forms: red, yellow, and green. The three values or meanings of these—stop, caution, go—provide the three signified elements. Societies use many other semiotic systems, such as gestures. Some scholars have treated clothing, eating practices, or rituals as semiotic systems, but the most complex semiotic system of human society is language.

The complexity of language leads investigators to approach it variously. Some make their way into it by concentrating on form; others on meaning. Traditional grammarians concentrated on meaning, using a semantic approach to grammar; nouns, for example, were defined by their reference. According to one traditional grammar, that of English by George Lyman Kittredge and Frank E. Farley, the sentence is made up of parts of speech, such as the noun, "which is the name of a person, place, or thing," and the verb, "which can assert something (usually an action) concerning a person, place, or thing."[3] Contemporary linguistics relies much more heavily on form. Structuralists, for example, define nouns primarily by their form. "The noun is a word-class; like all form-classes it is to be defined in terms of grammatical features."[4] Generative transformational grammarians identify elements of sentences by position in a string, applying labels like "NP" and "VP" rather than functional labels like "subject" and "predicate." Some contemporary linguists, such as the proponents of Montague grammar, however, take meaning greatly into account. One's approach to the study of language as a semiotic system then sets the direction for the linguistic theory selected.

Surface Structure versus Deep Structure

Whatever their approach to language and semiotics, linguists regard language as a system. Classical grammarians were especially interested in its morphology, identifying parts of speech and establishing their systems of inflection. Greek, Latin, and Hebrew grammars present us with many paradigms. In this century the major efforts have been directed at, first, the phonological system and, more recently, the syntactic system. In these efforts scholars may concentrate initially on the physical events of language, but through these they attempt to comprehend the system as controlled by the brain. The system in abstract representation is referred to as "deep" or "underlying structure," and representatives closer to actual utterances are referred to as "surface structures."

Linguists vary considerably in their views of surface and deep structure, especially concerning the relations between these two constructs as well as the abstractness of deep structure. Such views must be examined with regard to the additional conception of grammars as consisting of components.

Most hold that there are three components: a phonological, a syntactic, and a semantic. The phonological component has to do with sounds; the syntactic component has to do with sentences and their constituents; the semantic component has to do with the relation of linguistic entities to the world outside language, that is, to the conveying of meaning. Meaning is also conveyed through the syntactic component. Theories vary in their definitions of these components and in the abstractness they assign to each. Structuralists propose levels: first the most accessible (i.e., the phonological), then the morphological, syntactic, stylistic, semantic, and so on. Each of these they hold to be distinct. They also propose intermediate segments, such as the morphophonemic between the phonological and the morphological levels. Transformationalists by contrast tend to assume three components, with blurred distinctions between them.

In each component, surface and deep structures are identified. Individual theorists are most sharply involved with the component of central concern to them, attempting to clarify the bounds and interrelationships of surface and deep structure in this. Thus the structuralists in their concern with the phonological segment dealt at length with clarification of the phoneme concept. By 1930 phonetic instrumentation made it clear beyond doubt that language was not made up solely of groups of physical sounds; rather, these are classified and identified by speakers as an abstract unit, labeled "phoneme." Some linguists, such as Edward Sapir (1884–1939), regarded the phoneme purely as a mental unit. Others attached more importance to form. Still others, such as W. Freeman Twaddell (1906–), defined the phoneme as an abstraction based on sets of relationships. The disputes received much attention in the 1930s. Whatever the criteria used, linguists came to accept some kind of underlying unit in phonological study.

Phonemes in themselves do not convey meaning, but they serve to distinguish it. Thus the /r/ of *rot* and the /t/ of *tot* distinguish these words from each other, without themselves having meaning. Similarly the /n/ of *knot*, and so on.

Elements like *rot, tot*, and *knot* belong to the syntactic component. As linguistic entities composed of phonemes, they consist wholly of abstract units. But in the syntactic component they are regarded as surface elements that participate in deep structures. Each of them may stand in the following sequence, where the first two elements make up the subject:

The ____ annoyed her.

The entire sentence consists of two abstract elements: Subject Predicate, which may be further analyzed into Article Noun Verb Pronoun. The syntactic component is in this way analyzed for a surface structure and an underlying structure.

Treatment of these two constructs—surface structure and underlying, or deep, structure—and of the relationships between them has provided much of the basis for theoretical debate in the last three decades. Transformational theory took its name from the construct proposed to relate them: the body of transformational rules, discussed further below. Moreover, linguists differ, on the one hand, in limiting deep structures to syntactic constructs and, on the other, in including semantic entities. Yet all theories regard grammars of language as made up of components or levels, with differences between surface and underlying structures.

The Fundamental Importance of Relationship
Entities in each component are determined and regulated by relationships, which vary from language to language, not simply by overt form. Thus Chinese distinguishes unaspirated /p t k/ from aspirated /p' t' k'/, but English assigns both unaspirated and aspirated voiceless stops to the /p t k/ phonemes, distinguishing these in turn from /b d g/. In the same way, relationships determine the value of syntactic and semantic entities.

At the syntactic level, English distinguishes adjectives and adverbs, often overtly, as in *slow* : *slowly, good* : *well*, and by correspondence with these covertly, as in *fast* : *fast*. German lacks such distinction in many constructions, using the same form for the adverb as for the predicate adjective. Interrelationships within the syntactic structure thus determine the syntactic entities in the two languages. In much the same way, segments of sentences are identified by relationships, as Saussure illustrated by citing the ambiguous

French utterance: *sižlaprã* (*Course*, p. 104). This may be interpreted in two ways:

| si-ž-la-prã | 'if I take it' | Si je la prends. |
| si-ž-l-aprã | 'if I learn it' | Si je l'apprends. |

Whatever the interpretation, the units are singled out by divisions of sound-images corresponding to concepts, with the appropriate relationships.

The same principle applies in the semantic sphere. The meaning of English *cousin* is determined by its relationships to other elements in the kinship system. It has a wider meaning than does German *der Vetter* 'male cousin' or *die Kusine* 'female cousin' because its uses are not delimited by the feature (sex) that is found in the kinship terms *uncle, aunt,* and others. The semantic, syntactic, and phonological entities are all determined by relationships within their particular systems.

Syntagmatic versus Paradigmatic Planes

These relationships apply on a horizontal and a vertical plane. Any utterance is a string, as determined by the linear nature of language. In producing an utterance, a speaker chooses appropriate patterns and entities on each plane. English utterances include horizontal patterns such as Article Noun Verb Article Noun, or Auxiliary Noun Verb (as in *Do dogs bark?*). And when referring to animals, for example, they select from a "vertical set," consisting of items known as a paradigm, such as:

dog
cat
horse
pony

One choice from these possible patterns with appropriate entities yields:

The boy kissed the dog.
The dog kissed the boy.

This linguistic device is known as arrangement.

Differences may also be introduced on the vertical plane. Thus, if *m* rather than *k* were selected in the third word, the first sentence would be:

The boy missed the dog.

Differences could also be introduced on the vertical plane by selecting other lexical elements: *girl* rather than *boy, pony* rather than *dog*, and so on. This linguistic device is known as selection.

The two devices are often related to the two planes. Arrangement is said to apply on the syntagmatic plane, selection on the paradigmatic plane. Paradigms are sets of selection devices. If a language has six noun cases, like Latin, its selection is narrower than in languages like English and German, which have fewer cases. Users have less latitude of expression when confronted with a set of forms like Latin as opposed to English *friend*: *friend's* in the singular.

Nominative	amīcus
Genitive	amīcī
Dative	amīcō
Accusative	amīcum
Ablative	amīco
Vocative	amīce

The more specific selection categories permit the Latin user greater latitude of arrangement. Thus *amīcum amat puer* means 'the boy loves (his) friend' as clearly as does *puer amat amīcum*, whereas a shift in arrangement of the two nouns in English would bring about a totally different meaning. Selection and arrangement are then supplementary devices, maintaining a kind of balance in language, but not complete equilibrium.

Synchronic versus Diachronic Study

The lack of equilibrium, which is found throughout language, provides avenues for language change; this is not to say that it *causes* language change, which like any social change has multiple causes. Speakers tend to associate similar elements in sets. Thus a speaker of Latin would have maintained a set of forms contrasting nominative versus accusative:

	'rose'	'friend'	'foot'	'father'	'thing'
Nominative	rosa	amīcus	pēs	pater	rēs
Accusative	rosam	amīcum	pedem	patrem	rem

But the formal contrast was not found in some such sets:

	'city'	'horn'
Nominative	oppidum	cornū
Accusative	oppidum	cornū

In time the second situation prevailed. The Romance languages show a lack of contrast between the former nominative and accusative. The accusative has been generalized, as in French *pied*, Italian *piede* 'foot,' and French *rien* from *rem*. Such sets, and language in general, can be studied through time (diachronic study) or at one point in time (synchronic study). The Saussurian term "diachronic" is generally replaced by "historical"; "synchronic" is called "descriptive."

Like other branches of science, linguistics has varied considerably in its attention to these types of study. In the eighteenth century synchronic study was the favored approach. Then, with the discovery that Sanskrit and current Indic languages are related to German, English, Latin, Greek, and other languages of the West, historical linguistics attracted most linguists, so that historical study predominated in the nineteenth century. After Saussure, the pendulum swung back, so that historical linguistics went into decline. Saussure was aware of these shifts and their adverse effects. He looked forward to a period when both approaches would be in balance.

Nineteenth-century linguists held that explanation could be provided only by the knowledge of older forms. Thus "irregular" plurals like *men* and *mice* can be explained from phonological processes in effect a millennium and a half ago. But the knowledge of such processes is limited, especially when one concerns oneself with earlier periods of history and with areas such as Africa and the Americas, for which there are no early texts. The possibilities of historical explanation thus came to be limited, and linguists turned their attention to other studies.

Historical linguistics obviously is based on descriptive linguistics. A historian of English must have a descriptive grammar and a dictionary of medieval English and earlier forms of the language. The two approaches, historical and descriptive, are accordingly interrelated.

If descriptive linguists seek explanations of limited patterns like that in *write, wrote, written*, they must concern themselves with history. The demands made on linguists, however, are legion. A historical linguist must know older forms of related languages besides Middle English and Old English—Gothic, Old Norse, Latin, Greek, Sanskrit, even others like Old Persian, Old Armenian, Old Irish—in order to deal successfully with problems in English. Descriptive linguists in turn must have intimate knowledge of phonetics, understanding of formal logic, possibly of statistical theory, social structures, and so on. In practice then, the dichotomy between historical and descriptive linguistics remains strong, to the detriment of linguistic theories limiting their attention to only one of the two broad approaches.

Linguistic Study and Related Areas
Besides these competing demands, linguists are subject to other motivations. The divisions of intellectual life are artificial, though designed to admit depth of investigation. In the medieval period, intellectual life and universities were so structured that the study of language, or grammar, was distinguished from the study of extended texts, or rhetoric, and the study of reasoning, or logic. These three topics were the fundamental academic subjects that made up the trivium of the university curriculum.

In other periods, the distinctions have not been clearly maintained. In the seventeenth and eighteenth centuries the study of language and logic were closely associated. At the end of the nineteenth century, linguistics was closely associated with psychology. Various theoreticians show similar bents. Chomsky, for example, has classified linguistics as a subclass of cognitive psychology. But, like many recent linguists, he also applies practices of symbolic logic in his attention to language. Currently many linguists are combining the formerly discrete study of language and rhetoric, in the approach known as text-linguistics.

Schools of linguistics have a way of reflecting intellectual currents of their time, which often are stimulated by the excessive concentrations of their predecessors. After the overwhelming attention to historical linguistics in the nineteenth century, the structuralists virtually excluded history from their consideration. After the stern mechanism of Leonard Bloomfield and his followers, the transformationalists espoused mentalism. Each student must decide on an individual course of action. An eclectic approach is often characterized as dilettantism, but capable eclectics may make important contributions to the intellectual life of many generations, as did Cicero. To achieve whatever clarity is possible under the requirements for brevity imposed here, recent linguistic theory will be discussed below in accordance with the various schools.

III. Structuralism

The first major departure from traditional grammar based on Greek and Latin grammatical study is now widely known as structuralism. In contrast with previous approaches to language, it concentrated on form. Form was to be analyzed as rigorously as in the physical sciences. Science is "to deal only with events that are accessible in their time and place to any and all observers (strict behaviorism) or only with events that are placed in coordinates of time and space (mechanism). . . . Mentalistic terms do not figure in the procedure of physics, biology, or linguistics."[5] Mentalism, in contrast, assumes that special features of mind must be recognized if one is to understand language. Bloomfield's mechanistic view was in keeping with the prevailing positivism of the time. In this country Bloomfield crystallized this approach, especially through his book *Language* (1933). Its method led to severe restriction on the segments of language treated, as illustrated by Bloomfield with the nursery fable "Jack and Jill." For Bloomfield there are "two human ways of responding to a stimulus . . . speechless reaction: S $\ggg\!\!\rightarrow$ R" (i.e., stimulus arouses a reaction) and "reaction mediated by speech: S $\ggg\!\!\rightarrow$ r......s $\ggg\!\!\rightarrow$ R" (i.e., stimulus arouses a speech reaction, which in turn arouses a stimulus in the hearer, leading to a reaction) (*Language*, p. 26). A linguist notes such linguistic "reaction" and thereupon produces a description of language. First, the sounds are accounted for. Sounds are the elements that distinguish words, such as consonants distinguishing *Jack* from *Mac* or *Jack* from *Jan*, the vowels distinguishing *Jack* from *Jock*, and so forth. These then are arranged according to inner relationships that reflect the system or structure of a language.

Thereupon the linguist classifies the inflections, such as *went* versus *go*, *hills* versus *hill*, once again determining their structure. In practice this was the extent of linguistic concern.

Linguists at the time, roughly the 1930s to the 1950s, devoted a great deal of study to exotic languages, such as those spoken in the Americas and Africa. Describing the phonology and morphology of these is no small accomplishment. Description of events surrounding the speaker, the stimulus and response as well as the situation involving them, was left to others. For "to give a scientifically accurate meaning for every form of a language, we should have to have a scientifically accurate knowledge of everything in the speaker's world" (Bloomfield, *Language*, p. 139). The linguist deals with meaning only to discriminate forms; the study of meaning as such is the pursuit of the sciences and the humanities.

Characterizing the activities in accordance with the topics cited in Section II above, we may note that the *signifié* was largely disregarded. Yet the structuralists dealt with *langue*. They determined underlying forms in the systems of sounds and forms, labeling them "phonemes" and "morphemes." Relationships between these underlying elements were then set forth, though purely on a synchronic basis; any analysis taking historical matters into account was completely rejected, for the speaker was held to know only the language of the time. Diachronic study, to be sure, had its interests, but it was not to be merged with the chief interest, synchronic description. This attitude toward historical study has been maintained by subsequent influential schools.

Structuralism had a major impact on language teaching, especially the teaching of foreign languages—one of Bloomfield's continuing concerns. If an utterance was a response triggered by a situation, languages might well be taught by determining the most frequent responses, describing them accurately, and drilling students in their production and understanding. Moreover, the emphasis on phonology led to an attempt to equip students with a near-native command of the *sounds* of a language. Textbooks were carefully graded, with words and patterns selected by frequency counts and appropriately presented. The approach was highly effective, but it could also be reduced virtually to a parody when much of teaching was allotted to the tape recorder, leaving students to drone along after the patterns on the tape with little or no retention. As a result the entire approach fell into disfavor among many language teachers. Further discredit has come because of the structuralists' views on evaluations attached to patterns of language. Since a positivistic approach requires description of all data, including the everyday language of the untutored as well as the literary language of Shakespeare, all were accorded equal attention. When vocal members of the structural school applied this attitude to language standards, proposing that instead of adopting the language of respected users one should "leave one's language alone," the approach encountered severe criticism.[6] The criticism may have aroused most widespread attention with reference to *Webster's Third New International Dictionary* (1963), which omitted traditional labels, like "colloquial" and "vulgar," attempting instead to illustrate the status of particular usages through citations from literature, from well-known public figures, like Dwight Eisenhower and A. E. Stevenson, from journals, like *Time* and the *Times Literary Supplement*, from general commentators, like A. L. Kroeber and Van Wyck Brooks, as well as from other users. The approach met with considerable objection.

Literary texts were also analyzed under the theory. It was assumed that in eminent literary works form reflects content. Accordingly, close analysis of phonemic, morphemic, and syntactic patterning would securely disclose the meaning of texts. Among widely cited examples are Archibald A. Hill's analysis of Hopkins' "Windhover" and Roman Jakobson's analysis of Blake. Critics who object to this theory have provided examples of works in which capable form indeed mirrors content but in which this mirroring does not produce a respected literary work.

IV. Transformational Grammar

Although World War II and Bloomfield's untimely death interrupted development of linguistic structuralism, it was pursued by Zellig Harris

(1909–), the leading theoretician of the approach after Bloomfield. Harris continued the effort to identify characteristic structural features at higher levels. In analyzing sentences, he equated sequences like *Casals plays the cello* with *The cello is played by Casals*.[7] The relationships relating such sequences Harris called transformations. In the determination of transformations, meaning was used as a criterion for identifying equivalent patterns, but thereupon was excluded. Harris aimed to learn not "WHAT a text is saying, but HOW it is saying." In this way "something of the structure of the text" is to be determined ("Discourse Analysis," p. 1). The effort was pursued also at the level of texts, in discourse analysis, as it was called by Harris. Both the transformations and the conclusions on textual structure are based on surface patterns. Although the structuralists proposed underlying abstract phonemes and morphemes when dealing with phonology and with morphology, sentences were analyzed in terms of the simpler surface patterns known as kernels, such as *Casals plays the cello*. The appeal of this view of language was shortly to be superseded by that of a view introduced by one of Harris' students, Noam Chomsky.

In a sharp break with Harris and the Bloomfieldian approach, Chomsky came to relate surface strings with underlying abstract structures through a characteristic kind of transformational rule. Harris used transformational rules to relate a string like *Work altogether inferior is produced by him* with *He produces work altogether inferior.* As his own theory developed, Chomsky derived both such strings from a sentence rule: S→NP Aux VP.[8] The passive version is generated by a special rule, the passive transformational rule. Such a shift in the use of transformational rules reflected a mentalistic approach, which replaces the mechanistic view of Bloomfield. From the time of Chomsky's first publication, *Syntactic Structures* (1957), there was a major confrontation between the two approaches. After the Ninth Linguistic Congress (1960), descriptive theory looked to Chomsky for theoretical guidance rather than to Bloomfield and his followers.

This period coincided with massive expansion of American universities under federal support aimed to counter the challenge of sputnik. Vigorous new fields were favored. Energetic minds seeking challenges in their graduate study flocked to linguistics, even from areas like mathematics. The formalism introduced to relate the several kinds of rules provided problems of interest also to students who knew no language other than English. As linguistics underwent a tremendous expansion, the new recruits pursued their work in accordance with generative transformational theory.

This theory differed further from structuralist theory in its attention to language as an activity rather than a state. The structuralists took as their task the analysis and description of data in terms of a system. What interested the transformationalists, by contrast, were the processes that involve underlying abstract structures, to determine the phonetic form of sentences. For these processes they introduced metaphorical labels, such as "pied-piping," "affix-hopping," and, as illustrated below, "raising."

Moreover, whereas structuralists, especially in their attention to exotic languages, concentrated on phonology, transformationalists focused on syntax. A grammar is held to consist of three components: a phonological, a semantic, and a syntactic. In the production of utterances, the syntactic component is central. Speech is produced as underlying syntactic sequences are formed, such as S→NP Aux V in association with appropriate lexical entries, such as <produce><work>. Utterances result through treatment of such underlying features, in accordance with a grammar of the following design:

	Syntactic component	
Deep structures	Underlying syntactic rules	
	Lexicon	→ Semantic component
	Transformational rules	
	Surface structures	→ Phonological component

According to such a grammar the underlying syntactic rules, such as that illustrated above, and the lexical elements, like those above, would yield either the utterance *He produces work* or, if the passive transformation is applied, *Work is produced by him.* The syntactic, phonological, and semantic rules that make up the grammar of any language represent each process involved in the production of any utterance. Grammars are to be completely explicit, rigorous, and economical, accounting for language with as few rules as possible. Such a grammar, especially its total accountability, is referred to as "generative." The adjective in this sense, and also the prominent use of transformations, gave rise to the designation "generative transformational grammar."

In examining language, generative transformational grammarians view it as an *energeia*, in Wilhelm von Humboldt's words, rather than as a finished work, an *ergon*. The creativity of speakers is highlighted, as well as their capability of producing and understanding an infinite variety of utterances. The contrast with the approach of the structuralists may be illustrated with a sentence like *They imagine him to be highly successful*. Structuralists analyze the syntax for interrelationships of the constituents, treating the sequence *him to be highly successful* as a nonfinite clause, much as was done in traditional grammar. By the generative transformational grammar approach, such an embedded clause is derived from the abstract underlying forms of a sentence, which for clarity is represented here in something like its surface form. In the generation of the final sentence, the subject of the lower S[S²] (*He is highly successful*) is brought up and into the main sentence, by the process known as raising.

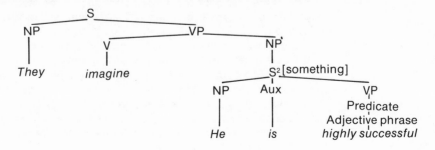

Considerable attention was devoted to raising and to other processes. Research focused on English, so that labels were taken from English grammar, such as the label "*wh*-words" for interrogatives of one kind. Processes and characteristics of English were often assumed to be universal. Thus the process of interrogation other than for *yes/no* questions was assumed to admit the placing of only one *wh*-word at the beginning of the sentence. And relativization was held to be expressed as in English, with some kind of relative marker. When further languages were investigated, however, some of these assumptions were demonstrated to be false; Slavic, for example, admits the placement of more than one *wh*-word at the beginning of a sentence. Other problems arose for the theory, such as the inability to account simply for even a single language like English in terms of the processes assumed. Thus with a long monograph on raising, produced after a decade of attention to the process, the subject reached an impasse, in part because of attempts to account for raising with verbs like *begin* in much the way as for verbs like *imagine, hope, expect*.

The author of this monograph, Paul Postal, is one of the outstanding transformational grammarians, and his work of 447 pages on one process is well-nigh definitive; yet a lengthy review article by an equally respected member of the school concludes with unhappy sections, one entitled: "Whatever Happened to Transformational Theory."[9] Postal, Bach, and others had for some time viewed the treatment of the semantic component in the so-called standard theory as erroneous. In the standard theory, this component is interpretive, relating the central syntactic patterns and lexicon to the outside world (as suggested in the model on page 13). The dissenting scholars placed the semantic component in central position, generating through a transformational syntactic component and a phonological component the actual surface structures. This approach came to be known as generative semantics, in contrast with the generative syntax pursued by Chomsky and his adherents. Yet this modification did little to solve many basic problems of generative grammar. In attempts to deal with these, the standard theory was modified and is still undergoing modification by its remaining proponents.

Generative transformational grammar in the meantime had been widely adopted, also by neighboring disciplines. With its emphasis on creativity it seemed ideal to account for the linguistic utterances known as literature. Attempts were made to illuminate metrics, problems of style, and other features of elevated writing, at times with little understanding of the phenomena discussed and less understanding of previous scholarship. Adherents of the approach were confident of the method, producing numerous exploratory works accompanied by expectations of subsequent clarification. The lofty expectations for transformational analyses may well be illustrated by Claude Lévi-Strauss's hope: "the day may come when all the available documentation on Australian tribes is transferred to punched cards and with the help of a computer their entire techno-economic, social, and religious structures can be shown to be like a vast group of transformations."[10] In time the high hopes were stilled, in large part through research in the discipline influenced most widely by generative transformational grammar, psychology.

With its explicit account of the generation of sentences, generative transformational grammar provided fresh avenues for investigating problems such as the acquisition of language by children, the use of language by bilinguals, the process of perception, and problems in language disabilities, such as aphasia. Psychologists began to devote enormous attention to linguistic research, for the study of language seemed now to provide best access to the proper aim of psychology—the understanding of the mind. The flourishing discipline called psycholinguistics is often dated from this time, though linguists were also deeply concerned with psychology in the nineteenth century. Structuralism also led to cooperation with other disciplines, as in an attempt to develop means for carrying out psychoanalysis on the basis of speech patterns, but the interrelationships between the disciplines were not nearly so many. In the psycholinguistic research it became clear that no support could be found in psychological investigations for the assumption of transformational rules. A central feature of the approach was thus undermined. Such problems, as well as the treatment of semantics, led to diminishing interest in the Standard Theory of generative transformational grammar. Today its founder is pursuing linguistic research with the use of virtually no transformations. Many of its other vigorous adherents turned to linguistic theories that are directed in the first instance at the semantic component.

V. Montague Grammar

Semantically centered theory has grown out of the study of logic, especially modal logic. Its adherents do not use semantics, as did the structuralists, simply to discriminate between different utterances or to interpret the syntactic component as do the proponents of the Standard Theory; they direct their primary attention to it. In their analysis of sentences they apply the rigorous procedures of linguistic philosophers, insisting on establishing truth values as well as determining semantic features. As a result, they apply the formidable notation developed in symbolic logic. Even an introduction to it would require an essay longer than the space allotted here. An example may therefore suffice to illustrate the shift in focus from the two previous dominant theories.

While generative transformational grammar focused on the processes yielding the sentence structure found in utterances like *One can imagine him smiling*, a semantic approach takes into account such properties as the control exerted by entities like "imagine," for the reference of *him smiling* is something true in the subject's imagination, not necessarily in actual life. In short, words like "imagine" express presuppositions. The person concerned may not have smiled at all; the speaker simply supposes that he did. Among topics of interest in the analysis of such elements is their scope. If the utterance continued, *but he merely frowned, replying that it didn't matter*, it is no longer within the scope of "imagine." It has a different truth value. By the semantic approach, all such properties of utterances must be precisely identified and stated.

Such an aim requires the development of means for representing explicitly the scope of all controlling segments, such as negatives. Even an apparently simple sequence like *Jane doesn't like blackberries* must be specified for the control expressed by *not*, for depending on the intonation the sequence may not be true of berries other than blackberries; *blackberries* would then carry the major stress in the sentence. Or the negative may indicate that Jane is not really fond of them but tolerates them, and *like* would then have the major stress. Or it may single out Jane from among a set, with major stress on *Jane*, contrasting her with her comrades who do like blackberries. For identifying such precise meanings, logicians have agreed on informal devices, such as expressions like *it is the case that . . . /it is not the case that . . .* but they also use highly formal notation. This kind of formal notation is formulated in Montague grammar, so that intricate analyses such as that concerning scope might be readily specified.

It has long been held that the procedures of modal logic could not be applied in the analysis of natural language, for natural language was assumed to be "illogical," permitting contrasts between linguistic and natural logic in expressions like *the trousers were too short*, where the plural is used of a single garment. This position was challenged by the logician Richard Montague (1930–71). His essays came to the attention of linguists concerned with a completely explicit account of language, including its semantic component. Since it is the primary semantic approach so far applied, "Montague grammar" is now used as a cover term. Students must, however, look toward other semantically centered theories, for not all investigators agree with Montague's Platonic approach.

Yet theories of language centering on the semantic component will no doubt occupy the center of attention for some time in the future. Only in this way can scholars concerned with perception and the functioning of the brain in general deal appropriately with all components of language. Moreover, computer processing has reached the point of functioning in natural language, rather than just in the reduced computer languages like FORTRAN, COBOL, and so on, which were devised to use computers for the manipulation of simpler symbol systems, such as the numerals. The theorists involved in such computer developments, in so-called artificial intelligence and cognitive science, require an analysis of language that will include all three components: the semantic, the syntactic, and the phonological. Accordingly the impetus from other scholars, as well as the linguistic aim of providing a thorough analysis of language, is leading to a position focusing on Montague grammar.

This approach, like generative transformational grammar, centers on *langue*. Now the *signifiant* and the *signifié* are accorded equal treatment, for no syntactic analysis is undertaken without accompanying semantic analysis. In contrast with generative transformational grammar, investigation focuses on the surface strings rather than on deep structures. Yet relationship is viewed as the basis for distinctive elements. And both the syntagmatic and the paradigmatic dimensions are taken into consideration, though only to the extent of the sentence. Like the two previous approaches, synchronic analysis is primary. Although the three approaches so far discussed have formed the central avenues to the study of language during the past four decades, others have been proposed having different aims, in part occasioned by dissatisfaction with restrictions on extent of materials considered by structuralism, generative transformational grammar, and Montague grammar.

VI. Sociolinguistic Approaches

Although the theories discussed to this point have the widest appeal among theoretical linguists, the basis from which they start has also occasioned severe criticism. The most stringently defined basis is that of Chomsky, though it differs little from that of Saussure or subsequent theoreticians. According to Chomsky, "linguistic theory is concerned primarily with an ideal speaker-listener, in a completely homogeneous speech-community" (*Aspects*, p. 3). This basis obviously separates linguistic theory from concern with social problems involving language. And it does not encourage other linguistic concerns, such as typology, historical study, the treatment of extended texts, and consideration of other forms of communication, such as gestures accompanying speech and animal communication. Many linguists are attracted by these topics; they also deal with them in keeping with the criteria for rigor, economy, and accountability proclaimed by linguists ever since the preeminent nineteenth-century theoretician William Dwight Whitney (1827–94). These standards require totally explicit rules in accordance with the generative approach. Of these further activities, linguists concerned with sociolinguistics may have made the most progress in this direction. Two of their procedures, which are central in this activity, will be presented.

One is the application of variable rules. These are parallel to rules for linguistic variants in highly formal grammars, such as the rules specifying a particular variant of the noun plural marker in English: [əz] after sibilants, as in *passes*, [s] after /p t k f θ/ as in *pats*, and [z] elsewhere as in *pads*. But while the controlling element in such rules is within language, the controlling element in sociolinguistic rules has a social basis, such as socioeconomic class, ethnic group, age, and sex. A widely cited example is the use of /r/ in New York City speech in words like *heard*. The social variable here is socioeconomic class: lower-class speakers tend to omit the [r]; middle- and upper-class speakers tend to maintain it. By developing rules that include such variables, sociolinguists can produce grammars with the rigor of linguists who base their rules on "ideal language." The task is also far more complex. Only occasional rules have as yet been produced for any language, leaving ample opportunities for future sociolinguistic research.

Sociolinguists have also observed that language is perceived in accordance with statistical procedures rather than as a fixed system. Thus, when speakers use characteristics like [d] in such words as *this* in a substantial proportion of utterances, their language is regarded as substandard, though virtually all speakers of English use the [d] variant occasionally, even those who are regarded as upper-class speakers. Such observations suggest that variation is a feature of the speaker's competence, not simply of performance. The study of language is therefore vastly more complex than envisaged in the strict theories presented above. Yet the impact of this conclusion has scarcely been felt.

With their attention to linguistic problems in social groups, sociolinguists find many areas of concern. Among these are the use of two or more languages by individuals, in bilingualism; the use of two or more dialects in society, such as black English, the English of Chicanos, and the English of established groups; and the attempts to tailor languages and writing systems for modern nations. Such linguistic problems are closely associated with important social issues, such as the integration of new speakers into long-established societies. Since this issue is well known from the recent history of this country, the similar situation in Europe may be cited where large numbers of "guest-workers" have been imported to the industrial nations; as they are being integrated into their new social setting—whether in Sweden, Germany, France, or elsewhere—some efforts are being made to determine and solve their language problems so that they can function more effectively. Even with modern educational techniques, the development of adequate procedures to overcome such language problems requires a long period of time and more funding than politicians, businesses, and school administrators like to provide.

Nations that are developing national languages include Israel, India, Indonesia, and China. The problems in China are especially complex, because the country is planning to abandon its ancient writing system, which requires extensive schooling, in favor of an alphabetic system that is more readily learned. The alphabetic system, however, must be aligned to one language, a situation that entails the teaching of one of the Chinese languages—Putonghua, formerly called Mandarin—to all citizens of China, including those who use the other mutually unintelligible Chinese languages and speakers of Thai, Korean, Altaic languages, and so on. The planning must make allowance for the great length of time necessary to accomplish these changes, as much as a century. It must also take into consideration attitudes toward language, which are generally deep-seated, as language-based protests in countries like Belgium and India attest. Similar planning will be required for the various new nations that have emerged during recent decades, like those in Africa that propose to select one of their indigenous languages rather than a European language as the national tongue. Sociolinguists, therefore, face a maze of problems that can be solved only in cooperation with practitioners of other disciplines.

Solutions, however, require investigation of the numerous languages in these areas, as well as social attitudes toward the old language, toward the newly selected language, and so on; the introduction of a general language is more effective if instructors know the indigenous languages. Renewed impetus in this way has been given to field work on languages in areas that are inadequately known, such as Australia, New Guinea, Southeast Asia, and Central America. That work in turn leads to scrutiny of languages for their types and for their history, inasmuch as differentiations between dialects and languages of one family have a historical basis.

VII. Typological Linguistics

A typologist classifies entities in accordance with selected characteristics. Such classification—whether of digging implements, habitations, or entities of language—has long been pursued in the human sciences. In the nineteenth century attention was given to the structure of words: languages with little or no inflection, like English and Chinese, were labeled "analytic," and those with considerable inflection, like Greek and Eskimo, were labeled "synthetic." Such classification was elaborated, but it dealt with surface characteristics and accordingly did not provide important insights into language. In time, attention was directed at syntactic structures, which now make up the central typological concern.

Typological study has disclosed two major language types, based on the arrangement of the clause: verb-object (VO) languages, like English and the other European languages, and object-verb (OV) languages, like Turkish and Japanese. Because the study of linguistics has centered in Europe, virtually no attention has been given to OV structures, which are characteristic of approximately half of the known languages. It is now clear that many characteristic language structures are associated with the arrangement of the clause.

In VO languages, for example, relative clauses are placed after the antecedent or head-word; in OV languages they appear before the head-word. Two simple clauses may illustrate the different clause structures of English and Japanese (Japanese marks the subject with postposed *ga* and the object with postposed *o*):

'John saw Hanako.'   Jon ga Hanako o mita.
'Hanako bought the book.'   Hanako ga hon o katta.

When the second sentence is relativized, the contrasting sequences are as follows:

'John saw Hanako, who bought the book.'
Hon o katta Hanako o Jon ga mita.
(or)
Jon ga hon o katta Hanako o mita.

Other nominal modifiers, like possessives and adjectives, occupy the same position with regard to nouns in strict VO and OV languages.

Further characteristic constructions have to do with prepositions and comparatives. While VO languages contain prepositions, OV languages have postpositions; in contrast with English *in Tokyo* Japanese has *Tokyo ni*, where the postposed *ni* is comparable to *ga* and *o* in the sentences above. In comparative constructions English places the standard after the adjective:

John is bigger than Hanako.

Japanese, by contrast, places it before the adjective:

Jon wa Hanako yori ookii.   ('John, Hanako from/than big [is].')

Both patterns observe the same arrangements of governing elements to "objects," as do clauses including a verb and an object.

These and further constructions disclose general observations about language. The two sets of constructions illustrated here involve two of the basic processes of language: modification and government. It is readily obvious even from these few constructions that a language has one principle of government: either the governed element precedes (OV) or it follows (VO). Among other implications, this situation illuminates the rapid acquisition of language by children; once the governing arrangement is clear, many constructions in the language are achieved by the child. The recognition of a central core in clauses also illustrates the basic principle of modification. Modifiers are so placed that they do not disrupt the OV or VO unit. Nominal modifiers are illustrated above. Verbal modifiers, such as interrogatives, might also be exemplified. In OV languages like Japanese, the verbal modifying element (*ka*) follows the verb, just as the nominal modifying element precedes the noun; in English, and more clearly in verb-initial languages, the interrogative element precedes the verb (*did*). The following are examples, based on one of the sentences given above:

'Did John see Hanako?'   Jon ga Hanako o mita ka?

Generalizations like these are being explored in typological study with reference to various constructions and also to their further implications. At the same time further languages are being investigated for their typological structure. The findings have provided a major contribution to the historical investigation of language.

VIII. Historical Linguistics

Of all forms of linguistics, the historical approach developed the most advanced theory in the nineteenth century. Notable findings resulted. Possibly the most brilliant was the assumption (prediction) of Ferdinand de Saussure in a publication of his student days that Proto-Indo-European included sounds for which there were no direct reflexes in any of the dialects (1879). These sounds were identified a half-century later when the recently discovered Hittite was examined.[11] Among other results of historical linguistic research, languages were classified in relation to one another. Yet the theory dealt only with the sounds and morphological elements of language, by no means with the component often held to be central—syntax. The typological observations noted above now make historical syntax possible.

Treatments of the syntax of ancient languages like Latin and Greek, to be sure, were produced in the nineteenth century and later, but these merely described the patterns, without attempting to explain them. As a simple example, Latin grammars recognize comparative constructions like *te maior*, literally 'you-from bigger,' but do not explain either the constructions or their presence as relics. It is now clear that such comparative constructions observe the OV pattern. Like other relics, they provide evidence of the earlier patterns of the language. Because similar OV patterns are found in the other early Indo-European dialects (Hittite, Greek, Sanskrit, even a dialect as late as Old English), one must conclude that Proto-Indo-European was OV in structure, or largely OV. This conclusion clarifies many of the problems in the syntax of the Indo-European family and permits us to grasp the historical development of its syntax as the nineteenth century did its phonology. Thus the arrangement of adjectives before nouns in English is also a relic OV construction. English has not developed as far in VO structure as have French, Spanish, and other Indo-European languages that arrange adjectives after nouns.

In this way, historical theory now allows insights into many syntactic patterns. Among these are absolute constructions, such as the first "clause" of the following sentence:

The fortress having been occupied, he governed the country.

Such absolutes are widely used in Latin, Greek, and Sanskrit but are frowned on in other languages, such as English. Historical linguists have long sought an explanation for them. They were proposed for the parent language, Proto-Indo-European, but they could not be reconstructed because each of these languages employs a different case for the absolute construction: Latin, the ablative; Greek, the genitive; Sanskrit, the locative. Insights gained from typological investigation provide a solution. Absolute constructions are much like relative clauses. These, as noted above, must precede nouns in OV languages and follow them in VO. At times in the history of languages they may, however, have either order. This was true of Classical Latin, Greek, and Sanskrit, as anyone reading Classical texts recognizes. If a language is ambivalent in structure, its speakers have no fixed rules for arrangement of relative clauses. Absolutes then arise, which have no fixed requirement for arrangement with regard to another noun in the larger sentence.[12] Many other syntactic constructions can now be accounted for, on the basis of the new understanding of historical developments.

Historical theory can accordingly be applied now to all components of language, the syntactic and semantic as well as the phonological. Many language families need to be explored, for most historical work has been carried out in the Indo-European family, an area that still has many unsolved problems. Theory must also be extended to features connecting sequences longer than sentences, that is, to features of texts.

IX. Text-Linguistics

In general, linguists view the sentence as the unit of language. Yet many sentences cannot be adequately interpreted outside their context, such as the one cited above: *But he merely frowned, replying that it didn't matter.* The antecedent of the pronoun *he* was presumably given earlier. Moreover, the force of *but* can be only generally determined. Moreover, the adverb *merely* suggests a qualification, which is opaque without further context. Concerned with such problems, some linguists assume texts rather than sentences to be the proper units of analysis, and they are devising strict procedures to deal with them.

Zellig Harris long ago proposed an approach to such analysis, which he named discourse analysis. Today the greater bulk of such work is going on in Europe and the Soviet Union, where it is known as text-linguistics.

Like sociolinguists developing a generative approach, text-linguists have formulated rules, in an attempt to account fully for given texts. Again the task is enormous. One problem is the definition of text. Even units like "sentence" and "word" are difficult to define. "Text" might conceivably be defined as one instance of a literary genre, such as a tale in Boccaccio's *Decameron*. Yet the entire work is itself something of a unit, and therefore a text. Oral sequences, such as conversations, are even more difficult to apportion into texts. No satisfactory solution to this problem has been provided.

A text-linguist may, however, choose to put off providing a principled answer, in the meantime identifying texts by arbitrary criteria; further questions then have to do with the characteristic constituents of texts. Sentences, the units of linguistics proper, have long been identified by characteristics of arrangement, selection, sandhi, and intonation. Seeking their own characteristic constituents, text-linguists assume coherence in texts brought about by such constituents as "the set of descriptions of objects referred to in the text," "the set of thematic units," "the net of time reference," and so on.[13] In effect, many linguists pursuing this approach devote their attention to such matters as the use and sequence of tenses, the placement of relatively free elements such as adverbs, the use of particles, and other characteristics that serve to relate sentences in texts, among them substitutes and ellipses.

Such characteristics are among the linguistic features that have been investigated in stylistic and literary study and in the ancient discipline, rhetoric. These activities distinguish among text genres, identifying each genre's distinctive features. They differ, however, from text-linguistics in not attempting to be generative. In other words, they do not seek to produce a formal model for texts by which a text is explicitly specified by rules. Yet text-linguists build on literary studies of the past, notably Vladimir Propp's study of the folk tale. One of their goals is to develop a theory that will permit them to account for all the properties of a text, not merely its distinctive structure but also its relationship to the outside world and to speaker-hearers—that is, its meaning and its position in a social situation. These requirements bring text-linguists into the sphere of semiotics, which has even broader aims.

X. Semiotics

While the theories discussed thus far are confined to human communication, semiotics embraces the use of signs in general. Study of bird-song and other devices used by animals to communicate makes up a part of its concern. So also do nonverbal communication systems of human beings, such as gestures, clothing, furniture, types of habitation, and other expressions of inner life. The scope of semiotics is accordingly vast. As noted above, Saussure advocated the inclusion of language study in such a general science. He was preceded in proposing a semiotic science by the American philosopher Charles Sanders Peirce (1839–1914), who is now recognized as its founder.

According to Peirce, semiotics involves the study of signs and of the behavior accompanying their use. To explain the phenomena, he proposed three subdivisions: (1) syntactics, the study of signs and their interrelationships; (2) semantics, the relationships of signs to the outside world (roughly, their meaning); and (3) pragmatics, the relationships between signs and their users. If one includes within pragmatics value systems, then semiotics is the fundamental discipline of the humanities. Any literary work, for example, results from an attempt to communicate, which is singled out from other communication because speaker-hearers attach a high value to it. Accordingly literary criticism, and sociology, economics, political science, and other disciplines concerned with the nonbiological and nonphysical aspects of the universe are embraced in semiotics. For such a science to attain credibility, a notation filling a role similar to that of mathematics for the physical sciences must be available. Hopeful scholars are counting on symbolic logic to meet this need.

In the meantime semioticians discuss various situations: the different songs of sparrows on the coastal plains of Argentina and at higher elevations; the relative positions of speakers as they converse; the sign languages used by the deaf. These studies are of more than just specialized interest: the discovery of dialects among some species of birds contributes to insights into the formation of human dialects; posture, gestures, and so on are conventional, like human language; sign language may disclose more clearly than oral language the functioning of the mind in communication, for the symbols are held to be more direct than are those of speech. Moreover literary scholars seem to derive stimulation from the explorations of semioticians. Yet the general vagueness and weakness of theory suggest the exploratory stance of an incipient activity, if the broadest in sphere of those undertaken for the understanding of language.

XI. Selected Linguistic Activities

Although theory has been the most prominent concern in linguistics, as the pages of leading linguistic journals like *Language* attest, linguists are engaged in many practical activities. Among these are language teaching, lexicography, applications to social and psychological problems, study and elucidation of literary texts and of languages of the past. Some of these activities have been touched on above; specific examples are given here.

Most introductory teaching of the less common languages as well as the teaching of English to speakers of other languages (TESOL) has been in the hands of linguists. These concerns continue the pattern established at the beginning of World War II, when only the major languages of Western Europe—French, German, Spanish—were widely taught in American universities and, less widely, in high schools. Suitable textbooks as well as teachers for other languages were nonexistent. Suddenly a large number of languages became essential for military, diplomatic, and intelligence purposes: Chinese, Japanese, Arabic, and many others. The concern for data at the time had accustomed linguists to learning new languages and writing descriptions of them. In an effort coordinated by the American Council of Learned Societies, linguists applied their skills to describing and teaching these languages; Bloomfield himself participated in the preparation of both the

Dutch and Russian handbooks. Many of the texts were subsequently published by a commercial publisher. When the teaching of these languages was introduced into universities after the war and even more dramatically after sputnik, linguists generally took charge of the programs. They have continued to play a large role in the huge expansion of programs for teaching English as a second language, first as English came to be widely taught throughout the world and later as increasing numbers of foreign students came to this country for training. Other situations have maintained the demand, as when large numbers of Vietnamese came to this country. They have learned their new language and culture in large part through texts prepared by linguists, now coordinated by the Center for Applied Linguistics.

Such activities attract linguists in part because they provide possibilities of acquiring new data. Many linguists with such concerns are attached to the Summer Institute of Linguistics. Having undertaken to translate the Bible into every known language, these linguists provide grammars, dictionaries, and texts from unknown or poorly known languages in all parts of the world. In this work they follow a theory developed largely by Kenneth L. Pike (1912–). Since involvement with such languages demands attention to patterns of culture and to social needs, members of this group concern themselves with the development of writing systems, problems of literacy, and the presentation of the most-valued texts of one culture to a different culture. These activities have directed attention to translation and to lexical systems that often fail to mesh with other lexical systems like our own. In a series of publications Eugene A. Nida (1914–) gives many examples based on deep acquaintance with translation resulting from his work with the American Bible Society. A densely packed bibliography of fifty-six pages in his *Toward a Science of Translating* gives evidence of linguists' participation in this growing field. Their efforts are directed primarily at techniques and tools, such as the preparation of dictionaries.

Lengthy undertakings with little glory for the participants, as Samuel Johnson eloquently noted, dictionaries are compiled quietly, usually at established centers. Fascicles of the *Middle English Dictionary* continue to appear from the University of Michigan under the editorship of Sherman Kuhn (1907–), as do volumes of the *Akkadian Dictionary* from the University of Chicago. Another large project is the *Dictionary of American Regional English*, which after long sponsorship by the American Dialect Society was crystallized at the University of Wisconsin under the editorship of Frederic R. Cassidy (1907–) and is soon to begin publication. The work parallels that of many linguists on geographical dialects of American English.

Planned by the Linguistic Society of America, an American dialect atlas was inaugurated in 1930 under the direction of Hans Kurath (1891–). Collection and publication under the original design covered no more than New England. Subsequently linguists have continued to investigate the dialects of other regions of the country from bases at various universities. For many of these regions ample collections now exist; they will most likely continue to be available largely in files rather than in the earlier large and costly volumes of the American dialect atlas.

A notable feature of this atlas was its concern for social as well as geographical variants. Attention to social varieties of language increased greatly as minorities achieved higher economic status and as schools were integrated. Most of the teachers were at a loss in dealing with forms of English regarded as substandard. Linguists took on the investigation of these forms, at the same time combatting views on supposed language deficits, which by some were also linked to mental inferiority. After more than a decade of such investigations and many discussions with teachers and teacher groups, elementary schools are finally beginning to recognize the existence of such varieties of language. In the fall of 1979 one elementary school in Ann Arbor, Michigan, acknowledged black English, not teaching it but noting that it is a distinct form of English that must be recognized by teachers. Further linguistic investigations are continuing as school systems expand their concern with bilingualism, often through legal requirement. Many of these investigations are directed at forms of Spanish spoken in this country and at the English of such Spanish speakers. As a result of their work on these problems, linguists have begun to play larger roles in positions outside the academic world.

Linguists have taken on similar responsibilities in applications of psycholinguistics, such as the treatment of problems in language learning and in aphasia and other speech disabilities. These problems offer many opportunities for research, since they are poorly understood, as the vague term "dyslexia" indicates. But involvement in this work is increasing slowly, in part because linguists have been accustomed to act from positions in the academic world, in part because of the deep-seated assumption that attention to language does not require a scientific specialist—probably because the exercise of language is regarded as an art rather than a form of behavior.

This attitude is also prominent among literary students, for many of whom linguistics is not worth consulting in their efforts to understand literature. Linguists by and large have not made their way into departments of English and of the European languages, even for the teaching of composition or rhetoric. Yet some linguists, such as Roman Jakobson and Archibald A. Hill, have gained attention through literary study. For the most part, however, literary analysis is carried on with little participation by linguists. Linguists may have made more headway in the study of metrics, though this field is largely in the hands of specialists. The study of Greek and Latin, and of other ancient languages undertaken chiefly for cultural and scholarly purposes, has not been highly receptive to linguists; in this area the linguists may be to blame, for they have frequently not mastered the tremendous body of descriptive material assembled in the past.

Like scientists in general, linguists are attracted primarily by fields that offer problems. A final example may be the language of the deaf, SIGN, as it is now widely known. The study of SIGN has attracted considerable attention because it is a language unencumbered by the articulatory organs. Gestures may have a more intimate relationship between events in the outside world than do conventional vocal signals. Investigations of SIGN provide some of the perspective that one obtains by mastering a new literature or a different culture. It has been noted above, for example, that languages generally place the subject before the verb and almost always before the object; most languages are SOV and SVO, with VSO languages far behind in frequency. In sign languages, however, it seems to be useful to make the object known first, then the subject, and finally the verbal activity relating them. Yet, although this may be the natural order, sign languages have been strongly influenced by the languages surrounding them; American sign, for example, has come to observe an SVO order, for many of its users are not profoundly or congenitally deaf and use the order of their spoken language for the sign system. Such investigations are still highly preliminary, as are also any applications.

Linguistics is finding new areas of concern, many of which will require hard work and dedication before they are recognized as useful fields of inquiry and application. A simple example is the production of tests. These have largely been constructed without any regard for the language in which they are presented. Tests to "measure" intelligence and even manual skills, then, have rated their takers by their mastery of language rather than mastery of the capability supposedly measured. It has been difficult to persuade the producers of such tests that the tests are biased, as controversies regarding IQ tests demonstrate. A more complex example is the use of machine translation. A purely engineering task, which requires minute analysis of language far beyond that in grammars and dictionaries of the past, machine translation was undertaken in part because computer specialists regarded it as a scientific problem. The resulting activity has been severely criticized, on the grounds that undue sums of money were expended. Compared with other scientific undertakings of similar difficulty, machine translation research has received very little funding. Scholars in the intellectual milieu from which linguistics developed are so accustomed to pursuing problems without mechanical equipment that the attempt to employ such equipment for the manipulation of language seems to strain unduly resources that are presumed to be available.

Since oral communication is the basis of social interaction, whether in practical, commercial, recreational, artistic, or literary matters, linguistics will continue to be central in academic and research activities. Recognition of its possible roles, however, may continue to require time.

XII. Conclusion

Linguistics, then, is by no means monolithic today. It includes a diversity of theories based on the sphere of data embraced, on the philosophical positions of its proponents, and on their aims. It also involves applications, some of which have been noted above. Its contributions can best be determined by those involved with language or communication for purposes other than theoretical clarification. Literary scholars, for example, may well look to linguists for an understanding of language, but they will not find evaluations of the patterns that distinguish eminent forms of language known as literature. Language teachers must also know the patterning of sounds, sentences, and semantic sets of the native languages of their students, as well as the language to be taught, but they will have to determine their teaching methods on other than purely linguistic grounds. Moreover, since language provides the means for virtually all human communication and education, all citizens may well wish to understand the mechanism through which they inform themselves and others, but a linguist cannot determine for them whether they should support general bilingualism, spelling reform, or other applications of linguistic findings that may seem to benefit society. Linguists are in various degrees concerned with applications and the impact of their work, but their primary aim is the understanding of language.

Notes

1 See Holger Pedersen, *Linguistic Science in the Nineteenth Century*, trans. John W. Spargo (1931); rpt. *The Discovery of Language* (Bloomington: Indiana Univ. Press, 1962).

2 Ferdinand de Saussure, *Course in General Linguistics*, trans. Wade Baskin, rev. ed. (London: Owen, 1974), p. 6, hereafter cited as *Course*.

3 George Lyman Kittredge and Frank E. Farley, *An Advanced English Grammar* (1913; rpt. Folcroft, Pa.: Folcroft, 1973), pp. 3–4.

4 Leonard Bloomfield, *Language* (New York: Holt, 1933), p. 202.

5 Leonard Bloomfield, *Linguistic Aspects of Science*, International Encyclopedia of Unified Science, Vol. I, No. 4 (Chicago: Univ. of Chicago Press, 1939), p. 13.

6 See Robert A. Hall, Jr., *Linguistics and Your Language* (Garden City, N. Y.: Anchor-Doubleday, 1960).

7 Zellig Harris, "Discourse Analysis," *Language*, 28 (1952), 19.

8 See Noam Chomsky, *Aspects of the Theory of Syntax* (Cambridge, Mass.: MIT Press, 1965), hereafter cited as *Aspects*.

9 Emmon Bach, rev. art. of *On Raising*, by Paul Postal, *Language*, 53 (1977), 621–54.

10 Claude Lévi-Strauss, *The Savage Mind* (Chicago: Univ. of Chicago Press, 1966), p. 89.

11 See Jerzy Kurylowicz, "ə indoeuropéen et ḫ hittite," *Symbolae Grammaticae*, 1 (1927), 95–104.

12 See Winfred P. Lehmann, "Contemporary Linguistics and Indo-European Studies," *PMLA*, 87 (1972), 976–93.

13 See Wolfgang U. Dressler, ed., *Current Trends in Textlinguistics* (Berlin: de Gruyter, 1978), p. 13.

Selected Bibliography

Bach, Emmon. Rev. art. of *On Raising*, by Paul Postal. *Language*, 53 (1977), 621–54.

Bloomfield, Leonard. *Language*. New York: Holt, 1933.

———. *Linguistic Aspects of Science*. International Encyclopedia of Unified Science, Vol. I, No. 4. Chicago: Univ. of Chicago Press, 1939.

Chomsky, Noam. *Syntactic Structures*. The Hague: Mouton, 1957.

———. *Aspects of the Theory of Syntax*. Cambridge, Mass.: MIT Press, 1965.

———. *Language and Mind*. New York: Harcourt, 1972.

Dressler, Wolfgang U., ed. *Current Trends in Textlinguistics*. Berlin: de Gruyter, 1978.

Hall, Robert A., Jr. *Linguistics and Your Language*. Garden City, N. Y.: Anchor-Doubleday, 1960. (Rev. ed. of *Leave Your Language Alone*. Ithaca, N. Y.: Linguistica, 1950.)

Harris, Zellig. *Structural Linguistics*. Chicago: Univ. of Chicago Press, 1951.

———. "Discourse Analysis." *Language*, 28 (1952), 1–30.

Hill, Archibald A. *Introduction to Linguistic Structures*. New York: Harcourt, 1958.

Jakobson, Roman. *Selected Writings*. 2nd ed. Vol. I: Phonological Studies. The Hague: Mouton, 1971.

Kittredge, George Lyman, and Frank E. Farley. *An Advanced English Grammar*. 1913; rpt. Folcroft, Pa.: Folcroft, 1973.

Kurath, Hans. *Handbook of the Linguistic Geography of New England.* 2nd ed. New York: AMS Press, 1973.

——, ed. *Linguistic Atlas of New England.* Providence: Brown Univ. Press, 1939–43.

Labov, William. *Sociolinguistic Patterns.* Philadelphia: Univ. of Pennsylvania Press, 1972.

Lehmann, Winfred P., ed. *A Reader in Nineteenth-Century Historical Indo-European Linguistics.* Bloomington: Indiana Univ. Press, 1967.

——, ed. *Syntactic Typology.* Austin: Univ. of Texas Press, 1978.

Montague, Richard. *Formal Philosophy.* Ed. Richmond H. Thomason. New Haven: Yale Univ. Press, 1974.

Nida, Eugene A. *Towards a Science of Translating.* Leiden: Brill, 1964.

Paul, Hermann. *Prinzipien der Sprachgeschichte.* 5th ed. Halle: Niemeyer, 1920. (*Principles of the History of Language.* Trans. of 2nd ed. [1886] by H. A. Strong. London: Longmans, Green, 1891.)

Pedersen, Holger. *Linguistic Science in the Nineteenth Century.* Trans. John W. Spargo. 1931; rpt. *The Discovery of Language.* Bloomington: Indiana Univ. Press, 1962.

Peirce, Charles Sanders. *Collected Papers.* Ed. Charles Hartshorne, Paul Weiss, and Arthur W. Burks. 8 vols. Cambridge, Mass.: Harvard Univ. Press, 1931–58.

Pike, Kenneth L., and Evelyn G. Pike. *Grammatical Analysis.* Dallas, Tex.: Summer Institute of Linguistics, 1977.

Postal, Paul. *On Raising.* Cambridge, Mass.: MIT Press, 1974.

Propp, Vladimir. *Morphology of the Folktale.* Trans. Laurence Scott. Ed. Louis A. Wagner. 2nd ed. Austin: Univ. of Texas Press, 1968.

Sapir, Edward. *Language.* New York: Harcourt, 1921.

Saussure, Ferdinand de. *Mémoire sur le système primitif des voyelles dans les langues indo-européennes.* Paris: Vieweg, 1879.

——. *Cours de linguistique générale.* Ed. Charles Bally and Albert Sechehaye, with Albert Riedlinger. 2nd ed. Paris: Payot, 1922. (*Course in General Linguistics.* Trans. Wade Baskin. 2nd ed. London: Owen, 1974.)

Trubetzkoy, N. S. *Grundzüge der Phonologie.* Travaux du Cercle Linguistique de Prague, 7. Prague: Cercle Linguistique de Prague, 1939. (*Principles of Phonology.* Trans. Christiane A. M. Baltaxe. Berkeley: Univ. of California Press, 1969.)

von Humboldt, Wilhelm. *Über die Verschiedenheit des menschlichen Sprachbaues und ihren Einfluss auf die geistige Entwickelung des Menschengeschlechts.* 1836; rpt. Bonn: Dümmler, 1968.

Whitney, William Dwight. *Language and the Study of Language.* 6th ed. 1901; rpt. New York: AMS Press, 1971.

Textual Scholarship

G. Thomas Tanselle

That the establishment of texts is a basic task of scholarship has long been recognized, at least for certain classes of material. One of the central preoccupations of the Renaissance humanists was the production of accurate texts of Greek and Roman authors, and the tradition of scholarly attention directed to textual problems in classical and biblical writings has continued to the present. There has also been a general recognition of the need for editorial work on certain more recent authors, such as Shakespeare, whose writings, intended for the stage, reached print through various—and not equally trustworthy—routes. It should be clear, however, that all texts, regardless of when or how they were produced, may contain errors and that they all require the services of scholarly research aimed at discovering those errors. No text, in other words, whether it is in an author's own manuscript or a printed edition proofread by the author, can be assumed to be free of textual error; all texts must be approached in the same critical and inquiring spirit that scholars are accustomed to employ in dealing with other kinds of data. The reason for the widespread corruption of texts is the obvious but profoundly important fact that authors, in making public what is in their minds, must utilize various means of physical transmission that lend themselves to mechanical errors and to the intervention of the opinions of others. Authors may slip when putting their own words on paper, whether they are using a pen or a typewriter; their copyists or typists may make further mistakes in transcription (or may make intentional alterations, on the sometimes mistaken assumption that they are correcting errors); and publishing-house editors and printing-house compositors may be responsible for additional changes, both inadvertent and intended. The points at which textual corruption can enter are legion. Errors and nonauthorial revisions made at one stage are not necessarily caught at the next; indeed, corruption is generally cumulative as the process of transmission continues, with texts becoming increasingly divergent from the original the more steps they are removed from it.

If one wishes to know what a writer intended to say, therefore, one cannot simply accept any text that is convenient to hand but must take some pains to investigate the textual history of the work. Although the branch of scholarship that specializes in this activity has had a long history, it is fair to say that only since the middle of this century has the editing of post-Renaissance writing occupied the interests of a sizable number of scholars or been the subject of vigorous methodological debate among literary scholars in general. The major organized effort that got under way in the 1960s to edit certain central nineteenth-century American authors, and the accompanying establishment of the Modern Language Association's Center for Editions of American Authors (CEAA)—later, with increased scope, the Center for Scholarly Editions (CSE)—have served to focus unprecedented, and much needed, attention on editorial matters. The discussion and disagreement that the CEAA editions have aroused, though not always well informed, have been salutary in causing more people than before, both inside and outside the scholarly profession, to give some thought to fundamental textual issues. Yet there are still many experienced scholars who, though scrupulous in other respects, do not question the accuracy of the texts they quote in their writings or assign in their classrooms. And there are others to whom the question occurs but who do not regard it as a matter of sufficient urgency to induce them to become informed on the subject. Not everyone, of course, wishes to become a specialist in textual matters, and, as A. E. Housman observed some sixty years ago, "Not to be a textual critic is no reproach to anyone." But one can legitimately expect scholars—who must perforce utilize texts—to be sufficiently acquainted with textual scholarship to enable them to ask the proper questions about the editions and texts from which their insights derive.

I. Editing and Scholarship

Textual scholarship, like most other kinds of scholarship, is historically oriented: it is concerned with establishing what particular writers intended to have in the texts of their writings at particular times. When scholars speak of textual "corruption," they are referring to readings not intended by the author of the text. Whether or not those readings are corruptions from an aesthetic point of view is an entirely separate question. Obviously, when authors revise their work, they do not necessarily improve it, but scholars must have as their goal the establishment of what the authors preferred, not what each scholar personally considers superior. It is important to understand at the outset the distinction between editing as a scholarly activity and editing that is aesthetic, rather than historical, in its orientation. Editors in publishing firms, for instance, attempt to "improve" the manuscripts that come to them, according to some aesthetic principle: fidelity to every detail of the author's wording and punctuation is not a primary consideration. In such "creative" editing, editors become to some extent collaborators with the authors; and scholarly editors thus sometimes find themselves engaged in undoing the work of creative editors who have gone before.

The texts that result from scholarly editing may of course be analyzed by literary critics of varying persuasions; not all critics, however, are careful to choose scholarly texts to work with, though few would be willing to say that the authors' textual intentions are irrelevant to their purpose. When the so-called New Criticism was the dominant approach to literary analysis, some students were puzzled by the existence within their departments of scholars who went to great lengths to establish the texts intended by various authors, at the same time that other members of those departments sought to avoid an "intentional fallacy" in their interpretation of texts. Although it is true that some New Critics did not inquire closely into questions of textual authority, few went so far as to claim that a text should be entirely disembodied from all historical context. Yet these are the logical alternatives: either to analyze a text as the product of a particular time, place, and person—in which case one needs to have the text in precisely the form its author intended—or else to analyze it purely as an aesthetic object—in which case its fidelity to what a given writer said at a specific time is irrelevant (indeed, "corruptions" would be desirable if they produced a more satisfying aesthetic whole). As it turns out, most discussions of literature (certainly most of those conducted in the academic world) have some historical perspective and therefore cannot responsibly avoid a concern for the authenticity of the text. But one must recognize that the historical approach to editing is not the only legitimate one and that another kind of editing, which aims at bringing texts into conformity with a particular aesthetic standard rather than with the authors' intentions, is conceivable—and is, indeed, routine—for certain purposes.

Without a firm grasp of this distinction between scholarly and creative editing, clear thinking about textual matters is not possible. One example of the muddle that can result is provided by a passage in Félix Boillot's *The Methodical Study of Literature* (Paris, 1924). A present-day textual scholar will smile upon seeing the table of contents of Boillot's work, in which the title of the first section of the second chapter, "Establishing the text," is followed by the words, "Rarely needed." But the book is an exposition of the French method of *explication de texte*, particularly as a system for use in the classroom, and one may in fact wonder why Boillot conceded that research to establish the text was ever needed. In this chapter he says, "For literature lectures proper, the best available edition is generally used and that is quite sufficient" (p. 31); the emphasis, in other words, is on the exercise of explication, and a text suffices for that purpose even if it is not the product of careful textual research. His next sentence, however, follows oddly: "Besides, most authors of recent date have carefully supervised the publication of their own works and thus saved the scholar unnecessary labour." Aside from the erroneous assumption that most modern works do not require scholarly editing, what strikes one about this statement is its implication that the author's intention is significant after all. The two statements together betray a confusion about the relationship of editing to criticism: if a text that conforms to its author's intention is desired, then one cannot simply accept "the best available edition" as sufficient (whatever "best" means in this case); on the other hand, if all that is required is an object upon which to practice explication, the question whether the author "supervised the publication" is beside the point. Boillot's work may be outdated but is worth noticing because its confused views regarding textual study are similar to those still expressed by many people.

It should be clear that any scholarly or historical study of a piece of writing must involve a consideration of what the most authoritative text ought to consist of. It should be equally clear that, whenever two or more pieces of writing are taken up together because they are by the same author or from the same period, a historical consideration has been introduced; from that point on, the texts utilized must conform to the author's intentions, even when the aims of the inquiry are entirely explicatory. Thus for most purposes of literary criticism, an accurate text is essential; but the accuracy of a text, like that of any other historical fact, cannot be taken for granted and can be established—within the limits set by the extant evidence—only through research. All serious readers, whether of writings normally considered "literary" or of any other kind of writing, therefore need to have before them authoritative texts. Textual scholarship is often associated with literary study because its greatest advances have been made by those whose immediate concerns were the study of literary works (including classical and biblical texts). But it is a fallacy to think that the close study of literature demands a level of textual accuracy that is unnecessary in other fields: the line between "literature" and other writing, after all, is not a precise one, and scholars in all fields must know as exactly as possible what any text they consult was meant to contain, for nuances of expression, sometimes turning only on punctuation, are significant whether or not a piece is belletristic. (In diplomacy and law, for instance, the punctuation of texts may be of crucial importance.) Textual study is obviously a field with boundaries that extend beyond those of literary scholarship: its boundaries overlap those of any field that involves the written, printed, or recorded word. It is certainly one branch of literary scholarship; but what is said about it in that connection applies to scientific, political, philosophic, religious, and legal writings as surely as it does to the work of poets, essayists, dramatists, and novelists.

II. Approaches to Editing

The published results of textual scholarship can take various forms, such as articles or notes (or even footnotes) that comment on the textual history of particular works or that suggest emendations to be made in specific texts or editions. But the goal toward which such publications are directed is the production of dependable scholarly editions, containing accurate texts supplemented by editorial commentary or apparatus documenting those texts. Although editions exist in great variety, each of them falls into one of two large categories. An edition is either a *noncritical edition*, which aims at reproducing a given earlier text as exactly as possible, or a *critical edition*, which contains a text resulting from the editor's informed judgment at points where questionable readings occur—a text that may therefore incorporate readings drawn from various other texts or supplied by the editor. One often hears editions referred to in terms that suggest the audience for which they were prepared, such as "classroom editions" or "editions for the general reader." There is no doubt that some of the contents of editions may vary according to the intended audience, but if the heart of an edition—indeed, the purpose of its existence—is the text it contains, the primary classification must be the division between editions containing unaltered texts and those containing texts that incorporate editorial emendations. All too frequently in the past when scholars or critics have supplied introductions to texts intended for classroom use, and perhaps offered some explanatory or historical annotation as well, they have been billed on title pages and in advertising as the "editors" of those texts, when in fact they may have given no attention to questions of textual accuracy, and the texts may have been selected by the publishers as those most convenient and economical to reproduce. Such usage blurs the distinction between "edition" and "text": these so-called editors have assembled certain materials for an edition and perhaps have seen it through the press, but they may have given little or no attention to the text it is to contain. This practice is declining as awareness of textual matters is becoming more widespread, but there is still too little general understanding, even in the academic community, of the need for textual work. An edition is the totality of a publication that contains a text as its centerpiece but that may contain many other materials in addition to the text. Some such editions may be extremely useful and may be the products of careful scholarship, but they do not always involve textual scholarship. Of course, rather than establish a new text, scholars may wish to use an already established authoritative text if they are satisfied with the textual scholarship that led to it. But to do that they must investigate the textual situation and come to a rational decision about it; what is irresponsible is to prepare an edition, regardless of the audience it is intended for, without giving serious attention to what should be the central concern of the whole enterprise, the text itself. The question of appropriate editions for different audiences deserves to be considered, but the first order of business is to understand the kinds of edited texts that can be prepared.

Furthermore, just as there are two fundamental kinds of edited texts, critical and noncritical, there are also two types of material to be edited: that intended by its author for publication and that not intended for publication. It would be a mistake to make a simple equation between these two types of material and the two kinds of texts finally produced, but it is a necessary preliminary to editorial thinking to recognize the existence of these two categories of material. Writings such as letters, journals, and notebooks are generally not written with publication in mind; they are designed to serve private purposes and therefore need not conform to the public conventions normally imposed on writings that are meant to be published. These private writings can be as eccentric as the writer wishes, the only restriction on that freedom being the specific purpose the document is intended to serve: if, for instance, a letter is meant to be comprehended by its recipient, it must follow certain mutually understood conventions (though they do not, of course, have to be the ones expected by the public at large). When private documents, because of their intrinsic interest or the significance of their creator, are judged by a scholarly editor to be deserving of publication, their essential nature is not altered: they are still documents not intended for publication, and a scholarly editor has no right to guess what the author would have done if faced with the prospect of publishing them. Indeed, this speculation would be beside the point, for the purpose of publishing such documents is to make available as much as possible of the evidence that they preserve. One can argue, therefore, that false starts, cancellations, insertions, and slips of the pen are important characteristics of these documents and that an editor who eliminates such features is altering the nature of the document and is obscuring evidence of potential significance for interpreting the author's state of mind and motivation. There is a good argument, in other words, for resisting the urge to smooth out the texts of such writings in order to give them the appearance that published writings usually have.

The situation is different, however, for writings of the kind normally intended for publication—works such as novels, poems, plays, essays, and treatises. For works of this sort, the author's intention is not necessarily fulfilled—is not, in fact, likely to be fulfilled—by the reproduction of one particular document. A given manuscript or printed edition may contain slips and blunders as well as readings altered in the publishing house or subsequently revised by the author. Each of these documents is of historical interest, and each might be worth reproducing for that historical interest alone. But works intended for publication demand something more: the raggedness that is characteristic of the texts of private papers is alien to the nature of works intended for publication, and an author's intentions with respect to such works are normally best fulfilled by a single text constructed so as to eliminate nonauthorial and superseded readings. Individual drafts or editions may be edited as historical documents, but a piece of literature (that is, any work, on whatever subject, intended for a public audience) is not being given its intended form until the evidence present in those documents (and in any other relevant material) is utilized to produce a single new text. One must keep in mind the distinction between the text of a *work*—an abstraction that may not have received a satisfactory embodiment in any one physical document—and the text of a *document*, which stands on its own as a historical fact and is by definition whatever appears in that particular document.

Noncritical Editions

These considerations understood, one is prepared to examine somewhat more closely the two kinds of editions. A noncritical edition—or, more precisely, an edition with a noncritical text—serves essentially the function of making the text of a particular document (manuscript or printed) more widely available. (Some editions of this kind are also called "diplomatic," in reference to the branch of paleography known as diplomatics, which deals with the transcription of handwritten official documents or diplomas.) The text of such an edition does not incorporate emendations based on the editor's critical judgment; instead the edition reproduces for greater accessibility the text of a document that is either unique (as a manuscript is) or relatively difficult to come by (as many printed texts are). That text (words and punctuation) must of course be reproduced exactly, but the physical features of the original document will come through in varying degrees of fidelity according to the method chosen. Since no substitute can duplicate an original in every physical detail, some compromise is inevitable, but obviously the least compromise is involved when the reproduction is photographic (or xerographic or reprographic in some form). For manuscript material, this kind of reproduction has the advantage of showing many potentially significant details (such as the formation of the letters, the relative precision or carelessness of the hand at different points, or the exact form of ambiguous punctuation marks) that cannot be rendered in print. It has the disadvantage of not giving the reader the benefit of the editor's experience in deciphering the hand—unless, of course, a transcription accompanies the photographic reproduction. Such a combination is probably the ideal way of presenting the text of a manuscript but is not always economically feasible. One should recognize, in any case, that the transcribing of a manuscript (whether printed with or without an accompanying photograph) is not a mere mechanical activity; even though it is noncritical in the sense that it does not involve emendation, editorial judgment is nevertheless called upon throughout. Manuscripts are more likely to be difficult to read than to be perfectly clear and straightforward, and informed judgment is required to determine just what actually does appear on the page. Sometimes, for instance, unless one is thoroughly familiar with the writer's hand and habits of expression, it is difficult to know which of two words a given group of letters is intended to be; it is similarly hard at times to decide whether a word with an insufficient number of humps is actually a misspelled word (to be transcribed as such) or a hastily scrawled representation of the correctly spelled word (to be transcribed in its correct form). Such problems at once illustrate the kind of evidence that a transcription conceals as well as the scholarly contribution that a careful transcription makes. Even if the document is a scribal copy rather than an original in the hand of the author, the goal is still to preserve whatever evidence the document provides. In preparing a transcription—a noncritical text—the knowledge and experience of the editor are brought to bear not on correcting the text of the document but on determining what in fact that text consists of.

The situation is somewhat different when the document is printed or typewritten, though the editorial aims of course remain the same. (Obviously there is also an intermediate category in which printed or typewritten documents contain handwritten alterations.) In these cases the individual letters and marks of punctuation are normally unambiguous, and little loss of evidence occurs when such texts are newly typeset or typewritten, utilizing the same or different typeface designs. For this reason various methods have been employed over the years in noncritical editions of these texts. Sometimes editors prepare "type facsimiles," in which an effort is made to provide a new typesetting that corresponds as closely as possible to the original in physical details as well as in text: the type designs and sizes, the spacing, the lineation, and so on are matched as nearly as can be (the series of Malone Society Reprints edited by W. W. Greg is an example). Less expensive and tedious to produce are "diplomatic reprints," in which no attempt is made to follow the physical details of the original: the text (words and punctuation) is reproduced exactly, but not necessarily with the same typefaces, lineation, and the like (as in Edward Arber's series of English Reprints). Both these methods naturally involve the possibility that typographical errors may be introduced into the text in the process of resetting and not be caught in proofreading; a preferable approach, and the one that necessitates the least sacrifice of evidence, is of course the use of photographic or xerographic reproduction. Facsimiles using photographic processes have long been available (such as the collotype Shakespeare Quarto Facsimiles prepared by W. W. Greg and later by Charlton Hinman). And as the range of such processes has increased and the relative cost of some of them has decreased, there has been progressively less reason for employing any other approach. The proliferation in recent years of photographic facsimiles of books—indeed, the emergence of firms specializing in such materials—has made this form of publication a familiar one to practically all students and has had a profound impact on the logistics of scholarly research.

One must be aware, however, that photographs of texts do not automatically guarantee accuracy. All photographic reproductions (whether of manuscripts or printed texts) need to be carefully collated, before publication, with the originals, to make sure that all the letters and punctuation visible in the original are visible in the reproduction and that no additional marks—especially those that could be interpreted as part of the text—have somehow found their way into the photograph. (In this process one will also observe any marks that may be more puzzling in the photograph than they are in the original—as when ink shows through from the other side of the paper—so that they can be explained in notes.) Another difficulty that must be borne in mind is that, whereas a manuscript is by its nature unique, a printed book is likely to exist in more than a single copy; therefore textual variation may occur among those copies, as a result of such events as stop-press alteration or type wear during the course of printing, the insertion of cancel leaves or gatherings after printing, or alteration made between impressions of an edition. All copies are of course historical artifacts, and any one of them could serve as the basis for reproduction. But since some of the surviving copies may be defective or may contain readings superseded by readings in other copies, there are likely to be certain copies more desirable for reproduction than others. A scholarly editor will wish to locate as desirable a copy as possible to reproduce, and the process will entail some investigation into the printing history of the book. It may even turn out that no single surviving copy would be as satisfactory as what could be obtained by photographing different pages from different copies. The classic instance of this approach is Charlton Hinman's Norton Facsimile of the Shakespeare First Folio, based on his analysis of eighty copies and incorporating all known revised states of individual pages by including photographs from thirty different copies. His edition is still noncritical, in the sense that it consists of photographic reproductions of the pages of the 1623 edition and does not make any alterations in the text found in those pages, but the choice of copies from which to draw particular pages required careful judgment, based on extensive research and knowledge.

Noncritical editions thus entail thought and decision, even though textual emendation is not considered in them. Two other points about noncritical editions are worth emphasizing. One is that, however much or little material is provided to accompany the text, a precise identification of the document from which the text comes is essential. When the document is a printed book, the specific copy must be identified (and when certain pages come from different copies, those must be specified). A second point is that while noncritical editions are particularly suited to writings not intended for publication, individual texts of writings intended for publication obviously may be handled in this way also. Noncritical editions of the texts of early drafts or other manuscripts of a novel, for instance, or of particular printed editions, can serve to make available documents of historical or literary importance. The editor preparing such editions, however, is concerned with presenting not a literary *work* but discrete stages in its history.

Critical Editions

Whereas noncritical editions aim at preserving the texts of particular documents, critical editions aim at constructing, by means of the editor's critical judgment, texts that come closer to attaining some desired standard than any of the surviving documentary texts happen to do. Defining the standard to be followed is therefore crucial. Of the various directions that editorial intervention could take, the one of scholarly interest is that which leads toward the text intended by the author. Because no preserved document may contain a text that fully reflects its author's intentions, the critical editor undertakes the task of deciding, after an assessment of all available evidence, which preserved text is most authoritative and what alterations are required in it so that it will conform still more closely with the author's wishes. The goal is fidelity to what the editor understands to be the author's intention; the editor's critical acumen, therefore, is put to the service of historical reconstruction. The resulting text can never be definitive in the way that a noncritical text can; being the product of critical insight, it can always be challenged by those who assess the evidence differently. More than one carefully reasoned and well-informed opinion may be possible about certain textual cruxes, and more than one critical text of a piece of writing may therefore legitimately exist. This potential lack of certainty is an inevitable aspect of a process involving judgment, but it in no way detracts from the importance of the undertaking. For writings intended for publication, in particular, noncritical texts of the relevant documents, useful as they are, cannot as a rule provide the kind of reading texts these works deserve; but critical texts can approach the goal of presenting them as they were designed to be presented to a reading audience.

Scholarly critical editors, with authorial intention as their guiding standard, are faced with three broad categories of potential emendation: (1) choosing which reading is to be preferred at points where variations occur among the texts that have claim to authority; (2) detecting erroneous readings, and thinking of appropriate corrections for them, at points where no variants occur to call attention to the problem (or in cases where only one authoritative text exists); and (3) deciding whether certain practices of punctuation, spelling, and capitalization are to be regularized.

The last two of these require less discussion than the first. Detecting erroneous readings at points where there are no variants is one of the primary responsibilities of the critical editor, but it has not been written about as much as other editorial duties because it is not amenable to theorizing or systematizing. Some corrections of this kind are obvious, as when they rectify mere slips of the pen or typographical errors. Others, however, come only after repeated close readings of the text and long familiarity with the author, for the errors they correct are by no means immediately apparent. An error that makes a kind of sense and that requires concentrated attention for its discovery may remain undetected for years or through a succession of editions. Once it is pointed out, readers often wonder why they had not noticed it before; similarly, the correct reading, when the editor hits upon it, seems so natural and so clearly right that it scarcely leaves room for doubt. An emendation of this sort is the product of imagination and insight and therefore does not occur with great frequency; locating subtle errors, difficult as it is, often is easier than knowing what to replace the errors with. The conservative editor will make a correction when a reading in the text is one the author cannot have intended and when a replacement for it can be found that resembles it enough so as to suggest how the error occurred and that at the same time alters the sense to what the passage requires. Editors can never be sure when this part of their work is finished: another careful reading of the text may reveal another error, hitherto overlooked. Yet they must keep their ingenuity from getting out of control; some of these emendations may indeed be ingenious, but they must also be convincing in their restoration of the author's intended wording. Instruction in this process is of little use; the proper preparation, as with most editorial tasks, is immersion in the works of the author being edited.

On the question of regularizing, there are two issues for the editor to consider, though they ultimately become one. First is the matter of modernizing. Although there are some situations in which it is probably justifiable to attempt to bring the punctuation, spelling, and capitalization of a text into conformity with present-day usage, this approach has no place in any edition intended for a scholarly audience. If the aim of a scholarly critical edition is to establish the text intended by the author, modernizing can be no part of the undertaking. Preserving such features of a text as its punctuation, spelling, and capitalization is not mere antiquarianism; these are elements in an author's style and convey nuances of thought. Any serious reader of an author will wish to get as close to that author's thought as possible, and the inevitably imprecise and haphazard process of modernizing cannot but take one farther away. (In any case, the need for modernizing has been greatly exaggerated by over-zealous editors who have assumed that readers are in greater need of assistance than they actually are; most readers, whether scholars or not, do not find unfamiliar spelling and punctuation an obstacle, at least for texts from the sixteenth century on.) If scholarly editors are therefore concerned with so-called old-spelling editions ("old-spelling," in this sense, referring to unmodernized punctuation as well), a second issue they face is whether or not to regularize within the conventions that the author apparently wished to follow. It is difficult, of course, to establish conclusively that an author always intended to follow a given form, and unless an author's preferred usage is clearly ascertainable, the difficulty with regularizing is the possibility of choosing the form that the author did not favor. Furthermore, whether an author preferred consistency is itself a matter that cannot be taken for granted.

Although some authors, particularly of the twentieth century, undoubtedly desired consistency in punctuation, spelling, and capitalization, it is by no means clear that such consistency has always been regarded as something desirable. For many texts, then, regularizing may amount to a kind of modernizing. Since these elements of a text can affect meaning, an editor must be extremely cautious about imposing a consistency that might conceal nuances and that might move the text further from the author's intentions. Consistency in these matters, in other words, can never be thought of as an automatic rule in scholarly critical editing; eliminating an inconsistency demands the same critical judgment that is brought to bear on other problems of emendation.

The third large area of possible emendation—consisting of variant readings among texts—is the one that has stimulated the greatest volume of theoretical discussion and is in fact at the heart of critical editing. Whenever a difference occurs between any two texts, one is always faced with the problem of determining whether the later reading is an authorial revision (or correction) or whether it is an unauthoritative alteration (like a compositor's slip or a change made by a publisher's editor), introduced either inadvertently or consciously in the process of transmission. Sometimes evidence exists to settle the question (as when a set of marked proofs shows what alterations the author made at this stage); more often the surviving evidence is inconclusive and requires the editor's judgment for its interpretation. A rationale for making these decisions is the central element in any editorial plan for a critical text. The history of editorial scholarship is a history of shifting views regarding how much freedom can be accorded editors in deciding among variant readings. R. B. McKerrow, who laid the foundations of the twentieth-century tradition of critical editing in English, reacted against what he thought was the excessive subjectivism of nineteenth-century editors and certain early twentieth-century editors. Although some of his views shifted during his career, his general position was that, if one accepted any readings in a revised text as authorial, one had to accept all the verbal alterations in that text (except, of course, those that were patently compositorial errors). W. W. Greg, recognizing McKerrow's undue fear of eclecticism, sought to give more weight to editorial judgment regarding individual readings, without at the same time allowing that judgment to escape the controls imposed upon it by the necessity of operating within the framework of authorial intention. In his study of editorial problems in Shakespeare in the 1930s and 1940s, Greg was working his way toward the mature position he enunciated in "The Rationale of Copy-Text" at the English Institute in 1949. This essay is unquestionably the most influential document in recent editorial history; it has been employed so widely since it appeared and has been the subject of so much debate that a knowledge of it is a prerequisite to understanding what has been happening in editing since the middle of this century.

Greg's rationale grew directly out of, and was supported with examples from, his work in English Renaissance drama. Like McKerrow, he held that a critical editor's copy-text (the text to be followed except at those points where an emendation is deemed necessary) should normally be an early, rather than a late or revised, text: the text of the edition closest to the author's final manuscript (or, by implication, that manuscript itself if it survives). This position rests on the observation that the texts of successive editions of a work generally show progressive deterioration; they may also contain genuine authorial revisions, of course, and these should be identified and preserved, but in other respects the later texts are likely to contain departures from earlier texts introduced by the compositors in the process of resetting (and not thereafter caught). In Greg's view, this early copy-text should be emended with any readings in later texts that can be convincingly shown to be authorial. Unlike McKerrow, however, Greg did not believe that the significant variants in a given text had to be regarded as a unit; the editor was under no obligation to accept variants simply because they occurred in a text containing other variants that were judged to be authorial. What Greg's method provides editors is a procedure to follow when they would otherwise be undecided: when in doubt, he was saying, stick to the copy-text. By emending the copy-text only when one has compelling reason to do so, one is probably neglecting a few authorial revisions in the later texts, but by adhering to the copy-text in cases of doubt one is maximizing the chances of retaining readings that were the author's at one time—for a wholesale acceptance of the later readings in order not to miss any of the author's revisions would normally mean importing into the text a far greater number of readings that were not the author's at all. So long as one can assume, when the evidence is inconclusive, that later texts exhibit a progressive deterioration, the logic of Greg's position is unassailable.

Greg clearly recognized in his analysis that textual authority is often divided (the authority of certain readings in a later text does not mean that the earlier text no longer has any authority), and he went a step further in describing the nature of this division. An editor examining variants will frequently have less basis for deciding how to handle variants in punctuation and spelling than those in wording; in any case, Greg argued, such variants in later texts are less likely to carry authority, because compositors often imposed their own styles of punctuation and spelling on a text, and authors, if they proofread these texts, were inclined to pay less attention to such matters than to the wording itself. Greg therefore set up his now-famous distinction between "accidentals" (punctuation, spelling, capitalization) and "substantives" (words). The terms he chose are somewhat misleading ("accidentals" is particularly unfortunate), for he was well aware of the fact that punctuation, spelling, and capitalization play a role in meaning (and thus have their "substantive" aspects), and he did not intend to suggest otherwise. His distinction, as he said himself, was practical, not theoretical. In practice, he was suggesting, persons associated with book production have often behaved as if accidentals were less important than substantives—and it is behavior that concerns the editor. If compositors have tended to feel that they had greater freedom with regard to accidentals and if authors have tended to concentrate on substantives in their proofreading, these patterns of behavior have a direct bearing on an editor's textual decisions. The upshot of this reasoning is a generalization about divided authority: an early text may retain authority for accidentals, even when the authority for substantives has shifted to a later text. This neat division, however, cannot be rigidly held to, for there are often some classes of indifferent substantive variants about which it is difficult to reason, and the safest course in those cases, as generally with accidentals, is to retain the copy-text readings. The only reason that a rationale for selecting a copy-text is needed, after all, is that there is rarely sufficient evidence for determining with confidence the relative authority of every variant. If there were, no text of presumptive authority would be needed to fall back on in cases of doubt, since there would be no cases of doubt. That ideal situation can rarely obtain, however, and thus the choice of copy-text becomes a central editorial decision. (This choice is of course not the same as deciding what copy is to be marked up for the printer. In fact, however, when the copy-text is a printed text, a xerographic copy of it is normally the best choice for printer's copy, but obviously there are situations—as when the copy-text is a manuscript text—that require other arrangements. In any case, preparing printer's copy is a practical and mechanical matter; selecting a copy-text is a matter of editorial theory and policy.) Greg's rationale is an answer to the question of how to select a copy-text, and it is a generally satisfying answer because it does not place arbitrary limits on editorial judgment.

One can readily see how the conditions of Renaissance dramatic publication underlie Greg's approach: few of the manuscripts survive, the printed texts often derived from playhouse documents that were several steps removed from the author's manuscript, and the instability of spelling and punctuation encouraged compositors to make variations according to convenience and inclination. Clearly the texts Greg had worked with required a method that sought to reconstruct, insofar as the printed texts would allow, the text of the author's fair-copy manuscript (or the text the author would have wished to appear there, for such a manuscript may never have existed). But this goal is certainly appropriate for texts of other periods as well, even though the conditions under which texts are produced and published do not remain static, and the essentials of Greg's approach would seem so basic as to be readily adaptable to materials other than those with which he was immediately concerned. Fredson Bowers, who has been the great champion of Greg's rationale, has demonstrated—both in theoretical essays and in actual editions of writers as diverse as Dryden, Fielding, Hawthorne, Stephen Crane, and William James—that Greg's approach is effective in handling a wide variety of kinds of writing from different periods. When the CEAA was established in 1963, it adopted Greg's rationale in its guidelines for editors; in more recent years Greg has been utilized by various editors of British texts as well, and he is increasingly being turned to by editors in fields other than literature. As a result, Greg's rationale has by now probably been employed for more editions of nineteenth- and early twentieth-century texts than for texts of the period for which it was originally envisaged.

This situation has not pleased everyone, and the debates over Gregian editing have well upheld the ancient tradition of editorial contentiousness. Of the criticisms that deserve to be taken seriously, most fall into one of two categories. The first is the argument that Greg's rationale is not, after all, applicable to all periods. The most provocative form of this argument asserts that compositorial fidelity to copy in some later periods negates Greg's basic assumption that texts inevitably deteriorate in successive editions. It must be recognized, however, that in the periods in which compositorial fidelity is higher the function of the publisher's reader or editor is also more fully developed, with the result that textual alterations may still be introduced in the publication process, even though they may originate at a different point in that process. There would still be a need, therefore, to try to get behind the first-edition text, and one cannot rule out this kind of publishing-house alteration when that text is reset for a later edition. When one has reason to believe, from the evidence in a particular situation, that a later text is most likely to reflect the author's wishes respecting punctuation and spelling as well as wording, there is nothing in Greg's rationale to prevent one from selecting it as copy-text (and thus according it presumptive authority). But whether it is safe to say for any period that as a general rule the odds favor a later, rather than an earlier, text is questionable. The matter certainly requires further investigation, but the chances for unauthorized alteration during the process of publication (of first and of later editions) seem great enough for all periods that Greg's approach may prove to be the most cautious one in cases (of any period) where the evidence is inconclusive.

A second category of criticisms of Greg concerns the matter of authorial intention. Greg's emphasis on the author's "final intention" as the goal of scholarly editing would seem to be appropriate for most written works. But Greg did not define the concept of authorial intention, and, if editors are to have an adequate framework within which to think about some of the more complicated questions of intention that arise, his remarks do need to be supplemented. The most basic point to recognize is that authors' descriptions of or claims about their intentions—however interesting biographically those statements may be—cannot be taken by editors as the primary evidence for authors' actual intentions. Obviously authors do not always do what they announce they are doing or think they have done, and editors have to proceed on the basis of the intentions that authors manifest in their works. Editors of course need to have as much external evidence as possible to inform their judgments, but determining the intended reading at a given point in a text finally turns on their critical understanding of the context of that reading, on inferring the author's intention from the text itself. An even more difficult problem involves how to decide what a "final" intention is. When authors make revisions, the later readings can generally be regarded as representing the authors' later intentions, and scholarly editors must respect those revisions even if they consider them artistically unwise. But final intentions are not always a matter of chronology. If authors make revisions as a result of external pressure, or what they conceive to be external pressure, it seems wrong to say that the new readings supersede the earlier ones, even though the authors themselves made the changes. (One thinks, for example, of the second ending of *Great Expectations* or the toning down Melville engaged in for the revised edition of *Typee*.) Similarly, the whole relationship between authors and publishers' editors requires sensitive analysis by the critical editor. One is interested, after all, in what the author, not the publisher's editor, wrote; but one must attempt to assess whether the author and publisher's editor engaged in an active and willing collaboration or whether the author merely acceded to various changes as the more prudent or practical course, without really regarding them as desired improvements. To say that an author expected certain alterations to be made by a publisher's editor and was prepared to accept them is not the same as to say that the author desired those changes.

A related question concerning the chronology of intentions is how to handle revisions that alter the nature or effect of a work and thus could be said to produce a new work, not simply a new version of the same work; the revisions come later in time and must be accepted as elements in the new conception, but they do not invalidate the earlier readings, which were integral parts of a different work embodying a different "final intention." Greg recognized that in such situations the two texts would have to be edited separately, but he did not pursue the matter, since the issue was not a pressing one for the materials he was working with. As a result, editors of certain later writings may find his references to intention inadequate for preparing them to deal with differing intentions that may exist at different stages in the post-publication history of those writings. One must try to distinguish between revisions that refine or develop the conception of a work as it already exists (revisions that might, for convenience, be called "horizontal") and revisions that push a work into a different level, in effect creating a different work ("vertical" revisions). When the author's revisions are of the former kind, a single critical text, incorporating those revisions, suffices, but when they are of the latter kind—as is the case, for example, with some of Henry James's revised texts for his New York Edition or Wordsworth's "The Ruined Cottage" as the first book of *The Excursion*—separate critical texts are called for, representing different and distinct conceptions of the work. The latter situation is likely to involve a large number of revisions, but it is the nature rather than the quantity of the revisions that is crucial in determining whether a "new work" has emerged. One could argue that theoretically any revision produces a different work. Nevertheless, the distinction between two classes of revision is a real one, even if the dividing line is not always clear, and in practical terms it makes sense to regard this distinction as separating those revisions that can satisfactorily be incorporated into an eclectic text through a process of critical editing from those that cannot be so incorporated without doing violence to one or more versions of a work deserving of perpetuation as independent entities (and not simply in the form of notes to another text). These questions of intention are difficult and rarely yield conclusive answers, but they go to the heart of scholarly critical editing. And it should be clear that a critical edition is itself a critical study, for it, like a volume of literary criticism, depends for its success on literary sensitivity as well as on historical, biographical, and textual knowledge.

III. The Process of Editing

Only when editors have thought through these various issues, and have therefore carefully defined their aims in relation to the whole range of conceivable editorial approaches, are they ready to begin the actual process of editing. Situations will differ, but in general the process—at least for scholarly critical editing—can be thought of as having five distinct, but interdependent, steps. Some of the points made below are not directly applicable to noncritical editions, but the editorial commentary to accompany a noncritical text (indeed, the very choice of the text to be presented) will benefit from the investigation and thinking entailed in these five steps. Each of them has been much discussed in print, and they are commented on here in the most summary form.

Locating the Relevant Materials

The first task is to identify and assemble the necessary materials, which fall into three classes. (a) First come all texts of the work to be edited that have any claim to authority—that is, any manuscripts, typescripts, or printed editions directly connected with or authorized by the author and any other copies or editions that may have drawn on authoritative documents now lost or damaged. Editors must routinely scrutinize any texts produced during an author's lifetime, but some posthumous texts may also require examination, and sometimes posthumous texts are the only ones extant. (Obviously, editors may wish to look at various nonauthoritative editions as well, simply for their suggestive value in calling attention to certain problems and possible solutions.) The process of identifying relevant texts can be greatly facilitated by the existence of bibliographies and catalogues, but frequently editors must in effect create their own bibliographies; indeed, the research underlying bibliographies and editions is so complementary that they are best developed in conjunction with one another. (b) One must also have at hand any texts quoted from, or used as sources for passages in, the work being edited. Although one would not automatically correct misquotations from source passages (if, for instance, the author seems to have intentionally misquoted or has based a discussion on a misquotation), one nevertheless cannot make informed textual judgments without knowing how quotations or paraphrases relate to the texts from which they are drawn. It is important, therefore, whenever possible, to identify the precise edition of a work used by the author. (c) In addition, editors must inform themselves about and seek out any materials bearing on the history of the composition, printing, and publication of the work to be edited (such as letters, diaries, printers' ledgers, publishers' account books, and scholarly studies of those documents). Editors must also— it should go without saying—have a thorough knowledge of the author's life, times, and other writings.

Collating the Texts

After the relevant, or potentially relevant, texts have been identified and located, they must be compared letter by letter and punctuation mark by punctuation mark to determine what variants, if any, exist among them. This tedious process can at times be somewhat alleviated by mechanical or electronic aids, and great advances in the technology of collating are inevitable in the coming years. At present there are several devices for speeding up the comparison of copies from the same edition (that is, from the same typesetting), the best known of which is the Hinman Collator; and progress is being made in utilizing computers for the collation of texts from different editions (some editors have experimented with optical scanners for reading the texts directly, and others have had the texts typed out to make them machine readable). However the collations are performed, they should be repeated until they can reasonably be regarded as error-free. In collations of printed books, different copies should be used each time in order in increase the chances of locating variants within editions (and of recognizing defects of individual copies), and there should always be some collations among copies of the same edition; when an edition has gone through two or more impressions, the most efficient course is to collate copies of the first impression against copies of the last to appear during the author's lifetime, when these can be identified, and then to track down the first appearances of the variants in any intervening impressions, but one must be alert to the possible existence of duplicate sets of plates. It is impossible to generalize about how many collations are sufficient, and a limit to the process will generally be determined on practical grounds. But editors will wish to continue collating until they can feel reasonably confident that all the relevant evidence has been recorded. (When the new edition reaches the proofreading stage, there will be an opportunity for a few further collations: numerous proofreadings will naturally be required, and in some of those readings the proofs may be compared with additional copies of the earlier editions.)

Determining the Relationships among the Texts

Although sometimes one may have a good idea of the principal relationships among the texts before collating them (especially when the texts occur in dated printed editions or impressions), the results of collation are necessary for understanding in detail the genealogy of the extant texts and for confirming any relationships inferred through external evidence. Knowing how each text relates to the others (information that is often schematized as a family tree, or stemma) is obviously essential for judging the relative authority of those texts at points of variation. Establishing the genealogy of the texts can in some instances be extremely complex, especially when (as with many classical texts) one has to deal with scribal copies standing a number of removes from the author, or when there is no single surviving common ancestor of the various extant texts. Elaborate theories for working out relationships among texts have been proposed, chiefly in connection with the editing of classical or biblical writings, but most editors of works from the Renaissance and later periods have not found it necessary to turn to these theories to any significant extent. In recent years Vinton Dearing has been concerned with showing connections between this kind of textual criticism and the editing of post-Renaissance works; certainly many editors need to be more fully aware of this tradition of editorial literature so that they may judge how and to what extent it might serve them. Another body of technical knowledge that can play an important role in working out the relationships among texts is that concerned with analytical bibliography. Although the genealogy of texts does not necessarily coincide with the chronology of the physical documents that contain them, editors obviously must find out all they can about the production of those documents. Physical details present in manuscripts and printed books (the ink and paper, the recurrence of particular damaged types, the characteristic spellings of certain compositors, and so on) can provide evidence that helps one to learn how those manuscripts and books were produced and thus how much authority to assign to their texts or certain readings within the texts. Analytical bibliography has been most highly developed in connection with the editing of English Renaissance dramatic texts (the work of Charlton Hinman is the culmination of this tradition), but books of all periods (including the twentieth century) contain evidence waiting to be recognized, though the differing conditions of printing and publishing in different periods may necessitate different techniques of analysis. Editors are sometimes inclined to avoid this kind of research, just as descriptive bibliographers often feel that collating texts goes beyond their responsibility, but these pursuits are so interrelated that no boundaries between them can be defended. In any event, working out the relationships among texts, whether it is a simple task or one requiring considerable time and ingenuity, is a central duty of an editor.

Selecting the Copy-text

Once the relationships among the texts are established, one is in a position to decide which text is best qualified to be the copy-text—the text that one will adhere to except when there is compelling reason to adopt a different reading. Because only rarely does a situation occur in which every—or almost every—choice among variants is certain, the selection of copy-text will in most instances have a considerable effect on the characteristics of the critical text finally produced. The considerations underlying that choice reflect one's editorial aims, and different choices can at times be defended for different purposes. The kind of thinking involved in choosing a copy-text for a scholarly critical edition, illustrated by Greg's rationale, has been described above.

Emending the Copy-text

The copy-text will require emendation by the editor wherever it can be shown to be in error or wherever the corresponding reading from another text supersedes the copy-text reading as a reflection of the author's intention (or, of several intentions, the one settled upon as the aim of the edition). The process of emendation has, like that of choosing a copy-text, been commented on earlier. Clearly, the insight and learning demanded by emendation make it the ultimate test of a critical editor.

IV. The Forms of Editions

After preparing a text, the editor can offer it to the public in a variety of forms. If a reliable text is presented without any editorial remarks whatever, it is no less reliable for that, but the publication will be far less useful for scholarly purposes and will thus show far less sense of scholarly responsibility. The reliability of a text, like that of any other product of scholarly research, cannot simply be taken on faith; the published results of the research should be documented so that users will know, and be able to examine for themselves, the evidence on which the work was based. For an edition of a text, documentation can consist of editorial commentary, footnotes, lists, or a combination of these. At a minimum, every edition—whether the text it contains is critical or noncritical—should include a statement identifying the source of the text (the precise manuscript or copy of an edition used) and indicating how that text has been treated by the editor (whether it is reproduced exactly—and by what means—or whether certain categories of alteration have been editorially introduced into it). There is no excuse for any edition, whatever its intended audience, to appear without this minimal kind of documentation.

But, for scholarly purposes in the broadest sense, including those of serious readers who are not professional scholars, fuller documentation is desirable—and, for critical editions, is required, because readers need to be informed of every emendation made by the editor in the documentary text. What further documentation there should be and what form it should take are questions that will be answered differently depending on the nature of the material and on the audience envisaged for the edition. A basic decision that affects the form of the documentation is whether the text is to be presented as a "clear text" (without editorial symbols, footnote numbers, bracketed interpolations, and the like) or whether certain kinds of textual information, appropriately bracketed or signaled, are to be incorporated into the text itself ("inclusive text"). As a general rule, clear text is to be preferred for critical editions of works intended for publication: intrusions of editorial matter into the text in such cases would be out of keeping with the goal of presenting the author's intended text of a finished work. For noncritical editions of writings not intended for publication, however, editorial symbols and bracketed explanations may be necessary for indicating interlinear insertions, cancellations, and other idiosyncrasies of the manuscript or typescript (producing a "genetic text"): to relegate such information to notes and offer a smooth flowing and uncluttered text would be to misrepresent the nature of the document. (The edition of *Billy Budd* prepared by Harrison Hayford and Merton M. Sealts, Jr., for the University of Chicago Press in 1962 effectively illustrates this distinction: it presents both a genetic text of Melville's unfinished manuscript and a clear reading text of the literary work embodied in that document.) These general guidelines will not fit every situation and must sometimes be disregarded. If, for example, a particular individual's letters are full of complicated insertions and deletions and at the same time are likely to be widely read and quoted by a broad range of people, the advantages of a clear-text rendering (accompanied by textual notes) would probably outweigh the disadvantages. The text then becomes a critical text, because the editor is making decisions about how the new text will differ from the text in the document.

Whether or not some editorial apparatus is incorporated into the text, there will still be textual data or commentary that must be recorded elsewhere. Arguments can be made both for placing this information at the foot of each page (where it is close to the relevant passages of text) and for bringing it all together at the end of the text (where the evidence as a whole can be more easily surveyed). For editions offering clear text, it is often thought more appropriate to keep the text pages entirely free of editorial matter; an additional consideration supporting this position is that the text will then lend itself more readily to photographic reproduction for use in other editions, such as those for classroom use, and a wider dissemination of a reliable text may result. This thinking underlies the form of the CEAA and CSE editions of works intended for publication. The apparatus in those editions, though it varies from volume to volume in minor respects, contains certain categories of material that are now regarded as standard for full-scale scholarly editions: (1) a statement or essay setting forth the history of the composition, printing, publication, reception, and later reprinting of the work, indicating the reasons for the choice of copy-text and the principles followed in any emendation, as well as specifying the individual copies collated and the one used as printer's copy; (2) a set of discursive notes on the handling of any textual cruxes that require further explanation than is provided by the general guidelines in the textual essay; (3) a record of every emendation, in both substantives and accidentals, that the editor has made in the copy-text—every textual change, that is, but not alterations in such nontextual features as typographic design; (4) a record of revisions present in any pre–copy-text documents; (5) a record—sometimes called "historical collation"—of the variants present in the collated texts, generally the authorized texts during the author's lifetime (in most of the CEAA/CSE editions this record is limited to substantives, but whenever feasible accidentals should be included as well; the fact that the line between significant and nonsignificant variants does not coincide with the line between substantives and accidentals provides a constant temptation for editors to devise other ways of cutting down the length of these lists, but any system of selection based on the subjective criterion of "significance" will undercut the goal of putting the reader in the position of knowing exactly what is and is not recorded in the apparatus); (6) a hyphenation record, consisting of (a) ambiguous line-end hyphens in the copy-text that required an editorial decision regarding their retention or deletion and (b) line-end hypens in the newly edited text that should be retained when quotations are made from that text. All this material enables readers to reconstruct the copy-text and other relevant texts and thus to have at their disposal most of the textual evidence on which the editor's decisions were based, so that they can think through and reconsider those decisions for themselves. It is obviously not necessary for this material to appear in any prescribed form, so long as the form is clear, but the more standardized the presentation can become, the easier it will be for readers to move from one edition to another, for they will not have to adjust continually to a new system. Editors should therefore take previous editorial usage into consideration in planning a new edition.

The presence within an edition of all this textual evidence should not lead one to think that individual textual decisions or emendations are of less consequence than they would be if the reader did not have immediate access to the variant readings. The apparatus, one must remember, is documentation for the text, and its presence does not give one license to be casual about emendations. In some so-called variorum editions, it is true, the main text seems more a peg on which to hang variant readings than an entity in its own right: the earliest text is printed in full, and attached to it are notes listing all the later variants. (A different kind of variorum edition is a compendium of critical commentary on particular words, lines, or passages, with the text itself present largely for convenience of reference—though what that text should be remains an issue.) Such an edition is useful as a historical record, but it leaves unfilled the need for a reading text reflecting the author's intention; since it is economically unrealistic to envisage the publication of several scholarly texts of the same work, precedence should be given, for works intended for publication, to critical editions that provide as the main text a text that can be defended as one conforming to the author's intention (or the author's intention for one of the conceptions of the work, if vertical revision is involved). The opposite problem—valuing the apparatus too little—is also encountered. Some people have argued that an apparatus (particularly a full one of the kind described here) is of interest only to specialists and that the expense of printing complex lists is not justified when they can be made available, to those who wish to study them, in microform or in a record deposited in a research library. What such arguments fail to recognize is how important the material in an apparatus is to the activity of reading critically. Whenever serious readers or critics are struck by particular passages or phrases and wish to examine them carefully, they will be aided by knowing the history of those passages or phrases, by knowing whether any other words or punctuation (that could be attributed to the author) ever appeared in them. The value of having this information at hand, in the same volume as the text, is incalculable. Naturally, economic considerations may in some instances dictate the elimination of certain data from the printed record, but there is no adequate substitute for the availability of these details in print, and a full record should appear in scholarly editions when at all possible.

Nothing has been said about historical or explanatory annotation—notes or discussions that identify allusions, define unusual terms, and the like. Many scholarly editions do not include this kind of information, on the grounds that the essential function of a scholarly edition is to establish a text and that the textual apparatus must therefore take precedence. To the extent that textual and historical annotation can be separated, this position is defensible, although one would scarcely wish to see the latter excluded if it is feasible to present both. Actually, the provision of historical, linguistic, and other clarifying information is not easily separable from editing. In order to establish a text, the editor must investigate and understand the allusions and linguistic subtleties it contains and is then in the best position to elucidate them; discussing these points is a legitimate, often essential, part of an editor's explanation for retaining, or altering, a reading. The editor's focus cannot be narrower than the full meaning of the text.

The production of a full-scale scholarly edition is clearly a time-consuming and demanding process. For major authors and books, such work, when not already done or in progress, will have to be undertaken eventually. It is unrealistic, however, to expect that all authors of interest can be accorded this treatment, at least in the foreseeable future. Considerably less elaborate editions can therefore serve a useful purpose, when they are produced with a sense of professional responsibility. A photographic reproduction of a historic text, for instance, can simply be accompanied by a brief introductory note identifying the copy of the text used and explaining why that particular text is deserving of reproduction. The resulting publication will not be a great scholarly accomplishment, but it will be an aid to further scholarship and study—a far more constructive aid, indeed, than a reset text containing silent (or inadequately recorded) editorial alterations and undetected typographical errors. Similarly, classroom editions may legitimately concentrate on "explanatory" annotation rather than on the establishment of the text—provided that they take a responsible approach to the choice and treatment of the text to be included. All editions, whatever level of research underlies them, should show a respect for documentary evidence: they should be clearly labeled for what they are and should put their readers in the position of knowing what information is, and what is not, available within their covers.

Well-prepared editions and textual studies are unquestionably basic to other kinds of literary scholarship and criticism, for the text is the occasion for, and the ultimate focus of, literary and historical exposition and analysis. But that fact should not delude one into thinking that textual scholarship merely prepares the way for scholarly criticism and is not itself a part of the critical process. It is clear that successful editors—particularly those producing critical texts—must possess not only a large fund of knowledge but also a keen sensitivity to nuances of language and to literary values. Their work is a critical activity, and a critical *edition*, by virtue of the textual decisions it contains (and any discussions of those decisions), is also a critical *study*. But an edition, because it is an edition, exerts an influence more pervasive than most critical studies can have. The power of an editor is a sobering fact, which should make every editor all the more conscious of a heavy responsibility to the author, the profession, and the community of serious readers. Practically every decision an editor makes—even those that ostensibly deal with mechanical matters—can have far-reaching consequences. The choice of text to appear as the main text, the alterations to be made in it, the decision whether to keep the text pages free of symbols and apparatus—all such decisions have a great impact on the dissemination of the text and on the way it will be read for some time to come. If a critical edition embodies aesthetic decisions, it also affects aesthetic responses. The readings adopted from among the variants make the initial impact on readers and influence their reactions, even though a record of the rejected readings is made available. Textual scholarship is thus enormously challenging, and an immense amount of material—much of it of major significance—still awaits the attention of dedicated scholarly editors.

Further Reading

A convenient recent guide to the literature of editing and textual study appears in another MLA publication, *The Center for Scholarly Editions: An Introductory Statement* (1977), pp. 4–15 (also printed in *PMLA*, 92 [1977], 586–97). The availability of this guide makes it unnecessary to present an extensive record here. An earlier similar listing is T. H. Howard-Hill's "Textual Criticism and Bibliography: A Selective Bibliography for Students of English," *Shakespearean Research and Opportunities*, 7/8 (1972–74), 6–32. Included in the MLA survey is a list of the CEAA editions and some related editions (pp. 5–6); readers of the present essay who want to see examples of responsible modern editorial practice will find this list a useful starting point.

Some readers will wish to turn first to other general introductory essays, such as Fredson Bowers, "Textual Criticism," in *The Aims and Methods of Scholarship in Modern Languages and Literatures*, ed. James Thorpe, 2nd ed. (New York: MLA, 1970), pp. 29–54, and his "Scholarship and Editing," *Papers of the Bibliographical Society of America*, 70 (1976), 161–88; Center for Editions of American Authors, *Statement of Editorial Principles and Procedures*, rev. ed. (New York: MLA, 1972); the opening sections of *The Center for Scholarly Editions: An Introductory Statement*, pp. 1–4; Peter L. Shillingsburg, "Critical Editing and the Center for Scholarly Editions," *Scholarly Publishing*, 9 (1977–78), 31–40; and G. Thomas Tanselle, "Literary Editing," in *Literary & Historical Editing*, ed. George L. Vogt and John Bush Jones (Lawrence: Univ. of Kansas Libraries, 1981). (Also available from the MLA is a set of "Guiding Questions" prepared by the CSE for prospective editors, but useful as well for prospective readers of editions; it serves as a concise summary of the standards and procedures that characterize careful scholarly editing.)

The central essay by W. W. Greg, "The Rationale of Copy-Text," appears in *Studies in Bibliography*, 3 (1950–51), 19–36, and is reprinted in his *Collected Papers*, ed. J. C. Maxwell (Oxford: Clarendon Press, 1966), pp. 374–91. Fredson Bowers has been the leading figure in the recent history of editorial theory and practice, and a generous selection of his most important essays on editing (along with other essays useful for understanding the relations between bibliographical analysis and editing) are gathered in his *Essays in Bibliography, Text, and Editing* (Charlottesville: Bibliographical Society of the Univ. of Virginia, 1975), including his significant supplement to Greg in "Multiple Authority" (originally published in the *Library*, 5th ser., 27 [1972] 81–115). Of his essays published since this volume appeared, one that should be singled out is "Greg's 'Rationale of Copy-Text' Revisited," *Studies in Bibliography*, 31 (1978), 90–161. Relevant discussion also appears in his *Textual and Literary Criticism* (Cambridge: Cambridge Univ. Press, 1959) and his *Bibliography and Textual Criticism* (Oxford: Clarendon Press, 1964).

Five of G. Thomas Tanselle's essays on editing are reprinted in his *Selected Studies in Bibliography* (Charlottesville: Bibliographical Society of the Univ. of Virginia, 1979), including his survey of the reactions to Greg's approach, "Greg's Theory of Copy-Text and the Editing of American Literature" (originally published in *Studies in Bibliography*, 28 [1975], 167–229). To these should perhaps be added his "Textual Study and Literary Judgment," *Papers of the Bibliographical Society of America*, 65 (1971), 109–22; "Problems and Accomplishments in the Editing of the Novel," *Studies in the Novel*, 7 (1975), 323–60; and "Recent Editorial Discussion and the Central Questions of Editing," *Studies in Bibliography*, 34 (1981), 23–65. Other articles that should be consulted—such as Hershel Parker's "Melville and the Concept of 'Author's Final Intentions,' " *Proof*, 1 (1971), 156–68, and his "Regularizing Accidentals: The Latest Form of Infidelity," *Proof*, 3 (1973), 1–20—are systematically recorded in the CSE *Introductory Statement* mentioned above. One should also turn to that listing for references to various editions' editorial manuals; editorial studies focusing on particular periods, including the pioneer work of McKerrow and Greg; the literature that has grown up around the CEAA; reports on the uses of computers in editing; and basic material on the editing of historical, classical, and biblical writings.

Several anthologies conveniently bring together a number of significant papers and contain checklists of material about editing: *Bibliography and Textual Criticism: English and American Literature, 1700 to the Present*, ed. O M Brack, Jr., and Warner Barnes (Chicago: Univ. of Chicago Press, 1969); *Art and Error: Modern Textual Editing*, ed. Ronald Gottesman and Scott Bennett (Bloomington: Indiana Univ. Press, 1970); and "Textual Studies in the Novel," ed. Warner Barnes and James T. Cox (*Studies in the Novel*, 7 [Fall 1975], 317–471). There is also a published series of collections of the papers from the University of Toronto Editorial Conferences (1966–). Two studies that aim to be more comprehensive are James Thorpe's *Principles of Textual Criticism* (San Marino, Calif.: Huntington Library, 1972) and Philip Gaskell's *From Writer to Reader: Studies in Editorial Method* (Oxford: Clarendon Press, 1978), both of which express some reservations about Greg's rationale and the CEAA procedures based on it (for comprehensive reviews of the latter book, see *Analytical & Enumerative Bibliography*, 3 [1979], 105–16; and the *Library*, 6th ser., 2 [1980], 337–50). Examples of other discussions critical of Greg and the CEAA are Morse Peckham, "Reflections on the Foundations of Modern Textual Editing," *Proof*, 1 (1971), 122–55; Vinton Dearing, "Concepts of Copy-Text Old and New," *Library*, 5th ser., 28 (1973), 281–93; and Tom Davis, "The CEAA and Modern Textual Editing," *Library*, 5th ser., 32 (1977), 61–74. Dearing's *Principles and Practice of Textual Analysis* (Berkeley: Univ. of California Press, 1974) concentrates on methods for determining the genealogical relationships among different texts. Recent developments in the field can be followed through such periodicals as *Studies in Bibliography,* the *Library*, and *Papers of the Bibliographical Society of America*, and through occasional special issues of journals (such as *Studies in the Novel*) or special series of articles (such as "Redefining the Definitive" in the *Bulletin of Research in the Humanities*).

Historical Scholarship

Barbara Kiefer Lewalski

Most students of literature spend a good deal of time practicing historical scholarship. Whenever a scholar checks the *OED* for the meanings a particular word may have carried in an earlier era, or seeks out a possible source for a literary work, or pursues an allusion within the text to some contemporary event or earlier work of literature, or considers the impact of contemporary politics or philosophy upon a particular novel or poem, that scholar is using historical resources to understand literature better. Traditionally, literary history has been perceived as a counterpart to other kinds of history—political history, military history, history of science, history of art—that describe the chronological development of a specific kind of human activity within a given time period and in a particular country or countries. But while some scholars continue to write broad-scale literary histories on this model, many more use historical methods, historical contexts, historical materials, and historical information in a wide variety of literary studies that are not, formally, literary histories.

Fortunately, the high walls thrown up in the 1930s to safeguard the purity of literary criticism and literary interpretation from the supposed encroachments of literary history, and vice versa, have been largely demolished. In the 1963 version of this MLA publication Robert E. Spiller argued, in an essay entitled "Literary History," that the literary historian has a "separate and quite precise function" and that he should "leave to others the problems of literary theory and of methods of critical analysis and evaluation" (pp. 55–56). The title of the present essay, "Historical Scholarship," intends to recognize that the province inhabited by the contemporary historical scholar is more extensive and at the same time less clearly demarcated from its neighbors than the territory Spiller mapped out.

For several reasons, this is an auspicious moment for literary students with a bent for historical scholarship. With the decline of the old New Criticism has come a resurgence of concern for locating literary works in the world—taking account of their temporal identities, their interrelationships, the various contexts that help explain them, the historical continuities in which they participate. Moreover, literary scholars today customarily exhibit a higher order of methodological rigor than did their predecessors in such areas as source study, literary biography, the study of contexts. Also, a lively interest in the theory of literary history is now in evidence, stimulated in part by the debates among historians as to whether or to what extent to adopt methodologies from the several social sciences or from statistics, and whether or when to exchange their traditional narrative rhetoric for various analytic methods of setting forth structures and problems.

The interest in theory has also been stimulated by intramural debates among literary scholars, past and present. Some issues, joined several years ago between New Critics and traditional literary historians, are still controversial. One such concerns the matter of literary history. For Robert Spiller, literary history is a variety of national cultural history—"the expression *in literature* of a people during a period of time . . . the history of man as revealed in literature." For René Wellek, by contrast, literary history traces the development over time of specifically literary elements (styles, genres, themes, periods, influences, etc.), leading to "the history of literature as an art, in comparative isolation from its social history, the biographies of authors, or . . . the political, social, or even intellectual development of mankind."[1] Another issue concerns the implications of literary history for literary interpretation: in a famous exchange, Roy Harvey Pearce urged the "historicist" argument that reading a text requires recovery of the author's intention and of his historical and literary milieu, against Wellek's "presentist" assertion that the modern reader necessarily must and should read a literary work from the viewpoint of his own age and of literature as a whole.[2] More recently, Claudio Guillén has considered certain fundamental problems of literary history—issues of periodization, of literary changes and currents, of the emergence and development of genres—in relation to a structuralist view of literature as system, asserting that "to explore the idea of literary history may very well be the main theoretical task confronting the student of literature today."[3]

Continuing challenges to and reformulations of the traditional role of the literary historian are urged in the pages of such comparatively new journals as *New Literary History* and *Critical Inquiry*: from some structuralists whose synchronic analyses almost wholly ignore diachronic concerns, from some hermeneutic critics for whom literature can have no history because its texts have no determinable meaning or referentiality, from some Marxists for whom literary study is basically the sociology of authors and audiences and critics, and from some stylistic theorists for whom "literary history should . . . be a history of words."[4] As Ralph Cohen notes, much of the new theory views literary history as "a history of the relation of readers to works," concerned therefore with "the changing functions of literary features, with changes of conventions, with changes in the meaning of language codes."[5]

Historical scholars of literature do not often address issues of theory directly, though many have been affected by such debates, at least to the extent that they attempt to yoke systematic analysis to chronological narrative and to take some account of their own cultural conditioning by race, sex, or class. Most, however, assume as postulates basic to their endeavor that they work with texts whose meanings (in some degree at least) can be determined and that historical study, rigorously conducted, can lead to a truer (if always partial) understanding of literary works and their interrelationships, in their own terms and times.

I am concerned in this essay with what historical scholars of literature now do, and with the methods and assumptions involved in that work, rather than with speculations as to what history or literary history should be. (See the bibliography at the end of this essay for a list of several important theoretical works.) This decision arises from the recognition that literary-historical scholarship is not one thing but several and that each variety poses its own particular theoretical issues and problems. A survey of the field, with attention to such specific issues, is important for the practicing scholar; I suspect it is also a precondition for fruitful engagement with abstract theoretical questions about literary history.

The broad categories of literary study that are the special province of historical scholars have remained fairly constant over the years: literary biography, source and influence study, the investigation of contexts, the history of literary genres or of certain formal or thematic elements of literary texts, the literary history of an era or a nation. In addition, some literary scholars work in the general historical fields of the history of ideas, social history, and cultural history, using literary texts as primary subject matter. Within all these categories, however, certain shifts in emphasis have become apparent in recent years. One such shift is evidenced by the fact that some of the liveliest and most important contemporary works of historical scholarship are unabashedly hybrid, incorporating theory, criticism, and interpretation in proportions determined by the nature of the problems addressed. Another shift is from broad and inclusive chronological surveys to histories developed in large part by means of topical analysis or the discussion of particular literary texts. Yet another movement leads away from exclusively literary concerns to focus upon the ways in which a literary text is related to its culture, being shaped by and helping to shape that culture.

The wilder fantasies of literary scholars sometimes include stumbling across buried treasure—a lost cache of Shakespeare letters, an unpublished Hawthorne manuscript, a hitherto unknown (and good) poet. It does sometimes happen (see Richard Altick, *The Scholar Adventurers*). But the finder must be equipped by imagination and knowledge to suspect the worth of what he uncovers and to follow the clues it affords. The rediscovery of Thomas Traherne offers a case in point. Traherne's unpublished poems and prose meditations, entirely forgotten for two centuries, were uncovered in 1895 by a London book collector and first ascribed to Henry Vaughan. This identification seemed dubious on internal stylistic grounds to Bertram Dobell, who followed up his sound critical perception by careful literary detective work, culminating in the discovery of a poem from the manuscripts in question in a published tract undoubtedly by Traherne (*The Christian Ethicks*). The discovery of the important American colonial poet Edward Taylor illustrates another truism—

that the cultural presuppositions of a given era often determine what will be examined and what will be overlooked. The unpublished manuscripts of Taylor's poems were given to Yale by one of Taylor's descendants in 1883, but they were ignored because the colonial period was assumed to offer little or nothing of literary worth. In 1936 an early specialist in American studies, Thomas H. Johnson, discovered them when he investigated a remark he chanced upon in John L. Sibley's *Biographical Sketches of Graduates of Harvard University*, calling attention to Taylor's "series of 150 poems" called *Sacramental Meditations*. Such examples encourage us to expect to find literary works of value in hitherto neglected places (as is now proving to be the case with the writings of blacks and of women); yet in new fields as in old the important discoveries are likely to be made by those who have a shrewd sense of where to look and the knowledge to recognize and evaluate what they find.

When the scholar wakes up from fantasies of discovering brave new literary worlds, he or she will probably turn to one or another of the time-honored kinds of historical investigation. Though any classification is bound to be arbitrary and though major works of scholarship are likely to claim membership in several categories at once, it will be useful to consider these several kinds in their distinctness. This procedure will display the range of possibilities open to the historical scholar of literature and permit some attention to present emphases and directions within the various scholarly modes, as well as to their particular methods, materials, rewards, and difficulties.

I. Literary Biography

Literary biography has claimed attention as an important genre of literary scholarship ever since Samuel Johnson's famous *Lives of the English Poets*. Johnson's method, still used by some biographers, treats the writer's life and works almost as two discrete topics, with the biographer assuming by turns the roles of historian and critic. Modern literary biography, however, most often fuses these two concerns.

The basic question for any literary biographer must be: what kind of biography will best present what is and can be known about this author? In several important respects, the literary biographer will have to approach this issue exactly as any other biographer must—exploring some of the same kinds of material, employing many of the same methods, and confronting many of the same problems. In terms of research, the literary biographer must find and examine all the available material by or pertaining to the author: published and unpublished works, diaries, letters, manuscripts, working papers, public records, oral testimonies from family or friends if available, and information about the persons, places, institutions, and activities important for his subject's life. Also, like all writers of lives, the literary biographer must determine the genre of biography to write, and thereby also determine his own authorial stance and principles of selection. In a fascinating set of lectures on the biographer's art, James Clifford describes four distinct scholarly kinds: (1) the "objective" biography, which presents an extensive selection of documents with little interpretative comment; (2) the scholarly-historical biography, which presents selected facts in chronological order with some historical background but eschews unacknowledged guesswork, fictional devices, and psychological interpretation of the subject's personality and actions; (3) the artistic-scholarly biography, which is based upon exhaustive research but undertakes to interpret the facts and to present them in the most lively and interesting way possible, using artful literary devices but avoiding conscious distortion or direct invention; (4) narrative biography, which is grounded upon extensive research but presents the facts in narrative and dramatic form, using fictional techniques and allowing some play of the subjective imagination to fill in lacunae.[6] Moreover, literary biographers, like all others, must come to terms with the insights of modern psychology in the interpretation of human behavior and should find a way to do this without contributing to the spate of simplistic, jargon-ridden psychobiographies produced over the past several decades. Though few biographers appropriating psychological insights have approached the complexity and range of Erik Erikson's *Young Man Luther* (1958) or Leon Edel's *Henry James* (5 vols., 1953–72), the issue can hardly be avoided: as Frank Manuel has observed, the biographer or historian "can scarcely compose a narrative line without committing himself, implicitly or explicitly, to some theory of personality and motivation," and he is "probably always obliged to accept and express himself in the psychological language of his times"[7]—aided, one would hope, by a fine-tuned historical awareness.

Yet in at least one important respect the literary biographer's task differs from that of the biographer of a president, or a queen, or an explorer, or a scientist: in almost every case the writer's life is important only or chiefly because of the writing. Accordingly, if the biography is not to be merely superficial and anecdotal, the writing must somehow be made its central focus. W. Jackson Bate has stated this issue succinctly: "If we are to find our way into the inner life of a great writer, we must try to heal this split between 'biography' and 'criticism,' and remember that a very large part of the 'inner life' of a writer—what deeply preoccupied him, and made him a great writer—was his concern and effort, his hope and fear, in what he wrote."[8] The best modern literary biography attempts to do just that.

Another factor bearing upon the modern literary biographer's definition of his or her task must be the potentialities and challenges offered by the available materials. The biographer of Shakespeare faces a particularly difficult problem because of the paucity of sources: comparatively few documents relating to Shakespeare and his family, almost no personal writings such as letters or diaries, a literary production largely dramatic in genre and therefore especially resistant to biographical inferences, and a small corpus of dubious Shakespearean anecdotes, passed along in the tradition. In this situation Samuel Schoenbaum decided on two biographical projects differing markedly from the usual literary biography and giving scant attention to Shakespeare's *oeuvre*, though in the event serving it very well. The first book, *Shakespeare's Lives* (1970), traces the course of Shakespearean biography through the centuries, beginning with a precise account of the life records and proceeding to a judicious and entertaining report of what succeeding generations have made of them and of the various Shakespearean legends and myths. The result is a massive clearing away of accretions and ungrounded speculations. The second book, *William Shakespeare: A Documentary Life* (1975), is the positive statement, presenting in clear facsimile reproduction all the available documents pertaining to Shakespeare and deriving from these a straightforward and surprisingly substantial account of Shakespeare's external life. Schoenbaum explains that the material available "is insufficient for a portrait in depth of Shakespeare the man, . . . but those records we have, supplemented by the fruits of the historian's researches, enable us to enter into the quotidian life of a vanished age" (p. xi). The service of these biographical works to Shakespeare the writer should be to discourage further ungrounded speculation about the man behind the playwright and further unprofitable efforts to glean from the poems and plays biographical tidbits that, in the nature of things, cannot be verified.

In his highly acclaimed biography *James Joyce* (1959), Richard Ellmann faced almost precisely the opposite problem—a plethora of biographical materials of all sorts: personal papers, letters to and from a host of friends and acquaintances, manuscripts of works, the reminiscences of a large number of living witnesses (wife, family, friends, other writers and artists, casual acquaintances in several countries). Collecting evidence was accordingly an immense undertaking, and presenting it in appropriate relation to Joyce's fiction was even more difficult, because in all his works Joyce drew largely upon but also transmuted personal experience. Given this situation, Ellmann set exactly the right problem for himself and solved it magnificently:

> This book enters Joyce's life to reflect his complex, incessant joining of event and composition. The life of an artist, but particularly that of Joyce, differs from the lives of other persons in that its events are becoming artistic sources even as they command his present attention. Instead of allowing each day, pushed back by the next, to lapse into imprecise memory, he shapes again the experiences which have shaped him. . . . In turn the process of reshaping experience becomes a part of his life, another of its recurrent events like rising or sleeping. The biographer must measure in each moment this participation of the artist in two simultaneous processes. (p. 1)

Written in a style that is lucid, precise, and often eloquent, the biography displays on every page the interaction between life and work, the resemblance and yet the distance between Joyce and Stephen Dedalus, and the complex ways in which life is reflected in and transmuted by art.

W. Jackson Bate's impressive *Samuel Johnson* (1977) exhibits a different kind of response to the literary biographer's complex concerns. Any biographer might well hesitate before undertaking the life of the man who founded modern literary biography, who was himself the subject of the best known and perhaps the most readable literary biography ever written; whose life for the first fifty years or so is scantily documented but whose later years are recorded in superabundant detail by Boswell, the Thrales, and others; and whose physical disabilities and self-proclaimed melancholy demand a psychological analysis that has somehow to avoid being reductive. Bate brings it off brilliantly by writing a modern interpretative biography rather than a Boswellian anecdotal one, giving most of his attention to Johnson's less-known earlier years and working out carefully what the available information will yield about them, aided in this by James L. Clifford's pioneering study, *Young Sam Johnson* (1955).[9] Bate's book is almost a Johnsonian biography of Johnson, in that it portrays the inner man as literary creator and informs that portrait by humane and jargon-free psychological insights as well as by the kind of profound moral estimates Johnson himself so constantly made about his subjects, as authors and as men.

Another complex work, remarkable especially as an effort to extend the usual boundaries of literary biography, is the projected four-volume study of Dostoevsky by Joseph Frank, the first volume of which appeared in 1976, *Dostoevsky: The Seeds of Revolt, 1821–1848*. Although Frank sketches the events of Dostoevsky's private life, his basis for selecting or emphasizing material is its critical and interpretative relevance to Dostoevsky's writing. Frank's enterprise is grounded in the conviction that Dostoevsky's work is "a brilliant artistic synthesis of the major issues of his time" and that his genius resided "in his ability to fuse his private dilemmas with those raging in the society of which he was a part." Accordingly, Frank has eschewed a detailed account of the routine incidents of Dostoevsky's daily life and has undertaken instead a massive reconstruction of Dostoevsky's social-cultural milieu as the ground for his ideas and values, the matrix for those life experiences that he translated into art. The impressive first volume, focusing chiefly upon the intellectual circles with which Dostoevsky was associated in his youth and the artistic climate in which his first fiction was produced, augurs well for this experiment in fusing biography, literary criticism, and social-cultural history.

II. Sources and Influences

Another traditional variety of historical scholarship, now moving in new directions, is the study of sources and influences. Once a synonym for unimaginative plodding or single-minded pedantry, such study is now seen in relation to the creative process, the genesis of literary works, and the transmission or transformation of literary tradition. Modern source and influence study builds upon the principle, well stated by Northrop Frye, that literature is made not only from a writer's experience of life but also from his experience of other literature:

> If we ask what inspires a poet, there are always two answers. An occasion, an experience, an event, may inspire the impulse to write. But the impulse to write can only come from previous contact with literature, and the formal inspiration, the poetic structure that crystallizes around the new event, can only be derived from other poems. Hence while every new poem is a new and unique creation, it is also a reshaping of familiar conventions of literature, otherwise it would not be recognizable as literature at all.[10]

The basic issue for the modern student of sources must be to determine what—in reference to any particular literary text—a source is. In its broadest terms, source study asks what an author has used of what he has read (or seen or heard) in creating his plot, characters, themes, structure, imagery, or style: its guiding principles should be tact and a sure sense of relevance. In order to avoid mistaking commonplaces or casual resemblances for evidence of specific influence and thereby falling prey to what André Morize calls the "hypnotism of the unique source,"[11] the scholar needs to read voraciously in the literature, history, philosophy, science, and popular culture of his period and to know the literary and intellectual traditions upon which it drew. To develop a sense for what ideas or images were in the common domain he must know how people were educated, what they read, what they heard in churches or on the stage or in coffeehouses, what they talked about in salons or taverns. Only against such a background can the scholar undertake a judicious evaluation of parallels in ideas or structure or language between two texts to see whether they are sufficiently close and unusual to suggest influence. He will then try to determine whether external evidence can document the probability of influence—by finding direct references to the supposed source in notebooks or other personal records, for example, or at least by mapping out channels of accessibility through the study of library holdings, publication history, manuscript circulation, the personal contact of authors, or the like. Modern as opposed to older style source study recognizes, however, that the writer's appropriation of commonplace material may be as important to the genesis of a literary work as his debt to a specific author. The scholar's primary interest is in the process by which the creative imagination transforms both kinds of sources into new and unique forms.

One increasingly popular activity involves the collection and publication in one place of major sources for important literary works. The limitations of such collections are obvious enough: long texts must be excerpted; only the clearest parallels of language and imagery can normally be included; parallels of structure and genre are very difficult or impossible to present; and there is little space for careful critical analysis of the ways in which the sources have been used. Nevertheless, such collections provide a most important staging ground from which to proceed to further investigations and more sophisticated analyses. An invaluable scholarly resource of this kind is W. F. Bryan and Germaine Dempster's *Sources and Analogues of Chaucer's* Canterbury Tales (1941), which was the collaborative effort of several distinguished scholars of the MLA Chaucer Group. Another, completed by a single scholar, is Geoffrey Bullough's eight-volume *Narrative and Dramatic Sources of Shakespeare* (1957–75). The well-nigh insuperable selection problem Bullough faced was partially resolved by his decision to include only narrative and dramatic texts, but even so, the extracts included often cannot adequately present Shakespeare's debts to the sources in question. Bullough's valuable introductions discuss Shakespeare's creative uses of and departures from his chief sources, and a long concluding essay draws out the general principles— relating to external circumstances, personal artistic preferences, and overarching thematic concerns—that seem to govern Shakespeare's choice and treatment of sources. Such a collection and analysis affords an insight obtainable in no other way into Shakespeare's craftmanship.

Despite its early date (1927), John Livingston Lowes's classic, *The Road to Xanadu: A Study in the Ways of the Imagination*, is probably still the most successful source study in English literary scholarship. Lowe's brilliant detective work uncovered a prodigious wealth of sources for Coleridge's *Rime of the Ancient Mariner* and *Kubla Khan*, and he made that recovery the vehicle for critical interpretation of those poems. Lowes began with Coleridge's ninety-leaf notebook of 1795–98, which contained jottings from his reading. Then, with the help of the Bristol library records, he traced elements of Coleridge's imagery and vision to numerous books of natural history and science as well as to a host of travel books old and new (*Purchas his Pilgrimage*, the explorations of Frederick Martens, William Barents, William Bartram, Captain George Shelvocke, and many others). From persuasive external evidence and close stylistic analysis, Lowes made his investigation yield virtually a line-by-line reconstruction of the way in which the Coleridge poems came into being, as products of the poet's remarkable imaginative synthesis and transmutation of what he had read.

Literary scholars are more likely, just now, to engage these issues from the opposite perspective—influence—and they are reinforced in this by contemporary theoretical interest in literary influence and its effects upon writers. The basic question in such studies is, how does influence work? In a seminal essay, "Tradition and the Individual Talent" (1917), T. S. Eliot described literary influence as a harmonious interaction of the present with the past, in which the poet's historical consciousness of past literary tradition is "present" in his own work in such a way that "not only the best, but the most individual parts of his work may be those in which the dead poets, his ancestors, assert their immortality most vigorously."[12] Half a century later, W. Jackson Bate saw the issue in much more problematic terms, and his title, *The Burden of the Past and the English Poet* (1970) alludes to the melancholy engendered in the major eighteenth-century writers by their awareness of their own lesser stature as compared to the greater ancient and Renaissance poets. Bate credits them with responding creatively to this melancholy by marking out new territory for themselves—new genres and verse forms. He credits them also with nurturing the great Romantic poets of the next age, who were able to respond to Shakespeare, Spenser, and Milton as liberating rather than intimidating forces by reason of their "animating, creative desire to live and share in the same company" (pp. 131–32). By contrast, Harold Bloom's several provocative books focus upon the Romantic and post-Romantic poets. Bloom portrays them as standing in the shadow of Milton and proposes a psycho-poetics of literary influence on some analogy to the Freudian "family romance" (*The Anxiety of Influence*, 1973; *A Map of Misreading*, 1975; *Poetry and Repression: Revisionism from Blake to Stevens*, 1976). Bloom considers that poets regard their poetic "fathers" with Oedipal anxiety, as threats to their own development: if weak, the new poets will submit and imitate; if strong, they will misread the parent poet in a variety of ways so as to appropriate him to their own use or image, thereby clearing imaginative space for themselves.

Though theoretical conceptions such as these affect modern influence studies, historical scholars generally pursue questions of literary relationship rather than of psychological response. Some of the finest influence studies have investigated patterns of transmission across eras. Recognizing how profoundly and complexly the concept of "imitation" in educational and rhetorical theory affected literary consciousness from the Renaissance through the eighteenth century, Douglas Bush's *Mythology and the Renaissance Tradition in English Poetry* (1932, rev. ed. 1963) traces the manifold ways in which classical myths and stories (chiefly from Ovid) were adapted and transfigured in Renaissance literature without wholly losing the associations of the originals. A more recent example is Rosemond Tuve's *Allegorical Imagery: Some Mediaeval Books and Their Posterity* (1966). This inquiry into the backgrounds of Renaissance and especially Spenserian allegory makes a fundamental assumption about influence and demonstrates its relevance for criticism: that we are more likely to understand what allegory meant to the Elizabethans by looking closely at those medieval allegorical books they demonstrably read and enjoyed than by appealing to Romantic or modern conceptions of allegory.

Other studies consider the impact of a particular writer upon subsequent writers. George H. Ford's *Keats and the Victorians* (1944) illustrates one approach to such an inquiry—a detailed account of just how Tennyson, Arnold, Rossetti, Morris, Swinburne, and others regarded Keats and what they drew from him in terms of attitudes, style, and verbal reminiscences. Hyatt H. Waggoner takes another tack with regard to Emersonian influence in his *American Poets: From the Puritans to the Present* (1968). Defining Emerson's influence less in terms of specific literary debts than as a governing ethos characterized by the persistent probing of personal experience and the search for transcendent meanings, Waggoner claims that "Emerson is the central figure in American poetry . . . not only the founder of the chief 'line' in our poetry but essential for an understanding of those poets not numbered among his poetic sons" (p. xii).

Milton has been the subject of all kinds of influence studies, by reason of his large impact upon so many writers in so many genres and countries as well as his prominent place in contemporary theories of influence. Some address particular relationships in quite specific thematic or stylistic terms, as does Anne D. Ferry's *Milton and the Miltonic Dryden* (1968), or H. J. C. Grierson's *Milton and Wordsworth* (1937), or Joseph A. Wittreich's *Angel of Apocalypse: Blake's Idea of Milton* (1975). In much broader terms, Wittreich's recent books (ed., *Milton and the Line of Vision*, 1975, and *Visionary Poetics: Milton's Tradition and His Legacy*, 1979), identify Milton as the poet who crystallized and then transmitted to later English poetry a visionary or prophetic tradition derived from the biblical Book of the Apocalypse. Significantly, the title chosen by Balachandra Rajan for a collection of scholarly essays, *The Presence of Milton* (1978), intends to suggest the diversity and complexity of modern influence study by a term "ample enough to accommodate the many forms of relationship that arise from and declare the Miltonic continuity" (p. vii).

III. Contexts

The study of contexts for literature—scientific thought, intellectual history, theology, contemporary politics, the social milieu, the other arts—is perhaps the most popular among the varieties of historical scholarship. In a large number of scholarly books, monographs, and articles of this kind, historical investigation is undertaken primarily in the interests of interpretation and criticism. The basic issues for the student of literary contexts are, first, how to identify appropriate contexts and, then, what to do with them. This kind of scholarship calls for (1) careful definition of a rewarding context for the literary work or works and of its appropriate limits; (2) mastery of the materials and methods of the related discipline or disciplines; (3) a firm sense of relevance and proportion, so that the context does not engulf the literary texts or deflect the inquiry from its central concerns; and (4) tactful, judicious, and balanced application of the insights gained in a manner that preserves the integrity and complexity of the literature.

Contemporary politics, current events, and topical references constitute one such context, a context that is of special importance for works of satire, allegory, or rhetorical argument but that is often necessary to explain allusions or themes in other kinds of literature as well. One danger besetting this type of investigation is the forcing of contemporary applications upon recalcitrant material, as in the misguided attempts to find real identities for all of Chaucer's pilgrims or Spenser's knights and ladies; another is exaggerating the importance of topical reference to the writer's overall purposes. In his brilliantly conceived *Tudor Drama and Politics: A Critical Approach to Topical Meaning* (1968), David Bevington treats this vexed question. He notes the considerable amount of external evidence (including the comments of Elizabeth herself and her contemporaries) concerning the political import of many dramas, but sets aside as unproved or improbable many proposed specific equations between real and dramatic events or persons, as well as most theories about secret meanings in the various plays. Bevington concludes that "politics is germane to a remarkable percentage of Tudor plays, but in terms of ideas and platforms rather than personalities" (p. 25). In his view the plays address such questions as: how should men come to authority? to what extent may the populace demonstrate about just grievances? how far may powerful counselors enforce their "advice" on the monarch?

David V. Erdman reaches a different conclusion in *Blake, Prophet against Empire: A Poet's Interpretation of the History of His Own Times* (1954). This study demonstrates how pervasive in Blake's mythological poetry were actual historical references to the American Revolution, the French Revolution, the slave trade, the threatened Napoleonic invasion of 1803, and much more. Yet Erdman also avoids literalistic equations, recognizing that Blake's invented myths always universalize the particular. Erdman's investigative methods are those that any scholar dealing with political contexts must employ and adapt to his own concerns: "I have read the newspapers and looked at the prints and paintings and sampled the debates and pamphlets of Blake's time. As Blake would say, I have 'walked up & down' in the history of that time. And I have learned to read the idiom of current allusion with sufficient familiarity to detect its presence even in Blake's obscurer pages" (p. viii).

The contemporary social milieu affords another context, one that is of particular importance for the realistic novelist or dramatist. Dickens is a case in point, for his novels not only reflect and criticize contemporary manners, relationships, and institutions (sometimes with specific reformist intention) but have themselves been widely used by historians as evidence of Victorian social mores and conditions. Noting the growth of interest among literary historians in the social and economic environment from which particular works of literature have emerged, Humphrey House proposed in his influential book, *The Dickens World* (1941), to trace "the connexion between what Dickens wrote and the times in which he wrote it, between his reformism and some of the things he wanted reformed, between the attitude toward life shown in his books and the society in which he lived" (p. 14). House's method involves a detailed comparison between actual English conditions and locales and the way these are treated in Dickens' novels, giving special attention to contemporary history, economic circumstances, social change, and attitudes and institutions concerned with charity, religion, and politics. One methodological problem in such studies, as House himself noted, is the tendency to regard the novelist as a kind of journalist, thereby blurring the distinction between fact and fiction, between polemical and artistic intention. Despite this limitation the field has proved fruitful: House's very useful book was itself the inspiration for several more intensive surveys of specific aspects of Dickens' society, notably Philip Collins' *Dickens and Crime* (1962) and *Dickens and Education* (1963).

Science and scientific ideas constitute another important context for literature, sometimes studied to illuminate the specific allusions and assumptions of a particular writer, sometimes to indicate how such ideas find reflection in the literature of an era. Walter Clyde Curry's early but still valuable work, *Chaucer and the Mediaeval Sciences* (1926, rev. ed. 1960), shows how extensively and precisely Chaucer employs concepts from the medieval systems of physiognomy, medical science, astrology, dream lore, and alchemy, among others, to characterize several of his pilgrims and to advance the action of several of the tales. Not only has Curry recovered these systems for the reader, but he has also shown how they function in Chaucer's poems, "fully assimilated, and . . . absolutely essential to the finished work of art" (p. xviii). Marjorie Hope Nicolson worked upon the broader canvas. *The Breaking of the Circle: Studies in the Effect of the "New Science" upon Seventeenth Century Poetry* (1950, rev. ed. 1960) traces the impact of the cosmology of Copernicus and Galileo upon the literary imagination and imagery of major seventeenth-century poets. And *Newton Demands the Muse: Newton's Opticks and the Eighteenth Century Poets* (1946) examines the impact of Newton's *Opticks* upon the visual imagination and the rendering of light and sight in eighteenth-century poetry.

Other literary scholars have concerned themselves with the impact of philosophical ideas or texts upon a given writer or group of writers. Working with a single poet, Louis I. Bredvold in *The Intellectual Milieu of John Dryden* (1934) outlines the several currents of philosophical skepticism and fideism in Dryden's age, arguing that Dryden's skeptical intellectual cast of mind was reinforced and given direction by them. A broader and more complex study, Rosalie Colie's *Paradoxia Epidemica: The Renaissance Tradition of Paradox* (1966), discusses the various Renaissance ways with paradox (rhetorical, theological, ontological, epistemological), seen as deriving from ancient logic and rhetoric and from Christian thought. The argument proceeds by analyzing the great paradoxical writers of the period (Rabelais, Donne, Burton, and Milton, among others). Colie's method presents the context in organic relation to the literary texts rather than as a body of concepts to be first understood and then applied—a kind of synthesis particularly attractive to contemporary scholars.

Theological contexts have also been much explored, particularly for poets using religious subject matter such as Dante, Milton, the metaphysical poets, Gerard Manley Hopkins, but also for others. D. W. Robertson's seminal and controversial work on medieval aesthetics invokes Christian and, more specifically, Augustinian theology and aesthetics to explain much medieval literature and art, including Chaucer (*A Preface to Chaucer: Studies in Medieval Perspectives*, 1962). Also seminal but more limited in its claims, Louis L. Martz's *The Poetry of Meditation* (1954, rev. ed. 1962) examines various methods of religious meditation (Ignatian, Augustinian, Salesian, Baxterian) and makes suggestive applications of this material to several English religious poets usually termed metaphysical. In another kind, the several contributions to the volume *Literary Uses of Typology from the Late Middle Ages to the Present* (ed. Earl Miner, 1977) explore the changing ways in which the ancient biblical mode of typological or figural interpretation finds its way into the literature of various eras; the particular attraction of such a volume resides in its scope, its flexible approach to the context studied, and the employment of a range of methods variously appropriate to the several periods and kinds of literature.

Most kinds of historical investigation just discussed are used in preparing standard editions of literary texts, which usually provide historical annotations and expository notes as well as textual apparatus. John Butt, general editor of the Twickenham edition of *The Poems of Alexander Pope* (II vols., 1939–69), discusses this matter, observing that historical study is essential for Pope's poetry since "much of it is made out of echoes and imitations of earlier poets, to whose ideas Pope gives better expression, and much of his wit is to be understood only from the knowledge of the secret history of his time" (IV, ix). But the particular emphasis in the individual volumes of this edition is sensibly adjusted according to the kinds of poems requiring annotation. The editor of the *Dunciad*, supplementing the already voluminous commentary supplied by Pope himself, presents much information on Pope's dealings with his literary contemporaries, the editor of *Imitations of Horace* concerns himself especially with Pope's political affiliations, and the editor of *An Essay on Man* traces phrases and ideas taken from various intellectual works. Questions of authorship and attribution in such standard editions are mainly the business of textual scholarship. but some of the research needed to resolve such questions is necessarily historical. A good introduction to the problems involved is David V. Erdman and Ephim G. Fogel, eds., *Evidence for Authorship: Essays on Problems of Attribution* (1966).

IV. History of Literary Elements, Forms, Genres

Some more strictly historical kinds of literary research trace the development over time of various elements, forms, or genres of literature in one or more eras or countries. Among the elements that have been studied in a historical frame are individual words, images, *topoi*, motifs, themes, literary conventions, verse forms. The primary issues for literary scholars of this kind are how to identify and describe the continuities and changes in the element in question and how to assess the various casual factors bearing upon this development.

The *OED* traces "on historical principles" the etymology and evolution of meaning in English words from their earliest known use to the present, illustrating richly from literary texts. E. R. Curtius' *European Literature and the Latin Middle Ages* (1948; trans. Willard R. Trask, 1953) is an enormously valuable history of several *topoi*, organized something like an encyclopedia, with discrete entries. These include the *locus amoenus*, the Book of Nature, the inexpressibility topos, the world upside-down, the *puer senex*, and very many more of the most significant *topoi, sententiae*, and themes that originated in classical literature and were transmitted through the Latin texts and education of the Middle Ages into Western European literature. Maren-Sofie Røstvig's two-volume study, *The Happy Man: Studies in the Metamorphoses of a Classical Ideal, 1600–1760* (1954, 1958) can exemplify the history of a single motif or theme, in this case the *beatus ille* motif as it was derived by Renaissance writers from texts in Horace and Vergil and then used and transformed over a century and a half in various English country-house and landscape poems. Formal elements also have their histories: examples are George Saintsbury's formidable three-volume *History of English Prosody from the Twelfth Century to the Present Day* (1906–10), and George Williamson's *The Senecan Amble: A Study in Prose Form from Bacon to Collier* (1951).

The history and development of particular genres is also a perennial focus of the historical scholar's attention. Massive, comprehensive surveys such as Ernest A. Baker and Lionel Stevenson's eleven-volume *History of the English Novel* (1924–67) have given way to more limited studies that often undertake to trace the development of a particular subspecies of a given genre in a given period by a critical analysis of major works. Moreover, the most impressive recent genre histories are concerned with genre theory as well, defining the formal and thematic characteristics of the kind in question and accounting for the way it develops. Examples in the field of fiction are Jerome H. Buckley's *Season of Youth: The Bildungsroman from Dickens to Golding* (1974) or R. F. Brissenden's *Virtue in Distress: Studies in the Novel of Sentiment from Richardson to Sade* (1974). The range and varieties of method in genre history may be indicated by a few distinguished titles: J. W. Lever, *The Elizabethan Love Sonnet* (1956); Murray Roston, *Biblical Drama in England from the Middle Ages to the Present Day* (1968); C. S. Lewis, *The Allegory of Love: A Study in Medieval Tradition* (1936); D. A. Stauffer, *The Art of Biography in Eighteenth-Century England* (1941); Fredson Bowers,

Elizabethan Revenge Tragedy 1587–1642 (1940); Ian Jack, *Augustan Satire: Intention and Idiom in English Poetry, 1660–1750* (1952). The conjunction of theoretical, historical, and critical concerns in such works may lead to problems in organization and balance; other problems may arise from the treatment of complex works in terms of an exclusive genre-set, when in fact they incorporate mixtures of kinds.

Not surprisingly, the most impressive genre histories have approached the question of genre complexly, with attention to both formal and thematic characteristics and also to various cultural factors affecting the genre's transformations over time. C. M. Bowra's *From Virgil to Milton* (1945) outlines the principal characteristics of the literary epic, whose prototype is Vergil, and then indicates how the *Aeneid* and its chief successors (Camoëns' *Os Lusíadas*, Tasso's *Gerusalemme Liberata*, Milton's *Paradise Lost*) variously reflect, encapsulate, and criticize the ethos of their respective cultures. The study is both comparative and historical: it ignores the numerous minor Vergilian epics that would be included in any complete history in order to concentrate on the genuine masterpieces, uniting critical discussion of these to the account of the genre's development.

A quite different kind of genre history is György Lukács' theoretical analysis of the historical novel from a sophisticated Marxist perspective, tracing the course of its development in relation to the social and economic changes of the nineteenth and early twentieth centuries.[13] Lukács argues that the historical novel emerged from the realist social novels of eighteenth-century England, and he identifies Sir Walter Scott as the creator of its classic type. Scott was the first to derive the individuality of his characters from the specific historical reality of their age and to define the most satisfactory kind of plot as that in which major historical events and personages remain at the periphery while at the center are ordinary people upon whose lives the forces of history impinge. Eschewing a comprehensive survey of the historical novel, Lukács focuses upon its major practitioners—Scott, Cooper, Pushkin, Stendhal, Balzac, and Tolstoy, for example—and gives some attention also to parallel but more problematic developments in the historical drama. Looking beyond formal elements, Lukács locates the essence of the historical novel in its strong commitment to the portrayal of man's life in history—"the social and human motives which led men to think, feel and act just as they did in historical reality" (p. 42). So conceived, the historical novel is not a special genre with rules of its own but a realistic novel having a conscious and fully developed historical awareness. Lukács expects this awareness, in its turn, to transform the contemporary social novel into "a genuine history of the present, an authentic history of manners" (p. 169).

Modern scholars are also finding it useful to extend accepted genre categories or devise new ones in order to accommodate newly recognized forms. An example is Theodore Ziolkowski's *Fictional Transfigurations of Jesus* (1972), which proposes to define and trace the development of a new genre comprising some twenty works, from *The True History of Joshua Davidson* (1872) to John Barth's *Giles Goat-Boy* (1966). Their common generic feature is a structure based to a determining degree on the events of the Gospels transposed to the terms of an entirely modern plot. Ziolkowski's proposition is that the parallels are formal, not thematic or ideological; the formal design is furnished by Jesus in the role of mythic figure or culture hero, even as Odysseus' voyage provides the formal pattern for Joyce's *Ulysses*. "Genre" probably is not the precise literary term for the "kind" Ziolkowski is describing, but his inquiry proceeds as a genre history and owes much of its success to the methods of genre history.

V. Literary History

Literary history in the strictest sense—chronological surveys of the literary production of a particular era or nation—has also taken new directions. One major issue for the contemporary literary historian is whether to attempt comprehensiveness (by some method) or focus upon specific patterns. Another is how to treat literary periodization (the identification of period characteristics, the reasons for period change).

The great works of comprehensive literary history from the nineteenth and early twentieth centuries were the products of the scholarly labors and unified vision of a single individual. Hippolyte Taine's *Histoire de la littérature anglaise* (4 vols., 1863–64), Francesco De Sanctis' *Storia della letteratura italiana* (2 vols., 1870–71), Georg Brandes' *Hovedstrømninger i det 19de Aarhundredes Litteratur* (6 vols., 1872–90), W. J. Courthope's *History of English Poetry* (6 vols., 1895–1910), and Vernon L. Parrington's *Main Currents in American Thought* (3 vols., 1927–30) are all multivolume works adducing various theories about national characteristics and historical conditioning as shaping forces in literature. Some European scholars have continued as individuals to write massive literary histories—for example, Antoine Adam's five-volume *Histoire de la littérature française au xvii*ᵉ *siècle* (1948–56), and Francesco Flora's five-volume *Storia della letteratura italiana* (rev. ed., 1959). But increasingly, because of the massive amounts of material requiring synthesis, inclusive literary history has become the province of cooperating groups of scholars, while individual scholars treating literary eras or periods often eschew comprehensiveness to explore limited but illuminating patterns.

One group endeavor is the projected twelve-volume *Oxford History of English Literature* under the general editorship of F. P. Wilson and Bonamy Dobrée (1945–). Each of the volumes or half-volumes is the responsibility of a single scholar, with the inevitable result that the individual volumes are uneven in quality and diverse in their methodology, assumptions, and approach, though each gives some attention to cultural backgrounds, major genres, important literary movements, and dominant authors, and each contains a substantial bibliography. Some are particularly distinguished: Douglas Bush's *English Literature in the Earlier Seventeenth Century, 1600–1660* (1945, rev. ed. 1962) is organized around genres and types of writing rather than particular authors, emphasizing thereby the sheer diversity of literary production in the age and reinforcing that emphasis with a very extensive bibliography. Bonamy Dobrée's volume, *English Literature in the Early Eighteenth Century, 1700–1740* (1959), also intends, in the author's words, "to give a general view of the literary activity of the period" (p. ix), but it focuses more directly on the great writers. Another cooperative enterprise, the *Literary History of the United States* (1946, 4th ed. 1974), was produced by more than seventy authors and a board of editors headed by Robert E. Spiller. It has two volumes, a history and a bibliography, both of them updated periodically. Because the several authors divided responsibility for particular chapters, the work as a whole does not in fact have the distinctive focus Spiller proposed when he described it as the record of a uniquely American literary tradition, which emerged from European origins but took shape in response to indigenous American experience. Spiller's conception of this literary history as "one kind of history of the United States" (p. ix), the portrait of a people in their literature, dictates consideration of literary texts less as works of art than as the means through which the culture of the American people was made articulate.

Much recent literary history by individual scholars undertakes to unite historical and critical concerns and to organize material in terms of significant patterns rather than straightforward chronology or inclusiveness. Hallett Smith's extremely useful *Elizabethan Poetry* (1952), subtitled *A Study in Conventions, Meaning, and Expression*, openly proclaims itself a hybrid: "This book is neither a systematic chronological survey of Elizabethan nondramatic poetry or a purely critical and evaluative judgment of it" (p. v). Smith observes that he is attempting to define the "series of ideals, values, commonplaces, or conventions" that make up the essential contexts for the era's poetry: "I am trying to explain, in part, the 'Elizabethan-ness' of Elizabethan poetry" (p. vi). Smith's method is to trace the development within the period of its most important literary kinds (some of them conventional genres, some not)—pastoral poetry, Ovidian poetry, sonnets, satire, poetry for music, heroic poetry—showing how particular works in each kind influence one another. The book offers a new model for literary history.

Another venture into a new kind of historical/critical analysis is Earl Miner's trilogy on seventeenth-century literature. The titles point to a concern for chronology, but especially for the identifying features of the dominant literary modes: *The Metaphysical Mode from Donne to Cowley* (1969), *The Cavalier Mode from Jonson to Cotton* (1971), and *The Restoration Mode from Milton to Dryden* (1974). As Miner makes clear in several places, these books examine the confluence of perceptions, attitudes, and values that characterize each mode. Yet the books also present historical movement, since each mode itself changes over time, and the order of predominance among them changes. Miner observes, for example, that after Donne and Jonson the lyric begins to take on narrative features, a reordering that presumes "a profound shift in human attitudes toward experience" and that "about 1640 conceptions of narrative experience begin to replace lyric conceptions."[14]

VI. History of Ideas; Social and Cultural History

Other fields of activity for the literary scholar are the history of ideas and cultural history. For the contemporary scholar in these modes, the issue is how to honor the uniqueness of the literary work while at the same time recognizing how it is embedded in society and culture. In the most exciting studies of this kind, the literary work is not studied as a document for tracing cultural history, but rather, the literary text is shown to embody that culture organically, in stylistic and formal aspects as well as in themes.

In the course of its long tradition, the history of ideas has accommodated various methodologies. For A. O. Lovejoy, the study of literature should be chiefly concerned with its thought content and the history of literature should be "a record of the movement of ideas" that are "in great part philosophical ideas in dilution."[15] Lovejoy's method involves breaking up complex philosophical systems into what he termed "unit-ideas" and tracing the origin, development, and appearance of these in many kinds of texts, literary and extraliterary. His *Great Chain of Being* (1936) traces and illustrates the concept in question in texts from Plato to Schelling, but focuses on eighteenth-century literature and thought; other Lovejoy essays address such topics as "Nature as Aesthetic Norm," "The Parallelism of Deism and Classicism," and (with George Boas) *Primitivism and Related Ideas in Antiquity* (1935).

Another form of the history of ideas is to be found in Perry Miller's influential book, *The New England Mind: The Seventeenth Century* (1939), whose declared aim is to present "rather a topical analysis of various leading ideas in colonial New England than a history of their development" (p. vii). Under such headings as "Religion and Learning," "Cosmology," "Anthropology," and "Sociology," Miller traces the origin, interrelations, and significance of Ramist rhetoric and dialectic, Augustinian piety, educational theory and practice, the conversion experience, the view of nature, and other components of American Puritan thought and experience. That these ideas constituted a unified body of thought virtually unbroken for three generations is cited in justification of the structural rather than chronological focus of the study, which Miller offers as "a chapter in the history of ideas" (p. vii). Conceived on similar lines—as analyses of the component ideas defining a particular era but also as portrayals of the *Zeitgeist* or spirit of the age—are Henri Peyre's notable studies, *Qu'est-ce que le classicisme?* (1922, rev. 1965), *Qu'est-ce que le romantisme?* (1971), and *Qu'est-ce que le symbolisme?* (1974).

An impressive recent contribution to the historiography of ideas, illustrating the special fusion of classical studies, art history, and Renaissance thought characteristic of the scholars of the Warburg Institute, is Frances Yates's *The Art of Memory* (1966). This is a history of theory and techniques for training the memory, based upon important texts from classical times through the Renaissance describing various memory systems—rhetorical, gothic, occult, cosmological. Because the memory systems taught their adepts to impress particular places (drawn from contemporary architecture) and images (drawn from contemporary imagery) upon the memory as a filing system for materials to be recalled, Yates's study also suggests the relation of the practical art of memory to general aesthetics in the various eras.

Histories of literary criticism are also a species of the history of ideas—ideas relating to aesthetics and poetics. René Wellek's four-volume *History of Modern Criticism: 1750–1950* is written from the perspective of a modern theorist and critic. Wellek explains that he began with 1750 because "in the later 18th century there emerge . . . doctrines and points of view which are relevant even today"[16] and that he sees his subject as involving a mix of aesthetics, theory, literary history, and practical criticism. Identifying his method as a variety of the history of ideas, Wellek treats the impact of the general intellectual climate and of specific philosophical systems upon critical theory, though he excludes as unmanageable the consideration of actual literary practice on the one hand or of social, political, and cultural causation on the other. In fact, Wellek seldom uses the pure history-of-ideas method of tracing key concepts or unit-ideas through several texts, preferring, as he explains, the more traditional practice of treating the major figures as individuals, summarizing and discussing the critical *oeuvre* of each in its entirety and rich diversity.

Bernard Weinberg's two-volume *History of Literary Criticism in the Italian Renaissance* (1961) constitutes a deliberate departure from the methods of those who, in Weinberg's terms, tend "rather to summarize texts than to analyze them, rather to disrupt texts (by isolating terms and passages) than to discover their structures, rather to construct chronologies than to write histories" (p. vii). His own method embodies the critical pluralism of the Chicago critics. The Renaissance texts on poetics are grouped into two categories: (1) general theoretical documents showing chronological developments, continuations, or mixtures of the great classical traditions of Plato, Aristotle, and Horace and (2) works dealing with the critical issues (as they developed chronologically) in the literary quarrels over Dante and Ariosto, Speroni and Guarini. Within these categories Weinberg undertakes to present each text as an entity: "to state . . . its central position, to give an epitome of its premises and its conclusions, and to discover the method by which it passed from premises to conclusions" (p. viii). The result is a history that proceeds by extended analysis of particular texts (and thereby makes available in considerable detail much material inaccessible outside the great libraries of Italy) but that also treats interconnections and developments by commenting on particular themes within the chronologically ordered sequences.

In recent years the notion that ideas can or should be detached for study from the material and social conditions that nourish them has come under increasing criticism, and not only from Marxist scholars. The effort to locate literature securely in its culture has led at times to the transformation of literature into sociology but has also produced some exciting and illuminating literary studies. A notable example is Raymond Williams' *The Country and the City* (1973), a sophisticated Marxist analysis of various literary works from the sixteenth to the twentieth century, works that present powerful images of country or city life (pastorals, country-house poems, landscape poems, urban satire, realistic novels, science fiction). The study shows how these texts reflect or contrast with the contemporary realities of life on farm or in village, in country house or city. Williams' underlying thesis, that capitalist society has caused dislocations in both country and city that are reflected obliquely or directly in literature, does not preclude careful attention to genre and classical tradition, where relevant, and to poetic texture. The special value of the study is its treatment of the complex ways in which literary images and social realities may interact in shaping human consciousness.

Other literary scholars have sought to make literary analysis itself the ground of cultural interpretation. Perhaps the most important and influential book of this kind in recent years is Erich Auerbach's *Mimesis*, subtitled *The Representation of Reality in Western Literature* (1946; trans. Willard R. Trask, 1953). The work begins with a now classic essay, "Odysseus' Scar," contrasting the passage in Book 19 of the *Odyssey*, in which the old housekeeper Euryclea recognizes Odysseus, with the biblical passage in Genesis xxii, in which God bids Abraham to sacrifice Isaac. These passages are shown to embody two contrasting styles, which have exercised a determining influence upon ways of perceiving and representing reality down to the present day. The Homeric style is characterized by externalized description, uniform illumination, smooth connections of parts, the foregrounding of all events, clarity of meanings, and little historical development or psychological perspective. The biblical style is characterized by multiplicity of meanings, abruptness, need for interpretation, a background in which much is left obscure or unexpressed, claims to universality, and the notion of historical becoming. The various permutations of these styles are then traced through passages in Petronius, Dante, Rabelais, Shakespeare, Cervantes, Molière, Schiller, Zola, and Virginia Woolf, among others. The texts chosen are all from "realistic works of serious style and character" (p. 491), and they are analyzed with great flexibility and subtlety so as to draw out the rich significance of these two "styles" in Western culture.

M. H. Abrams' *Natural Supernaturalism: Tradition and Revolution in Romantic Literature* (2nd ed. 1975) has a period focus, but within those limits it examines the specific organization and texture of a wide variety of literary, philosophical, and historical texts as embodiments of the culture that produced them. Abrams grounds his study upon a particular text—Wordsworth's "Prospectus" for his intended masterpiece, *The Recluse*, which he set forth in the "Preface" to *The Excursion*. The book is organized as a sequence of movements out from and back to specific passages in the "Prospectus," catching up in the course of those sweeps striking parallels in other Romantic poets, philosophers, writers of autobiography and romance, and political theorists. By this means Abrams points up common Romantic values, imagery, forms of thought and imagination, designs of plot or structure, conceptions of the authorial persona, and much else. Abrams' work is also, on a vast scale, a kind of influence study, tracing the secularization of inherited Christian theological ideas and patterns in England and Germany, two Protestant nations that were heirs alike to a biblical culture and to traditions of theological and political radicalism. Abrams positions his central literary text and his related contemporary texts in a wide historical frame, which reaches back to the Bible, to Christian exegesis, to devotional and confessional literature, and to philosophy and forward to those moderns in whom the Romantic values persist: his thesis asserts that "Romantic thought and literature represented a decisive turn in Western culture" (p. 14).

Paul Fussell's impressive study, *The Great War and Modern Memory* (1975) exhibits yet another way of fusing literary analysis, historical event, and the history of culture. The book's comparatively limited focus—the British experience on the Western front in the 1914–18 war as recorded in literature—permits the analysis of some complex interactions between literature and life in brilliant and suggestive detail. Fussell studies how the war experiences were remembered, conventionalized, and mythologized by literary means in literature and, conversely, how inherited myths set forth in the literary and rhetorical tradition often shaped the way in which actual events were perceived and recorded in documents, memoirs, and other nonliterary forms. This study of the interaction of literature and history in the generation and transmission of important cultural myths has fascinating implications for the conception of literary history.

The kinds of historical scholarship exhibited by Auerbach, Abrams, and Fussell persuade by complex presentation of the manifold ways literary texts relate to, exhibit, transmit, transform, undermine, or revolutionize the values of their culture, past and present. Some version of this task is the fundamental business of all historical scholars of literature, on whatever scale they can manage it and in whatever modes.

VII. Some Common Methods

No matter their interests or fields, historical scholars of literature share certain procedures and need to develop some special qualities. Some readers may be surprised by the assertion that the primary requirement for such a scholar is a speculative mind and a wide-ranging (though disciplined) imagination. But after all, the source and starting point of all scholarly work must be the discovery of a good problem—one that needs to be and can be solved. The scholar finds his or her way to such a problem by means of a lively curiosity, a healthy skepticism about received explanations adduced on less than overwhelming evidence, and an awareness of how new research, approaches, and techniques might be made to address old problems. The crucial role of the scholarly imagination (as well as the happy rapprochement of the disciplines of history, literary history, biography, and criticism) may be illustrated in the conception and execution of Christopher Hill's *Milton and the English Revolution* (1977). The distinguished historian seems to have asked himself two questions not hitherto formulated by Miltonists: can it be that Milton's fundamental ideas as manifested in his prose works and in his great poems are much more closely related to those of the radical fringe in seventeenth-century England than anyone has ever supposed? and how might recognition of such a relationship change our perception of the poet and his works? Often enough, as in Hill's case, questions of this kind will grow directly out of a scholar's previous work, and the very posing of the question will imply a tentative hypothesis, though if the question involves a new field and unfamiliar material, the hypothesis will probably come later. In either case, the scholar arrives at his working hypothesis by speculation or imaginative guessing, though he also needs sufficient flexibility to keep from being locked into his tentative formulations before all the evidence is in, as well as a scrupulous honesty that will force him to revise or abandon any hypothesis not truly supported by the evidence.

The next stages call for patience, carefulness, and scholarly discipline. A thorough survey of the state of the question must determine whether it has been addressed or partially answered elsewhere: the starting points are such general bibliographical resources as the *Cambridge Bibliography of English Literature* or the *Literary History of the United States*, the comprehensive annual *MLA International Bibliography* or the annual bibliographies published by the Modern Humanities Research Association; the annual bibliographies of particular literary periods or topics published in some of the scholarly journals; lists and abstracts of doctoral dissertations; and other bibliographical resources available for the particular topic. (Bibliographical searches of this kind are likely to be expedited in the near future by a greater use of computer technology.) The actual research involves searching out and examining likely sources of evidence: printed books, rare publications housed in the great research libraries in America and abroad, manuscripts in library collections or private hands, public documents and records of all kinds, private diaries and letters. For these activities the scholar needs sound judgment as to what may prove relevant, painstaking accuracy in transcribing materials (though photocopying now makes that task easier), and, again, imagination to spark the methodological searches. Any seasoned researcher can recount a score of literary adventure stories about finding his or her way by inspired hunch or lucky accident to valuable materials.

In the subsequent stages—analyzing the material, revising the hypothesis and the scope of the project as necessary, plotting the argument and adjusting its claims to the nature of the evidence—the literary scholar needs broad knowledge, sound judgment, and literary tact, in order to assign new findings their just place in the total order of what is known. Christopher Hill's study has some limitations in the matter of judgment and balance: he brilliantly uncovers new dimensions of Milton as a political poet but pays less attention than the case demands to literary convention and to the transformations wrought by a powerful creative mind upon both political experience and literary convention. Hill also exemplifies one attractive way of meeting the scholar's final challenge, the written presentation of the argument: his book is lucid, forceful, often witty, effective in marshalling evidence, and forthright in stating and arguing positions; the rhetorical style is engaged, personal, persuasive.

Most historical scholars of literature will also need at one time or another a rather formidable array of skills and related disciplinary knowledge. Certainly they need languages—not only the French and German usually required of Ph.D. candidates to assure their access to the scholarship and criticism published in those tongues but also, for any literary period before the modern era, Latin (in addition to a thorough knowledge of classical literature). Renaissance scholars also need Italian and should have Greek; students of Romanticism need to know German literature and philosophy well; medievalists require an array of Romance, Teutonic, and Celtic languages in their older forms and dialects; and literary scholars of all periods and kinds need at times to work comparatively, examining related works in other languages and literatures. Moreover, any student of a particular national literature needs to know from historical philology something of the way the language in question developed at various periods. There is more: the techniques of descriptive bibliography can help the scholar discover what the physical features of a book reveal about its provenance. Paleography will be required for reading manuscripts, particularly those from earlier periods. In addition, literary scholars need to know a good deal about the political, economic, and social history of their period of specialization, about its philosophy and theology, its visual arts and its music; they should also keep abreast of the advances in methodology in such related fields. Beyond all that, modern psychology and social theory can enhance understanding of literature, writers, and the creative process, and a rich fund of human experience will certainly do so.

Obviously, few literary scholars, however learned, can know or possess all this, and doctoral students can only make a start toward acquiring what they need to know according to the priorities suggested by advisers and the work of scholars whom they most admire. There is comfort in the fact that the historical scholar of literature can and must continue to develop the skills and disciplines needed for various projects as he or she undertakes them. In a very real sense, the essential training of a literary scholar takes place throughout a lifetime.

Notes

1 Robert E. Spiller, "Literary History," in *The Aims and Methods of Scholarship in Modern Languages and Literatures*, ed. James Thorpe, 2nd ed. (New York: MLA, 1970), p. 55; René Wellek and Austin Warren, *Theory of Literature*, 3rd ed. (New York: Harcourt, 1962), pp. 254, 264.

2 Roy Harvey Pearce, *Historicism Once More: Problems & Occasions for the American Scholar* (Princeton: Princeton Univ. Press, 1969), pp. 3–45; Wellek and Warren, *Theory of Literature*, pp. 38–45.

3 Claudio Guillén, *Literature as System: Essays toward the Theory of Literary History* (Princeton: Princeton Univ. Press, 1971), p. 420.

4 Michael Riffaterre, "The Stylistic Approach to Literary History," *New Literary History*, 2 (1970–71), 55.

5 Ralph Cohen, ed., Introduction, *New Directions in Literary History* (Baltimore: Johns Hopkins Univ. Press, 1974), p. 9.

6 James Clifford, *From Puzzles to Portraits: Problems of a Literary Biographer* (Chapel Hill: Univ. of North Carolina Press, 1970), pp. 84–87. Clifford's fifth kind, fictional biography in which the imagination is given full reign, clearly falls outside the domain of scholarly biography.

7 Frank Manuel, "The Use and Abuse of Psychology in History," *Daedalus* (Winter 1971), p. 205.

8 W. Jackson Bate, *Samuel Johnson* (New York: Harcourt, 1977), pp. xx–xxi.

9 See also James L. Clifford's second volume, *Dictionary Johnson: The Middle Years of Samuel Johnson* (New York: McGraw-Hill, 1979).

10 Northrop Frye, "Literature as Context: Milton's *Lycidas*," in *Milton's* Lycidas: *The Tradition and the Poem*, ed. C. A. Patrides (New York: Holt, 1961), p. 207.

11 André Morize, *Problems and Methods of Literary History* (1922; rpt. New York: Biblo and Tannen, 1966), p. 88.

12 T. S. Eliot, in *Selected Essays, 1917-1932* (London: Faber & Faber, 1932), p. 14.

13 György Lukács, *The Historical Novel*, trans. Hannah and Stanley Mitchell (London: Merlin Press, 1962), trans. of *Der historische Roman* (1937; rpt. Berlin: Aufbau, 1955).

14 Earl Miner, *The Restoration Mode from Milton to Dryden* (Princeton: Princeton Univ. Press, 1974), p. xiv.

15 A. O. Lovejoy, *The Great Chain of Being: A Study of the History of an Idea* (1936; rpt. New York: Harper, 1960), pp. 16–17.

16 René Wellek, *A History of Modern Criticism: 1750-1950*, I (New Haven: Yale Univ. Press, 1955), v. A projected fifth volume dealing with the first half of the twentieth century has not been published.

Additional Reading

On History and Literary History

Aaron, Daniel, ed. *Studies in Biography*. Cambridge, Mass.: Harvard Univ. Press, 1978.

Barzun, Jacques. "Biography and Criticism—A Misalliance Disputed." *Critical Inquiry*, 1 (1974–75), 479–96.

———. *Clio and the Doctors: Psycho-History, Quanto-History & History*. Chicago: Univ. of Chicago Press, 1974.

Bush, Douglas. "Literary Scholarship and Criticism." *Liberal Education*, 47 (1961), 207–28.

Cohen, Ralph, ed. *New Directions in Literary History*. Baltimore: Johns Hopkins Univ. Press, 1974.

Damon, Phillip, ed. *Literary Criticism and Historical Understanding*. New York: Columbia Univ. Press, 1967.

Edel, Leon. *Literary Biography*. 1957; rpt. Bloomington: Indiana Univ. Press, 1973.

———, ed. *Literary History and Literary Criticism*. New York: New York Univ. Press, 1965.

Ellmann, Richard. *Literary Biography*. Oxford: Clarendon, 1971.

Foerster, Norman, et al. *Literary Scholarship: Its Aims and Methods*. Chapel Hill: Univ. North Carolina Press, 1941.

Guillén, Claudio. *Literature as System: Essays toward the Theory of Literary History*. Princeton: Princeton Univ. Press, 1971.

Hexter, J. H. *Doing History*. Bloomington: Indiana Univ. Press, 1971.

Historical Studies Today. *Daedalus* (Winter and Spring 1971). Rpt. *Historical Studies Today*. Ed. Felix Gilbert and Stephen R. Graubard. New York: Norton, 1971.

Mazzeo, Joseph A. "Some Interpretations of the History of Ideas." *JHI*, 33 (1972), 379–94.

Nicolson, Marjorie Hope. "A Generous Education." *PMLA*, 79 (1964), 3–12.

Pachter, Marc, ed. *Telling Lives: The Biographer's Art*. Washington, D.C.: New Republic, 1979. (Essays by Leon Edel, Justin Kaplan, Alfred Kazin, Doris Kearns, Theodore Rosengarten, Barbara W. Tuchman, and Geoffrey Wolff.)

Pearce, Roy Harvey. *Historicism Once More: Problems and Occasions for the American Scholar*. Princeton: Princeton Univ. Press, 1969.

Stern, Fritz, ed. *The Varieties of History from Voltaire to the Present*. 1956; rpt. New York: Random House, 1973.

Thorpe, James, ed. *The Aims and Methods of Scholarship in Modern Languages and Literatures*. 2nd ed. New York: MLA, 1970.

———, ed. *Relations of Literary Study: Essays on Interdisciplinary Contributions*. New York: MLA, 1967.

Wellek, René. *A History of Modern Criticism: 1750–1950*. 4 vols. New Haven: Yale Univ. Press, 1955–65.

———. *The Rise of English Literary History*. Chapel Hill: Univ. North Carolina Press, 1941.

Wellek, René, and Austin Warren. *Theory of Literature*. 3rd ed. New York: Harcourt, 1962.

Primary Scholarly Resources

Altick, Richard D., and Andrew Wright. *Selected Bibliography for the Study of English and American Literature.* 6th ed. New York: Macmillan, 1978.

Bond, Donald F. *A Reference Guide to English Studies.* 2nd ed. Chicago: Univ. of Chicago Press, 1971.

New Cambridge Bibliography of English Literature. Ed. George Watson. 5 vols. Cambridge: Cambridge Univ. Press, 1969–77. Revision of the *Cambridge Bibliography of English Literature (CBEL).* 4 vols. Cambridge: Cambridge Univ. Press, 1940.

Literary History of the United States. Ed. Robert H. Spiller et al. 2 vols. New York: Macmillan, 1974. See especially Vol. II: Bibliography.

British Museum [now the British Library]. *General Catalogue of Printed Books to 1955.* 1959–68. With supplements.

The National Union Catalog. Library of Congress. Pre-1956 imprints. 1968– . With supplements.

Pollard, A. W., and G. R. Redgrave. *A Short-Title Catalogue of Books Printed in England, Scotland, and Ireland, and of English Books Printed Abroad, 1475-1640 (STC).* Oxford: Oxford Univ. Press, 1926. Rev. ed. W. A. Jackson, F. S. Ferguson, and Katharine F. Pantzer. 1976– .

Wing, Donald. *Short-Title Catalogue of Books Printed in England, Scotland, Ireland, Wales and British America and of English Books Printed in Other Countries, 1641-1700.* 3 vols. New York: MLA, 1945–51.

———, et al. *Short-Title Catalogue of Books Printed in England, Scotland, Ireland, Wales and British America and of English Books Printed in Other Countries, 1641-1700.* 2nd ed. 3 vols. New York: MLA, 1972– . Vols. I and II are in print as of 1980.

Oxford English Dictionary (OED). 13 vols. Oxford: Oxford Univ. Press, 1933.

Dictionary of National Biography (DNB). 22 vols. Oxford: Oxford Univ. Press, 1882–1953. With supplements.

Critical Inquiry. 1974– . See exchange among M. H. Abrams, Wayne Booth, and J. Hillis Miller in Vols. 2 and 3.

Journal of the History of Ideas. 1940– .

History and Theory: Studies in the Philosophy of History. 1960– .

New Literary History: A Journal of Theory and Interpretation. 1969– . See especially Vol. 1.

On Research Methods

Altick, Richard D. *The Scholar Adventurers.* 1950; rpt. New York: Free Press, 1966.

———. *The Art of Literary Research.* Rev. ed. New York: Norton, 1975.

Barzun, Jacques, and Henry F. Graff. *The Modern Researcher.* 3rd ed. New York: Harcourt, 1977.

Bateson, F. W. *The Scholar-Critic: An Introduction to Literary Research.* London: Routledge and Kegan Paul, 1972.

Beaurline, Lester A., ed. *A Mirror for Modern Scholars: Essays in Methods of Research in Literature.* New York: Odyssey, 1966.

Christopher, H. G. T. *Paleography and Archives: A Manual for the Librarian, Archivist, and Student.* London: Grafton, 1938.

Elton, G. R. *The Practice of History.* New York: Crowell, 1967.

Erdman, David V., and Ephim G. Fogel, eds. *Evidence for Authorship: Essays on Problems of Attribution*. Ithaca, N. Y.: Cornell Univ. Press, 1966.

Gaskell, Philip. *A New Introduction to Bibliography*. Oxford: Oxford Univ. Press, 1972; largely supersedes R. B. McKerrow, *An Introduction to Bibliography for Literary Students*. Oxford: Oxford Univ. Press, 1927.

Morize, André. *Problems and Methods of Literary History with Special Reference to Modern French Literature*. 1922; rpt. New York: Biblo and Tannen, 1966.

Stallman, R. W. "The Scholar's Net: Literary Sources." *College English*, 17 (1955), 20–27.

Literary Criticism

Lawrence Lipking

In the early 1960s, when Northrop Frye contributed a brilliant essay on literary criticism to a previous version of this volume, both his own work and that of a generation of critics seemed to have established some enduring critical truths. Many of the methods of literary criticism, including his own, remained controversial. Yet most critics tended to agree that their field had matured into a discipline, capable of defining terms, identifying and reprimanding certain fallacies and accepting a common body of principles. Frye's own statement of principles reflects that confidence. For the sake of convenience his argument may be reduced to four points.

1. "We have to avoid of course the blunder that is called the intentional fallacy in criticism. The question 'What did the author mean by this?' is always illegitimate. First, we can never know; second, there is no reason to suppose that the author knew; third, the question confuses imaginative with discursive writing. The legitimate form of the question is: 'What does the text say?' "

2. "The metaphor of the judge, and in fact the whole practice of judicial criticism, is entirely confined to reviewing, or surveying current literature or scholarship: all the metaphors transferred from it to academic criticism are misleading and all the practices derived from it are mistaken. . . . Criticism never leads logically to a value judgment: value judgments may be assumed at one end or emitted at the other, but the relation between them is rhetorical only. The source of the confusions involved here is the failure to distinguish criticism from the direct experience of literature."

3. The aim of academic criticism "is categorical and descriptive: it tries to *identify* a writer's work." To this end, "the primary understanding of any work of literature has to be based on an assumption of its unity. However mistaken such an assumption may eventually prove to be, nothing can be done unless we start with it as a heuristic principle."

4.   "The primary axiom of critical procedure is: Go for the structure, not for the content. This must be the invariable attitude of every genuine critic," because the social and moral benefits of studying literature come not from its content or "great thoughts" but from "the sense of the total form or *telos* of criticism as the theory of literature, studying literature as a coherent and unified order of words, and becoming in itself a coherent and unified body of knowledge by virtue of that order."

Frye's principles retain their interest; they have been debated but not refuted. Yet the confidence that they reflect has ebbed away. Indeed, a great deal of the development of literary criticism, in the past few decades, might be viewed as a direct reaction to each of his points, or even as a direct contradiction of each of the "truths" accepted by many critics not long ago.

1.   So far from being dismissed as a "fallacy," the study of the author's intentions now seems to some critics the surest single ground of interpretation. The question "What does the text say?" might be considered merely a dehumanized or falsely "objective" version of "What did the author mean?" since texts neither mean nor say in the absence of specific human beings to write and read them. Only by acknowledging the priority of the author's intention at the moment of writing, E. D. Hirsch has argued, can we hope to achieve any standard of validity in interpretation. And even critics who disagree with that position have shown an increasing interest in the author's conscious or unconscious meanings, in the author's readings or misreadings of previous texts. A new revitalization of Freudian theory, in recent criticism, opposes the distinction between the author's psychology and the meaning of the text. Biographical speculation has returned as a permitted analytical tool.

2.   The divorce of criticism from the direct experience of literature, and consequently from value judgments, now seems to many critics a way of anesthetizing or depoliticizing literature, cutting it off from its life in the responses of readers. Works of art do not exist, according to some current theories, until they have been perceived. Thus whole schools of criticism are now devoted to the experiences of readers, whether to determine the value of texts by their effects on those who read them, to define an implied reader within the text, to analyze the minds and feelings of readers, or to construct a general theory of reading. Although the metaphor of the judge may have lost its hold over academic criticism, the metaphor of a jury of peers—each reader responsible for constituting the text in his or her own way—would stand for a good deal of lively recent work.

3.   The aim of *identifying* a work of art by defining its theme or principle of unity now seems to many critics an illusion or mystification. Literary texts are notoriously difficult to categorize or paraphrase, and their tendency to evade definition may signify a fundamental resistance, within literature itself, to any principle of unity. Much current criticism sets out to demonstrate the multiplicity or radical indeterminacy of texts. The longing for unity, critics have argued ever since Nietzsche, betrays a nostalgia for outmoded beliefs: for a world ruled over by a single god, a personality fixed in a single identity, or a work of art deciphered by a single interpretation. On the contrary, no single interpretation can account for a work of art, and a critic who has fully accepted this lesson will cease to look for a principle of unity and instead will recognize and welcome the essentially arbitrary nature of critical activity. Such critics are willing to sacrifice the hope of certainty in exchange for an unrestricted, independent play of mind.

4.   In the wake of structuralism, a focus on structure rather than content now seems to many critics an artificial means of privileging literature and literary study by isolating them from moral and social concerns. The idea of a literary *telos*—an autonomous, coherent, and unified order of words—can easily merge with the idea of a literary canon—a closed corporation or hierarchy of accepted forms. Hence the emphasis on structure may well serve the interests of a latent conservative ideology. Marxists, feminists, and other socially concerned critics have drawn attention to the way that discussions of literary form can be used to neutralize or mask the underlying issues of power—such questions as, what books do we read? who chooses them? and what do we read them *for*? A discontent with formalism is now widespread. Some critics have reacted by affirming the priority of content over structure in the analysis of literature; other critics have sought some means of reuniting content with structure in a dynamic, mutually sustaining equality. But relatively few critics still agree with the final implication of Frye's vision of a *telos*: that all literary critics, no matter what their differences, are cooperating in a single great enterprise, or that all literary critics have interests in common.

What do these four points of disagreement indicate about the current practice of criticism? First of all, obviously, the prevalence of disagreement. It would be a mistake for a young critic to suppose that Frye's assumptions have been "replaced" by more recent ideas. Critical assumptions do go in and out of fashion, but those with vitality seldom vanish altogether. Just as the history of recent criticism might be dubbed, from the perspective of twenty years ago, "the return of the fallacies," doubtless many positions that seem fallacious today are awaiting their moment of return. Indeed, one might argue that the four areas of disagreement correspond to the most ancient divisions of criticism, an emphasis respectively on the author, the audience, the form of the work, and the relation of the work to the world it imitates. Yet the repudiation of so many "truths" does suggest that principles of literary criticism can less than ever be taken for granted. Whether or not criticism is in a state of crisis, it is surely in a state of contention.

The climate of disagreement spreads far beyond theory. Perhaps the most sobering document of current literary criticism is neither a book nor an article but the latest MLA Convention Program. The immense proliferation and fragmentation of topics supply visible evidence of critical divisions. Though all the participants belong to the same society, many of them seem not to belong to the same world of discourse. Certainly they do not agree on first principles. Whether we regard the program as a sign of healthy participatory democracy, of chaos, or simply of professional necessity, it demonstrates vividly how many scattered voices are trying to be heard at the same time. Nor do other practical tests of what critics believe disclose any better consensus. In many colleges and universities, for instance, the courses once labeled "Introduction to Literary Criticism" or "The History of Literary Criticism" have been dislodged by courses in special studies. No text has replaced Wellek and Warren's *Theory of Literature* as a standard introduction to the field, and there is currently no standard anthology of modern literary criticism.

Another sign of increasing specialization is the division in this book itself, which now separates "Literary Criticism" from "Literary Theory." The distinction responds to a shift in practice. In recent years the production of theory has begun to outpace the explication of texts, and claims for the importance of theory have become more aggressive. As critics grow more sophisticated about their methods and as criticism of classic works accumulates, the "innocent" reading of a text seems harder to justify or publish. The very assumption of critical innocence comes under suspicion; critical principles are no less dominant for being unconscious or implicit. Hence literary critics face strong pressures to declare their interests and presuppositions and to specify the implications of their chosen modes of procedure. A high degree of self-consciousness, a grudging or liberal deference to theory, now characterize a great many academic critics. If Randall Jarrell was right thirty years ago in describing his era as an "age of criticism," then today we are evidently living in an age of criticism of criticism.

The new prestige of theory may also witness a new relation between criticism and literary works of art. In the Anglo-American critical tradition, most of the major critics from Sidney to T. S. Eliot have also been important poets or novelists. Criticism has been intimately tied to creation, either (in Ezra Pound's words) "to serve as gun-sight" or as "Excernment. The general ordering and weeding out of what has been performed." But criticism no longer seems committed to those functions. Many reasons have been suggested for the change: the rising number of academic critics who have flooded out the smaller ranks of genuine poet-critics; the lack of great poets who might challenge and stimulate a criticism to explain them; the increasing influence of continental critics, whose traditions foster a greater stress on theory (many of the major European critics, from Hegel to Derrida, have begun with philosophy rather than literature); or even the desire of critics to rival poets, in the hope of establishing criticism as an autonomous art. Yet whatever the cause, the effect has been pronounced. Fifteen years ago, after a lecture on theory, I heard a poet repeatedly ask a critic the same belligerent question: "What does a critic talk about?" The poet believed there could be only one answer: "Poems. The texts of poems." But neither the question nor the answer would seem so obvious today. Several well-known literary theorists hardly ever write about works of literature (a few theorists, one sometimes fears, hardly ever find time to read them).

Most literary critics *do* write about works of literature and define themselves through that activity. The aim of literary criticism, from this point of view, is the analysis and interpretation of texts. Often this aim is considered to be quite straightforward and unproblematical. Critics engaged in practical tasks like reviewing, classroom instruction, or annotation may well regard themselves as servants of the text, patiently bringing its dark places to the light. Yet the questions raised by theory are not so easily disposed of. Even the most impartial description of a text requires a choice of methods or principles of description. Summarizing a story, we implicitly adopt the view that stories consist of a plot, an imitation of something in the world, a moral; we take, perforce, a critical position. In formal literary criticism this unconscious procedure works toward conscious expression. Thus the tension between theory and practice seems intrinsic to the nature of criticism. Even when critics define their aim as servicing the text through analysis and interpretation, they remain under a double obligation: one toward the text, the other toward the analytic method. In this respect criticism is an art of mediation. It travels between the text and the method chosen for describing it, between textual facts and interpretive hypotheses. Nor can this tension ever be resolved. Even the best hypothesis cannot disappear into the text or insure itself against a later competing hypothesis.

Indeed, the tension exists not only in the nature of literary criticism but in its name. On the one hand, "criticism" has always suggested the mastery of an acquired skill: the "art of discrimination" or the ability "to determine upon principles the merit of composition." In this sense criticism may be opposed both to creation and to passive appreciation, the production and consumption of works of art. Instead, the critic serves as a cicerone, describing, expounding, and judging artistic products. To perform this service properly requires experience and discretion. The critic must be familiar with a great many works of art, learned in the traditions, genres, and laws that govern their formation, and capable of drawing lessons from that knowledge. Quintilius, the ideal critic portrayed in Horace's *Art of Poetry*, applies his skill very firmly: "When you read something to Quintilius, 'Correct this, please,' he says, 'and this.' " Most later critics have dreamed of commanding the same authority. Though Frye rejects both the authoritarianism and the urge to judge, he obviously does view criticism as a skill: the ability to *identify* works of literature by comparing them with other works and with categories or principles of art.

On the other hand, "criticism" may be viewed less as a skill than as a continuous process or habit of mind. The ancient association of "criticism" with "cavilling" or "detraction" represents a permanent tendency: the spirit of contradiction or skepticism that will not rest content with any achievement. In this sense criticism may be opposed, as Arnold opposed it, to dogma. Instead of refining upon tradition or placing works of art, it endlessly asks questions and points out flaws. Nor does it submit to experience or learn discretion. The wisdom of received opinion no sooner establishes principles of criticism, like those summarized so well by Frye in 1963, than other critics descend to tear them apart. Each successive school of modern criticism has made the same strong claims, and each has met the same fate. Doubtless Quintilius himself, after he had applied his skill, was answered by corrections of his corrections, though the scene is not recorded ("critics," in the first sense, are notoriously sensitive to "criticism," in the second). Relatively little attention has been paid, in books on literary criticism, to the sheer disputatiousness, the love of questioning and arguing, that marks so much of the practice of criticism. "Cavilling" has always had a bad press. (Even Blake, who so much liked to pose profound, embarrassing questions, was not himself overly fond of "the idiot questioner.") Yet neither of the two senses of criticism has the right to exclude the other; they are interdependent.

Much of the development of literary criticism in this century, and especially in the last two decades, may be seen as a turn from the first sense of criticism to the second, from the application of traditional skills to a perpetual skeptical questioning. "Putting into question" has become a favorite phrase of contemporary theorists. Nor have many of the old assumptions about literature been allowed to stand unchallenged. Consider again the four areas of disagreement with which we started. In recent years each of these traditional subjects for debate has been declared not merely open to dispute but fundamentally illusionary or invalid—the result of a "mystification." Hence we read, in critics like Roland Barthes, of "the death of the author," whose assumed presence vanishes like a ghost as soon as we question it. Authors exist in the text only insofar as the text conjures them up for its own purposes, like that hypothetical "Cervantes" or "Cide Hamete Benengeli," not to be confused with any actual person, who participates in the fictional games of *Don Quixote* by claiming to write them. A critic who accepts this analysis (not all critics do) will hardly waste time debating the author's "intention." If the author is a fiction, the author's intention must be doubly fictional—a fantasy about a phantasm. And a similar logic will uncover similar vacancies in old-fashioned assumptions about the reader, about literary form, or about the world that art is supposed to imitate. Each of them may be regarded, under questioning, as a mystification (who *is* that reader? can form exist without content? do the "imitated" worlds of literature refer to anything outside literature itself?). Such questions have proved easier to ask than to answer.

A similar line of questioning may be turned against criticism itself. In relation to the other fields of literary study, "literary criticism" may be viewed from a double perspective. From one point of view it perches on top of a pyramid whose building blocks consist of texts and whose feet wear labels like "historical scholarship," "textual scholarship," "aesthetics," and "linguistics." "A further stage in the scholarly organization of literature" (as Frye called it), criticism assimilates the best findings of the other, partial disciplines (what is the best text? what is the historical context?) and completes them by subsuming them in a final act of interpretation. Criticism gives meaning to literary studies; only when we, as critics, have performed our task have we fulfilled the purpose of understanding and placing the text. Not surprisingly, critics have always been fond of this point of view. At times when hostility to criticism has threatened to belittle all literary studies that do not trade in facts, the appeal to critical superiority has had enormous polemical power. Nor is this appeal merely a matter of polemics. In practice as well as in theory, literary studies tend to become arid or even anti-intellectual when divorced from criticism. Moreover, the view of critics as persons who complete the other disciplines also requires them to *know* the other disciplines. A superior position involves burdens as well as privileges. If literary critics stand atop a pyramid, perhaps that testifies not only to their elite situation but to the difficulty of the climb and the precariousness of keeping balance.

From another point of view, however, the notion that literary criticism *completes* anything may seem far too paradoxical. The other disciplines of literary scholarship, it might be argued, do occasionally arrive at definitive results. We can speak of textual scholarship that will hold its place, if not for eternity, then at least for the foreseeable future; we can recognize examples of historical scholarship that, once having been done, will not soon have to be repeated. But when has criticism ever settled an issue for more than a day? Experience teaches us not to expect the verdicts of critics to last; today's authority will be tomorrow's whipping boy. From this point of view literary criticism seems less a "discipline" of scholarship than an exercise in taste. A process, not a product, it stands to scholarly fields as epicurism to cooking or opinion to science. More favorably, one might say, the process of criticism reminds other literary disciplines of their own limitations, not by completing them but by constantly offering other perspectives. In this respect it stands to scholarly fields as gastronomy to cooking or scientific method to science. Criticism does not give meaning to literary studies so much as it prevents them from hardening into premature meanings. It serves as a gadfly or conscience, and its best weapon is the many-sidedness of the text.

Both the aims and methods of literary criticism, therefore, may be seen as double. Criticism aims at interpreting texts or at defending them from simplistic interpretations; it uses the method of elevating particular observations into general principles or of confounding general principles by citing particulars. It erects a schema and notes an exception.

The doubleness of aim and method also affects almost every individual piece of practical literary criticism. Most critics work from two opposing premises or impulses. One premise is the hypothesis: a conjectural interpretation of a text, frequently accompanied by a challenge or assault on previous critical interpretations, and often by a suggestion that the new reading offers a model of a significant theoretical principle. Psychologically, such hypotheses are likely to be born quite suddenly, in the moment when the critic discovers, with a shock of recognition, a private key to the text. From that moment another motive also intrudes: the need to discriminate this interpretation from others, for without a minimal originality even the most worthy piece of criticism will lose its claim, not to soundness, but to publication. The hypothesis establishes its own chain of priorities. Principles of criticism become more or less relevant to it as they afford more or less support; previous criticism assumes a new order according to the extent of its agreement or disagreement.

Let us imagine, for example, that a critic of *The Sorrows of Young Werther* experiences an abrupt insight: the two halves of the book mirror each other, section by section, in perfect symmetry. At once many other features of Goethe's work spring into bold relief: the theme of returning or reprising the past; the author's own theory of *Wiederholte Spiegelungen* ("repeated reflections"); the two-part structures of *Wilhelm Meister, Elective Affinities,* and *Faust*. Soon the hypothesis takes on a life of its own. Reinforcing its position, it tries to encompass more and more of the text or of literature in general. The mirror effect may be seen in rhyming couplets, in the nature of mimesis, or as a universal formal archetype (the Old and New Testaments, Vergil's *Aeneid*, Blake's *Milton*, Shelley's *Prometheus Unbound*, and so forth). Support is enlisted from other critics and perhaps from other fields, like botany, geometry, or crystal formation. Eventually such a hypothesis may require a whole new theory of structure. It props itself up with every kind of evidence and fills all available space. To some extent, then, each piece of criticism or new hypothesis tends to be a microcosm of the field of literary criticism—the attempt at a conclusive act of interpretation.

At this point critics often do something disillusioning: they submit their work to mentors, friends, students, a spouse, or an editor. An experienced critic may simply put a piece in a drawer and reread it later. Many fine hypotheses never recover from this stage. A neutral observer, standing outside the enchanting logic of the hypothesis, is likely to notice flaws. Certain events in the first half of *Werther* are not echoed in the second half; the mathematics and the dating of letters do not quite work out; Goethe's own statements about the work can be interpreted differently; the evidence is too selective. Here the inventor of the hypothesis faces a choice: either to abandon the hypothesis, to defend it against its attackers on the grounds that they have misrepresented or misunderstood it, or to repair it. The last choice, however, may be just the beginning of the ordeal. Each revision of the hypothesis, each new selection of evidence, results in a fresh set of problems. Ultimately no critical idea is immune to challenge. Moreover, the effort to protect the argument against possible criticisms may well lead to ruinous consequences: either stretching and refining the hypothesis until it has become utterly, safely bland or losing the central thread in a patchwork of individual knots and stitches. A few critical pieces survive this process, but many more escape to the printer with the signs of compromise still upon them—stubbornly ignoring contrary evidence or revised almost to extinction. Criticism is the enemy of criticism. In this respect every critical interpretation contains a destructive element: a habit of skepticism or contradiction or disinterested inquiry that undermines every effort to reach a final conclusion.

The process we have been observing is not unique to literary criticism. Every scholarly inquiry might be held to follow a similar pattern: the formulation of hypotheses, the endeavor to refute them, issuing in still more conjectures and refutations. But the process seems peculiarly characteristic of criticism, for several reasons. First, the nature of a poem (as Coleridge argued) may be defined as a constant adjustment between part and whole, in which the unusual intensity of individual linguistic details must be made compatible with a larger design, and the larger design must reward attention to individual details. Hence the process we have seen in criticism, accommodating hypotheses to particulars and vice versa, may be thought an inevitable response to the internal dynamics of literature, reproducing the tension between part and whole in a contingent medium. "Like the motion of a serpent, which the Egyptians made the emblem of intellectual power; or like the path of sound through the air; at every step he pauses and half recedes, and from the

retrogressive movement collects the force which again carries him onward"
(*Biographia Literaria*, xiv). Coleridge's description of the reader's serpentine
motion of mind points to a second reason why the critic must be involved in a
pattern of unending hypotheses and refutations: every reader shares the same
involvement. Indeed, the formation and modification of hypotheses may be
thought to *constitute* a text, or at least our experience of a text. Moreover, the
text represents not only the object to be interpreted but the final evidence for
the correctness of that interpretation. Unlike the scientist or the historian, the
critic reaches no conclusions that cannot be immediately tested and judged in
the experience of the reader. That is a third reason why the process looms so
large in criticism: it cannot be avoided. Finally, one might maintain, criticism
only comes alive as a process. The interplay between hypotheses and
corrections may be regarded not as a means to an end, like the knowledge
sometimes attained by history and science, but as the end itself, like a work of
art. A criticism that arrived at incontrovertible judgments would cease to be
criticism.

    If criticism is destined to remain always in process, however, if critical
hypotheses can never be verified and critical certainty can never be attained,
what right has criticism to be considered a field of knowledge? Does every
reading or interpretation of a literary text have an equal claim to validity? Few
critics would say so. Yet the practice of criticism in recent years leaves
considerable room for doubt. Almost no hypothesis about a text, however alien
to common sense, seems too preposterous to attract some admirers. There is
no court of final appeals in criticism, no generally accepted rule about what
may be permitted. Many critics appear to have lost confidence in their ability to
distinguish a valid interpretation from one merely paradoxical or ingenious.
And other critics, it seems, have decided that the effort to refute hypotheses is
none of their business. Instead, a hypothesis must be pushed to its limit and
beyond, impatient of all restraint and heedless of any objections. "The road of
excess leads to the palace of wisdom." The originality and force of the
unrestrained interpretation, in this view, will more than compensate for any
distortions noticed by weaker minds. Nor is this reasoning unsupported by its
results. Many of the best and most famous critics have attained success not by
being accurate but by being extreme, boldly following their vision to its end. As
the posthumous reputation of Walter Benjamin has grown, in the last few
decades, scholars like René Wellek have begun to remark not only the
contradictions in his thought but also his carelessness; at times Benjamin
seems incapable of summarizing a story without changing the details or
missing the point. Yet such mistakes have apparently not diminished his rising
eminence in the least. Indeed, in some circles Benjamin is now regarded as the
greatest modern critic. The test of criticism, from this perspective, is not its
correctness but its ability to be interesting. If no hypothesis can shut off
criticism, then a good hypothesis will be known through its power to survive
and flourish after its refutation. Or so many critics believe.

    Are standards of criticism really so flexible? In practice the answer is no.
Even though critical descriptions can never close the book once and for all,
even though critical judgments remain relative rather than absolute, most
literary critics are still convinced that they can tell the difference between a

correct and an incorrect piece of interpretation. And so are most editors. If no interpretive hypothesis is absolutely right, some are nevertheless more nearly right than others. A good many hypotheses, at any rate, seem wrong. Even those literary critics who deny, in theory, the possibility of valid interpretation tend, in practice, to dismiss many interpretations that offend their sense of logic or their sense of the text. "Fallacies" have gone out of style; errors have not. And no survey of the aims and methods of literary criticism will be complete unless it takes account of errors.

The first source of error, so obvious that far too often it goes without mention, is simply not knowing enough. The interpretation of a text depends on having a proper text to interpret; the interpretation of linguistic details invites some attention to the nature of language; the interpretation of a historical document requires a minimum of historical knowledge. Literary criticism is not an island, separated from the other disciplines of literary scholarship. It takes from them and gives to them. Nor do most critics have much reason for complacency about what they know. It is a rare critical article, in my experience, that does not suffer from at least one error about a text, one historical mistake, or one misunderstanding of a word (the adverb "still," for instance, which once meant "always," has prompted dozens of published blunders). Whole arguments have been built on such errors. Indeed, one might maintain that whole fields—for example, studies of Diderot, *The Dream of the Red Chamber*, or Emily Dickinson—were perverted for many years by systematic misconstructions of what the author wrote. Ideally, literary critics like to regard their work as beginning where scholarship ends. But in practice much criticism has not reached the beginning of scholarship. Infested by errors, even the best designed critical analysis will sink like a termite-ridden boat.

Nothing causes more acrimony between critics and those who criticize them than accusations of faulty or sloppy scholarship. With good reason, critics tend to be defensive about such charges. The art of criticism, they may reply, does not concern itself primarily with matters of fact. Instead it exercises powers of discrimination, interpretation, and judgment that an obsession with facts might well destroy. Since the gathering of facts never reaches an end and since even the best scholars acknowledge large gaps in their own stores of information, meticulous scholarship often appears to be a way not of preparing a critical judgment but of avoiding it. Criticism, like any act of the mind, requires a leap of faith: a decision to stop accumulating materials and begin to put them to use. A good critic cannot afford to be pedantic. Even in the classroom (as I. A. Richards' experiments confirmed long ago) a fresh, sincere encounter with a naked text frequently results in more sensitive readings than those weighed down by historical and biographical details. Like skilled surgeons, critics need only a minimal amount of information about the history of their patients; the important thing is that they be alert and handy, and know what they are doing.

Plausible as it seems, however, this line of defense is not altogether convincing. The distinction between the facts about a text and the interpretation of a text cannot always be sustained; at many points they blur into one another. When a textual editor observes that criticism is weakened by attending to some text that the author did not actually write, doubtless the argument carries some weight. Not all critics would agree, to be sure. A few years ago I received a paper from a student who had hinged his reading of Keats's "Ode to a Nightingale" on a single, crucial line: "To thy high requiem become a god." But the last word, I pointed out, was "sod." After some research the student conceded the point, but not the argument. It was true, he admitted, that his interpretation had been based on a verbal substitution. Yet many well-known critics (he cited Kenneth Burke) consciously practiced the same technique. The worth of his criticism could hardly stand on such a gratuitous detail as a single letter. It deserved to be judged as if Keats *had* written "god," and then it would be found a highly original piece of work. The ingenuity of this argument impressed me; we compromised. But I was also impressed, as other, better-known critics have since impressed me, with his lack of shame. Few respectable critics feel comfortable when caught in a misquotation or an error of fact. When the case is gross, we lose some of our confidence in the critic; when it is repeated, we cease to trust the critic. Very good academic critics, fortunately, also tend to be very learned scholars who steer their way around mistakes. Yet no one is infallible. Not many critical articles can survive the scrutiny of an unforgiving specialist with all their facts intact. And critics with consciences often spend their lives haunted by their dependence on other people's research and other people's knowledge—with the pack of pursuing scholars only a step behind.

Yet many critics fear a second source of error much more: the errors induced by faulty reasoning. Even in the absence of universally accepted critical standards, criticism seems bound to standards of logic, argumentation, and consistency. Granted a premise, how well has the critic followed out its implications? Most readers continue to ask that question. Moreover, here again most critical pieces are vulnerable. The desire to prove a case can easily lead to special pleading or suppression of evidence. At one extreme such biased arguments reduce critics to manipulating private codes, like the cryptographers who used to find messages hidden everywhere in Shakespeare, though no two critics ever seemed able to duplicate each other's results. At another extreme, reason itself may be doubted. The complexity of literary texts—the need of the critic to confront matters as subtle or nebulous as tone, feeling, theme, the sounds and connotations of words, irony, symbolism, and quality—has driven some critics to despair of logic or to rely on impressionism. Even the style of criticism often seems calculated to rival, rather than to serve or explicate, the literary text. The tendency of artists to regard the critic as an artist manqué is justified, to some extent, by Wilde's formula of "the critic as artist," as well as by critics who hold themselves unaccountable to logical reasoning. Nor can it be denied that good criticism usually draws on some of the resources of art. But most readers of criticism would prefer to take their art direct and to go to criticism for commentary and explanation. Artists create; critics reason. And critics who accept argument as their mode of discourse must also accept its rules.

Errors of fact and errors of logic can be demonstrated more or less conclusively; by and large most critics agree on the need to shun them. A third source of error, however, is far more problematic and controversial: the errors that arise from principles of criticism themselves. Criticism, we have already suggested, contains elements of scholarship, of dialectical reasoning, and even of art. But it also contains an element of science: the definition and establishment of a coherent body of principles. Most critics regard their field as progressive. We like to think that, over the centuries, criticism has evolved and matured. We know how to read Shakespeare better than Thomas Rymer or Voltaire did, and we know how to read lyric poems and oral narratives with techniques unknown to our ancestors. The sense of progress has dominated criticism at least since the Renaissance. Almost every major critic of modern times has promised, in some early manifesto, a new establishment of criticism on fixed and certain principles. But the claim also implies, obviously, that most earlier criticism was based on mistaken principles. Insofar as literary criticism has succeeded in defining correct principles of analysis, then every critic who departs from those principles may be accused of error.

Yet the claims of criticism to be regarded as a science, with its own standards of correct or incorrect procedure, relevant or irrelevant evidence, continue to be viewed with a good deal of skepticism. Even the most rigorous critics rarely pretend to have discovered a method applicable to every critical situation. Most interpreters of texts pay lip service, at least, to such notions as eclecticism or pluralism: a willingness to acknowledge that competing principles of criticism may have equal validity according to the texts they consider, the problems they set out to answer, and the modes of discourse they choose to adopt. Nor would even the most progressive scholars always deny the validity of older critical principles in relation to their own times. Dante the critic will forever have something to teach us about Dante the poet. A critic who assures us that he or she has permanently settled the outstanding questions of the field is likely to be engaging not in science but in pseudoscience. The field accommodates a wide variety of valid questions and answers. The house of criticism has room for many mansions.

Nevertheless, it is both possible and necessary to accuse a great many critics of being mistaken in their principles. If no critic possesses the whole truth, neither is any critic entitled to pretend that his or her half-truths and quarter-truths have any authority over a text. Far too much criticism suffers from dogma. In practice, many critical articles compromise themselves in their opening few sentences, where it is all too easy to elevate a bland truism or an ingenious sophism into an imposing universal law. "All poetry is made of language." On the face of it, what could be more plausible or self-evident? Yet few pieces of criticism recover from such a beginning. Unless the critic is extremely careful, the self-evident observation will soon inflate into a monster of dogmatic assertion, employed less as an instrument for investigation than as a weapon against all other, equally plausible assertions ("all poetry is made of feelings"; "all poetry is made of structures"; "all poetry is made of ideas and images"; "all poetry is made of tensions"; "all poetry is made of the human need for order"; "all poetry is made of other poetry"; etc.). None of these premises is wrong, exactly; none is inadequate to sustain a valid critical analysis. Yet neither is any of them sufficiently, exclusively strong enough to eliminate the others. Experienced critics learn to beware of almost any statement in the form of "all poetry is. . . ." Categorical assertions soon deteriorate into special pleading, if not into outright error.

The most characteristic sort of critical error, that is to say, more often stems from exaggerating a right principle than from adopting a wrong one. The "intentional fallacy" became identified as an error, quite properly, because many critics thought they could substitute an inquiry into intentions for any other critical analysis. The identification of the "affective fallacy" and the "genetic fallacy" was a legitimate response to schools of criticism that gave a privileged and largely unexamined status to impressionistic reports of emotions and to simple explanations of the "causes" of literary works. Are questions about the intentions of the poet, the effects on the reader, the genesis of the poem, then, utterly barred to a responsible critic? Certainly not. They become dangerous when, and only when, too much is expected from them, when they cease to be one of many possible aids to interpretation and become the end or replacement of interpretation. A little critical learning is a dangerous thing. Critics who have become infatuated with a single principle have already established their policy toward the text: to bend it to their will.

Two plausible sorts of objection may be offered to this line of argument, and each of them deserves a hearing. First, it might be maintained that, by putting so great an emphasis on critical errors, I have prejudiced the right of the critic to follow imagination and intuitions wherever they may lead. "Correct" criticism, in any case, is impossible, and an obsession with avoiding error will only result in stilted and inhibited criticism. The insights provided by the best and most stimulating critics correspond intrinsically with their special "blindness": the narrow but powerful lenses that focus the vision while eliminating most of the field. Nor could it be otherwise. In criticism as in science, the instrument of analysis can never measure itself, and thus it inevitably introduces distortions of its own devising into whatever it surveys. No interpretation can be purified of its own shadow: the "hermeneutic circle" or principle of uncertainty that accompanies every investigation. But wise critics will take this principle not as a limiting factor but as a license to do what they wish. Since every interpretation depends on some bias, the test of interpretation must be how much its biases can help to illuminate. "Correctness" is not only an impossible but a pusillanimous ideal. Far better for critics generously to accept their involvement in error and to pursue their vision boldly to its ultimate brink of destruction.

Much of this analysis strikes a sympathetic chord. Certainly most criticism does not suffer from an excess of imagination, and the willingness of a critic to try new ideas and take new risks may be one of the reasons we admire him or her. Yet such efforts at originality can degenerate very quickly into a cynical and trifling self-promotion. The critic's impatience with logical constraints can easily extend to impatience with rival criticism or even with the text itself—a bar as well as a stimulus to vision. Moreover, the notion that, because no interpretation can escape some distortion, every interpretation is equally distorted clearly entails a logical confusion. The principle of uncertainty might be thought instead to put a special onus on the critic, as it does on the scientist, to avoid as many errors as possible. Nor does the argument that a preoccupation with error will inhibit criticism carry much weight, unless we believe that massive production of criticism is itself a positive good. Many readers would welcome almost any method of inhibiting criticism. If imaginative criticism is in short supply, then criticism that is both imaginative and relatively free from error should be even more precious. It does not seem too high a goal toward which to strive.

A second objection to my argument, however, may be thought more serious. By identifying critical errors with the exaggeration of a principle, rather than with its ultimate soundness or unsoundness, have I not prematurely waived the possibility of formulating a sound, consistent, and universally valid basis for literary criticism? The health of any field depends on the ability of scholars to learn from their mistakes. Why should it not be possible for critics to continue to learn, until someday the whole field of criticism will have attained a rigor and coherence unknown to us today? The present sophistication of criticism demonstrates how far we have come. Perhaps we are only beginning to understand the basic principles of the field.

Like any supposition grounded upon a hope or expectation of what may happen in the future, the call for a rigorously logical criticism can hardly be refuted in the present. Perhaps someday criticism *will* have become a science, equipped with scrupulous (if not infallible) rules of procedure. Perhaps someday critics *will* agree on most (if not all) of their principles. Everyone impatient with the current illogic and anarchy of much of the field would welcome that day. But it does not seem near. Indeed, according to my own account it seems much further away than most critics twenty years ago would have believed. Some of the principles that once seemed most secure have now turned into issues for debate. And even the starting place, in positing a universally valid criticism, is far from certain.

What might that starting place be? Contemporary theorists often put their trust in semiology, the system of signs from which literature is generated. But practical critics who continue to believe in the possibility of logically rigorous interpretation ordinarily subscribe to some version of Frye's third principle: "The primary understanding of any work of literature has to be based on an assumption of its unity." Here if anywhere, it might seem, critics of different persuasions can agree: the whole of a text is greater and more significant than any of its parts. Thus, according to John M. Ellis (*The Theory of Literary Criticism: A Logical Analysis*, 1974), "The object of literary criticism, then, is an interpretative hypothesis as to the most general principle of structure which can be abstracted from the combination of linguistic elements in a literary text." And Walter A. Davis (*The Act of Interpretation: A Critique of Literary Reason*, 1978) aims at a similar goal: "Put in the simplest and most exacting terms, the task of interpretation is to apprehend the purposive principle immanent in the structure of a literary work which determines the mutual interfunctioning of its component parts." Though one critic looks for a "general principle of structure" and the other for a "purposive principle immanent in the structure," both found their interpretations on a sense of the whole, an "integral totality." Critics begin by postulating the unity of the literary work, proceed by adjusting each part to the whole, and end by redefining the unity—the "structure" or "purpose"—in the light of what they have discovered. So Aristotle recommended, so Coleridge, and so most of today's interpreters.

As a formula for guarding the critic against partial or scrappy interpretations, the assumption of unity doubtless has practical uses. A critic who focuses on one or two details of a text always needs reminding that the significance of details depends on their function within a larger whole. When Keats changed a line in "To Autumn" from "While a gold cloud gilds the soft-dying day" to "While barred clouds bloom the soft-dying day," he was making choices that affect our reading not only of the line but of the whole poem (where the paradox of "bloom" on the "dying" might be thought central to the conception). The analysis of such a line obviously requires an understanding of its place within the total structure and meaning of "To Autumn." Similarly, no character in a story or play exists independent from his or her function in the work as a whole, and no literary theme floats free from the complications introduced by its particular embodiment. If the best explanation of any phenomenon is that which explains most, both in general and in particular, then the best literary criticism is necessarily the most comprehensive. Critics who emphasize one aspect of a text at the expense of all others—like composition teachers who mark nothing but grammar—only reveal their own limitations. A sound analysis begins and ends with the whole.

If so many interpreters agree on this principle, however, why do so few seem to carry it out? A number of reasons might be given—not least the human frailty that prevents us from doing the right thing even when we know what it is. But three more fundamental answers may be given priority. The first is simply that, while almost everyone tries to discover the unifying principle of texts, almost no one accepts anyone else's definition of unity. One person's whole is another's part. Both in theory and in practice, agreement on unifying principles tends to be rare. One critic looks for "structure," another for "purpose"; one critic for "plot," another for "theme"; one critic for "harmony," another for "tension." Nor do such theoretical differences tally in practice. If a dozen critics were given a sonnet by Shakespeare and requested to define its principle of unity, how many would arrive at the same interpretation? The answer need not be taken on faith: a glance at the Variorum will disclose that the probability of any two agreeing comes close to nil. No hypocrisy is involved in these multiple understandings of unity. The truth is that defining the general structure or purpose of a literary work presents almost insuperable problems. On the one hand it can easily lead to vacuous abstractions; on the other to a surfeit of particulars. Each critic tends to search out the strengths of his or her own definition and the weakness of others'. No wonder that the grounds of unity have proved so elusive.

A second, more radical answer might challenge, not the varying methods for defining unity, but the aim itself. What gives us the right to assume that every literary work *does* constitute a whole? On the face of it, a great many masterpieces—*The Satyricon, The Canterbury Tales, The Fall of Hyperion, Don Juan, Dead Souls, Bouvard and Pécuchet*, and *Felix Krull*, among others— seem flagrantly incomplete. None of these examples, to be sure, lacks critics to defend its wholeness. But such defenses merely raise the question of whether the unity of these works, or of any work, exists as anything but a speculation or an artificial postulate after the fact. Though the author may have regarded the work as incomplete, though death may have interrupted it, though the text may be labeled "A Fragment," though it may end in the middle of a sentence, nothing prevents the critic from repairing the deficiency by sketching the unity of the work in its essence or as it might have been. The search for such a principle, we are often told, responds to one of the deepest needs of the human mind. Yet its very universality may warn us of our tendency to discern a whole in anything presented for study—a body, a limb, or even a fingernail. In this respect the principle of unity pertains more to our way of seeing than to anything inherent in the object to be seen. We cannot *not* see unity. But few critics who insist on the obligation of criticism to define the work as a whole would admit that their ideal is so circular: a text perceived whole because the perceiver cannot help it. Most interpreters assume instead that the text possesses some kind of unity—a structure, purpose, theme, plot, meaning, emotional complex—independent of any particular reading. That case remains to be proved.

For practical critics, some skepticism about their own ability to define the principle of unity in the text may well be healthy. Literary works outflank us. Thoroughly interpreted in one direction, they reassemble around another interpretive core. And critics who regard their grasp of the whole with a certain modesty may gain in partial insights what they lose in authoritative pronouncements. Too many critical interpretations that begin with precise, individual acts of attention later push toward grandiosity. No law compels critics to pretend that their own part of the truth can stand for the whole. An interpreter who clarifies one obscure line in a famous poem has performed a greater service than a critic who forces every line to conform to a predetermined meaning. In the best interpretations an attention to parts and a grasp of the whole mutually reinforce each other in a delicate equilibrium. But in criticism a little below that level a modest determination to state what one knows, and only that, can bring its own rewards.

A third and still more radical challenge may be offered, however: a challenge to interpretation itself. Perhaps the difficulty of establishing the unity of a text reflects a more basic problem, the inherent instability not only of the interpretive process but of literary language. The reason that texts evade our efforts to identify them, on this analysis, may be that texts are designed for evasion. We recognize a work of literature precisely because it resists our best attempts to define it, because something is always "left over." Word and meaning, or signifier and signified, never quite coincide. During the last decade whole schools of criticism have arisen to follow out the implications of this gap. The dream of a unified interpretation, such critics would say, leads to inevitable disappointment. Because texts promiscuously interact with other texts and with an infinite supply of possible meanings, every effort to stabilize the conditions of literary discourse merely displaces the notion of significance from one arbitrary resting place to another. Too many readers mistake their own constructions and fictions for the presence of a text. Hence the proper task of criticism is to unsettle; not to yearn for an end to interpretation, but to emphasize and take pleasure in all the contradictory and self-canceling motions that an unbound text inflicts on a reader.

Whatever one thinks of this line of thought, in one respect it neatly complements the search for unity: as a constant reminder to the critic of where the analysis falls short. The ideal of "the whole text" serves to warn the reader that every detail counts, that even the most elegant interpretation is likely to be insufficient or incomplete. The work is larger than our views of it. Accepting that burden, we should expand our horizons and determine to see a little further into the most distant or perplexing regions of the text. Thus the principle of unity, like the principle that something in every text always escapes us, functions to criticize the critic. Not every piece of literary criticism is required to aim at a definitive interpretation, but the possibility of a fuller interpretation should drive critics always to demand more of themselves. The richness of the work asks us to make our perceptions fine.

Indeed, the aim of literary criticism, in relation to the practical critic, may be regarded either as knowledge of the text or of our instruments for perceiving it. Nor are these two incompatible. One of the most popular misconceptions about criticism, recently enjoying a new vogue, has contrasted two ways of dealing with a text: one a selfless dedication to investigating what the work contains in itself, the other a means to self-exploration that uses the work to probe the critic's own reactions. The division between "objective" and "subjective" criticism became especially fierce in the wake of I. A. Richards' experiments with *Practical Criticism* (1929), which revealed unforgettably the extent to which readers distort texts to make them conform to private interests. Depending on their own concerns, critics could employ these results to call for a new objective critical method or to claim a new critical license, on the grounds that every reader has hold of a different truth. An extreme version of this distinction would oppose criticism as "science" to criticism as "therapy." Certainly many critics have been happy to embrace one pole or the other. But a moment's reflection will expose the falseness of the dichotomy. Every act of criticism, however inadequate, bears upon both the text and the reader; it is all a matter of the direction in which we are looking. The fact is that our initial views of texts can be made to change and improve. Though critics can never see more of a text than their means of perception allow, the misunderstandings and perplexities caused by incompetent reading can always warn open-minded critics to refine their perceptions. Texts criticize us as we criticize them. Similarly, every act of criticism can be amended either toward a more accurate statement about a text or toward a correction of the critical instruments. Ideally these two things are one. Critical skill can be developed either by teaching readers more about the nature of a text or more about their own habits and shortcomings as readers. Self-exploration and exploration of the literary work combine in a never-ending, mutually reinforcing process. To know the text and to know thyself should be, for the critic, the same.

Neither sort of knowledge is easy. In practice and theory, the progress of literary criticism has been slow, and "the total form or *telos* of criticism" remains a visionary ideal. Even the best interpretation of a text, like the best understanding of its reader, seldom keeps its life for longer than a generation. Yet for all its insufficiencies and uncertainties, practical literary criticism holds its place near the center of humanistic studies. The very vulnerability of critics testifies to their continuing efforts to reform not only what they know but also their ways of knowing. Criticism is the literary discipline that tests the value of all the others: the principles of works of art, the applications of textual, linguistic, and historical studies, the usefulness of theory. Nor does it cease to test itself. The problems of criticism arise from the unending rigor, and the unending value, of such testing. Fifty years ago, summarizing the lessons of *Practical Criticism*, I. A. Richards expressed both its difficulty and its vitality. "The critical reading of poetry is an arduous discipline; few exercises reveal to us more clearly the limitations under which, from moment to moment, we suffer. But, equally, the immense extension of our capacities that follows a summoning of our resources is made plain. The lesson of all criticism is that we have nothing to rely upon in making our choices but ourselves." And *ourselves*, in this context, clearly represents nothing less than everything we know and everything we are. This lesson is still the burden and challenge of practical criticism.

Selected Bibliography

This bibliography does not pretend to be comprehensive. Instead it offers a brief list of two kinds of books: influential modern "classics" in the development of practical criticism, and recent attempts to reformulate literary criticism in the light of contemporary practice. Among anthologies, *Modern Literary Criticism 1900–1970*, ed. Lawrence Lipking and A. Walton Litz (New York: Atheneum, 1972), includes large selections from major critics, especially Pound, Eliot, Richards, and Frye; *Issues in Contemporary Literary Criticism*, ed. Gregory Polletta (Boston: Little, Brown, 1973), presents a variety of important debates; and *Textual Strategies*, ed. Josué Harari (Ithaca, N. Y.: Cornell Univ. Press, 1979), supplies "perspectives in post-structuralist criticism."

Barthes, Roland. *Critical Essays*. Trans. Richard Howard. Evanston, Ill.: Northwestern Univ. Press, 1972.

Benjamin, Walter. *Illuminations*. Trans. Harry Zohn. New York: Harcourt, 1968.

Bloom, Harold. *Poetry and Repression: Revisionism from Blake to Stevens*. New Haven: Yale Univ. Press, 1976.

Booth, Wayne. *Critical Understanding*. Chicago: Univ. of Chicago Press, 1979.

Burke, Kenneth. *Language as Symbolic Action*. Berkeley: Univ. of California Press, 1966.

Crane, R. S. *The Languages of Criticism and the Structure of Poetry*. Toronto: Univ. of Toronto Press, 1953.

Davis, Walter A. *The Act of Interpretation*. Chicago: Univ. of Chicago Press, 1978.

Derrida, Jacques. *Of Grammatology*. Trans. Gayatri C. Spivak. Baltimore: Johns Hopkins Univ. Press, 1976.

Ellis, John M. *The Theory of Literary Criticism*. Berkeley: Univ. of California Press, 1974.

Frye, Northrop. *Anatomy of Criticism*. Princeton: Princeton Univ. Press, 1957.

Hirsch, E. D. *Validity in Interpretation*. New Haven: Yale Univ. Press, 1967.

Holland, Norman. *Five Readers Reading*. New Haven: Yale Univ. Press, 1975.

Iser, Wolfgang. *The Implied Reader*. Baltimore: Johns Hopkins Univ. Press, 1974.

Reichert, John. *Making Sense of Literature*. Chicago: Univ. of Chicago
    Press, 1977.
Richards, I. A. *Practical Criticism*. London: Kegan Paul, 1929.
Rosenblatt, Louise. *The Reader, the Text, the Poem*. Carbondale: Southern
    Illinois Univ. Press, 1978.
Ruthven, K. K. *Critical Assumptions*. Cambridge: Cambridge Univ. Press, 1979.
Wellek, René. *Concepts of Criticism*. New Haven: Yale Univ. Press, 1963.
Wimsatt, W. K. *The Verbal Icon: Studies in the Meaning of Poetry*. Lexington:
    Univ. of Kentucky Press, 1954.

Literary Theory

Paul Hernadi

At the time when René Wellek and Austin Warren published their *Theory of Literature* (1949), few other academic critics chose to engage in systematic theorizing.* Most seemed content to learn from creative writers or philosophers what literature is and what literary studies ought to accomplish. As always, some writers and philosophers were willing to oblige. The playwright-novelist-philosopher Jean-Paul Sartre had of late responded to the first question, *Qu'est-ce que la littérature?* (1947). As for the second, W. K. Wimsatt and the philosopher Monroe C. Beardsley had just outlawed almost all trafficking in the cause or the effect of literary works as "The Intentional Fallacy" (1946) and "The Affective Fallacy" (1949).

Perhaps because the age-old lack of consensus among writers and philosophers has become ever more obvious, many scholar-critics today feel comfortable wearing theoretical assumptions on their sleeves. This state of affairs, together with the recent cross-fertilization of some brands of philosophy, linguistics, anthropology, sociology, psychology, and literary criticism, has led to a prodigious growth of European and American theorizing about literature. Some might even consider certain portions of that growth cancerous and recommend surgery. Ironically, however, valid arguments

---

* References are furnished in the appended Bibliographical Note and Bibliography. Some arguments presented in this chapter were more fully developed in my introductions to *What Is Literature?* (1978) and *What Is Criticism?* (1981), both published by Indiana University Press, and in two overlapping articles, "Literary Theory: A Compass for Critics," *Critical Inquiry* 3 (1976), 369–86, and "So What? How So? and the Form that Matters," *Interpretation of Narrative*, ed. Mario J. Valdés and Owen Miller (Toronto: Univ. of Toronto Press, 1978), 167–73. I am thankful to the copyright holders for permitting the use of some previously published materials, verbatim or revised, in the present volume.

against theory have to be theoretical arguments. Thus only more and presumably better theory can cure whatever is perceived to be wrong or excessive about literary theorizing today.

Surely no reader and especially no professional reader of literature is ever quite innocent of literary theory. Just to read a poem or a novel as literature or as a particular kind of literature places the text and the reading in a more or less explicit frame of theoretical reference. This is why René Wellek, having contrasted literary theory ("the study of the principles of literature, its categories, criteria, and the like") to literary criticism and literary history ("the study of concrete literary works . . . in isolation or in chronological order"), insists that the three are inconceivable without one another. The question is, then, to what degree we should deliberately scrutinize our theoretical presuppositions at a given stage of our development as increasingly experienced readers. Or, to put it in concrete pedagogical terms, whether students of literature—or of any other field—ought to be encouraged to get involved with the theory of their subject.

Presumably they should not, if we are to take a memorable session of early academic advising literally. Here is what the perplexed freshman in Goethe's *Faust* gets to hear at the end of a lengthy interview:

Grau, teurer Freund, ist alle Theorie,
Und grün des Lebens goldner Baum.

Gray, my dear friend, is all theorizing,
And green the golden tree of life. (ll. 2038–39)

The young man seems relieved. But the often quoted words are far from solving his problems or ours. Even if we disregard the warning signal of excessively colorful rhetoric—is life's tree green or golden?—the dubious reliability of the bad-mouther of "gray theory" needs to be noted. It is not Goethe, of course, and not even Faust, but Mephistopheles disguised in Faust's academic gown who thus concludes his devilish job of counseling and proceeds to inscribe the serpent's words from Genesis iii.5 into the reverently unsuspecting student's album: "You will be like God, knowing good and evil."

This is not the place to decipher the import of a profoundly ambiguous passage. But three fundamental dilemmas involved with that critical task may serve to illustrate the interplay of literary theory with other modes of literary study.

First, should we interpret the passage as part of the earliest pertinent document called *Urfaust* (1775–76), or as part of what Goethe published in 1790 as *Faust: A Fragment*, or as part of *Faust: Part One* (1808), or else as part of the posthumously published complete work (1832)? The theory of interpretation (for example, Friedrich Schleiermacher's celebrated course on hermeneutics) teaches us in general that the proper understanding of each part of a text relies on the proper understanding of the whole and vice versa. But a great deal of textual scholarship and much critical interpretation are required for deciding what are the proper parts and wholes that make up a particular version of this "hermeneutic circle."

Next, should we approach the chosen text in its intertextual context with reference only to other texts or in its extratextual context, that is, in the light of Goethe's "life and times," which are in turn interfused with other lives and times? Once again, theoretical considerations (such as Friedrich Nietzsche's concerning *The Use and Abuse of History*) should inform the literary critic's and the literary historian's pertinent decisions. But, as Quentin Skinner recently observed, "before we can hope to identify the context which helps to disclose the meaning of a given work, we must already have arrived at an interpretation which serves to suggest what contexts may most profitably be investigated as further aids to interpretation." The establishing of a relationship between text and context as part and whole is, therefore, "an instance of the hermeneutic circle, not a means of breaking out of it."

Finally, should we decide in what sense, if any, the quoted lines are true, good, or beautiful? More or less clear-cut principles for such evaluations can be laid down in theory. But, as Immanuel Kant noted in a related context, there are no generally valid rules to tell us how to apply rules. Hence individual readers and critics must take responsibility for each of their value judgments even if it is based on someone else's theoretical framework.

To the extent that all chapters of the present volume intend to provide the student of literature with rationales for choosing among methodological options, the book as a whole can be considered a "theoretical" *Introduction to Scholarship in Modern Languages and Literatures*. Since, however, contemporary literary studies reflect a great variety of conflicting opinion about both their own function and the very nature of their subject matter, I take it as the main task of this chapter to address the deceptively simple questions mentioned at the outset as pointedly theoretical, namely, what is literature? and, in the general sense of literary study, what is criticism?

My recent experience with editing books under those titles has taught me that disagreement is widespread among contemporary critics even concerning the *kind* of answer demanded or admitted by the two questions. As for defining literature, persuasive arguments can be advanced for taking either avenue at several major crossroads. Some critics prefer neutral, others honorific definitions; some base their concepts of literature on complete texts, others on a literary quality assumed to inform some or all discourses to varying degrees; some tie literature or the quality of literariness to texts and utterances, others to verbally triggered mental acts. Quite a few critics even doubt the feasibility of defining literature on any grounds whatsoever. The most philosophically minded opponents of definitions tend to argue that works, qualities, or responses considered literary merely exhibit what Ludwig Wittgenstein called "family resemblance" and that it is possible for two legitimate members of the literary "family" to have no single trait in common.

In any event, all critics in search of literature face a version of the classifier's dilemma: how can I tell what literature is before I know on what instances to base my definition; yet how can I pick out instances of literature before I have defined it? It is by pulling harder on one horn of the dilemma or the other that some critics stress the processes and others the principles of the formation of a literary canon—processes and principles, that is, of establishing what may count as evidence in discussions about literature.

A historian of literature and of literary theory can, of course, consider any set of "principles" as temporarily emerging from, and eventually receding into, the historical process. From the vantage point of theory, however, any particular view of a historical "process"—or of *the* historical process as a whole—results from one of many possible conceptualizations of what Hayden White calls the "unprocessed historical record." Should we therefore attempt to answer questions like "What is literature?" by proposing that literature is all that has been called literature at one point in time or another? That solution quickly loses its initial attractiveness as we realize the need for distinguishing terms from concepts. For a long time, the term "literature" and its foreign cognates were mainly used to refer to the entire body of preserved written documents whereas the term "poetry" and its cognates were mainly used to refer to poems, plays, and fictive narratives. Since current usage is different, we cannot literally apply the principle, "literature is what has been called literature," to pre-nineteenth-century critical discourse. And once the literal application of that "historical" principle has been ruled out of order, we must return to the "theoretical" task of defining, in the light of our own literary and critical experience, what makes a text or reading literary in our sense of the word. Only after the accomplishment of that task can we usefully explore what term, if any, approximates our concept of literature in earlier parlance or, for that matter, in the vocabulary of other twentieth-century readers.

Chart 1 attempts to correlate, with a good deal of simplification to be sure, some of the most influential theoretical frameworks proposed or endorsed during the last decades. It places the literary work, like any other uttered or utterable discourse, at the meeting point of the rhetorical axis of communication and the mimetic axis of representation. Strictly speaking, communication takes place between the writer or speaker and the reader or listener, whereas representation activates the relationship of a verbal construct with what it conceptually signifies and perceptually evokes. But the full contexts of communication and representation are larger. On the one hand, writers, speakers, readers, and listeners inhabit the world as their source of motivation and their field of action; on the other, every instance of employed language and all information conveyed through locutionary acts partake in the world as a reservoir of signs and as the totality of facts and fictions representable by signs. This is why Chart 1 shows the work—a thing said and made—surrounded by the world in all directions.

Despite the first impression such a chart might create, no work is suspended in a timeless net of simultaneous relationships between author, reader, language, and information; each of those four apparently sturdy entities is, after all, subject to continuous change. The youthful author of *The Comedy of Errors*, for example, can hardly be regarded as identical with the mature author of *The Tempest*. Likewise, the sophomore reading *King Lear* for the first time is, one hopes, no longer the same reader when returning to the play in preparation for a term paper. Even language and what it represents are far from being stagnant. In a matter of years, the slang term "cool" could end up conveying just about the same positive value judgment as "hot" used to convey, and the originally fantastic worlds evoked by the early science fiction of Jules Verne have become describable as characterized by a kind of prophetic realism.

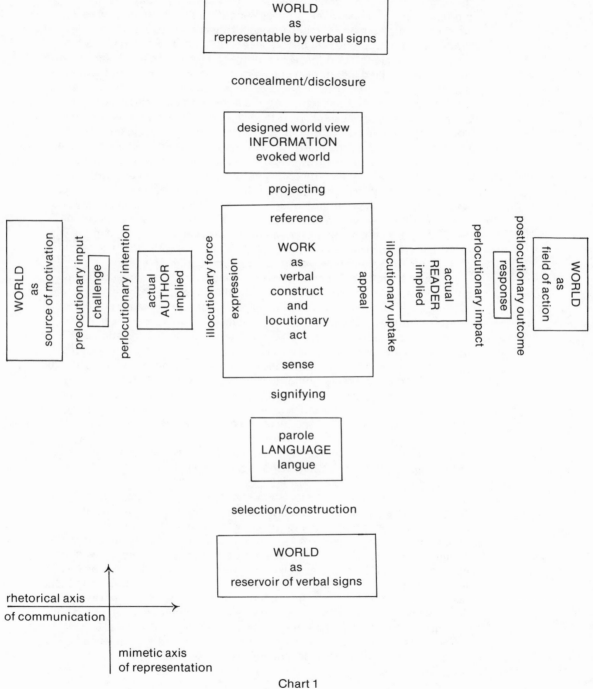

WORLD
as
representable by verbal signs

concealment/disclosure

designed world view
INFORMATION
evoked world

projecting

reference

WORK
as
verbal
construct
and
locutionary
act

sense

WORLD
as
source of motivation

prelocutionary input

challenge

perlocutionary intention

actual
AUTHOR
implied

illocutionary force

expression

appeal

illocutionary uptake

actual
READER
implied

perlocutionary impact

response

postlocutionary outcome

WORLD
as
field of action

signifying

parole
LANGUAGE
langue

selection/construction

WORLD
as
reservoir of verbal signs

rhetorical axis
of communication

mimetic axis
of representation

Chart 1

Ferdinand de Saussure's distinction between *parole* and *langue* has greatly helped linguists to clarify the difference between a fixed, concrete instance of employed language and a permanently changing system of verbal signs and combinatory rules. The more recent literary distinctions between the implied author of a work and its actual author and between implied and actual readers rely on a strikingly similar principle. For example, the respective authors implied by *The Comedy of Errors* and by *The Tempest* are in a sense fixed, concrete manifestations of the actual author whose permanently shifting potential of manifesting himself in literary works or otherwise was only partially realized between 1564 and 1616; his full potential has for ever remained virtual. The congenial readers or spectators implied by the respective plays are in turn "roles" that actual readers or spectators are invited to slip into. To cite an extreme instance, even a book like *Mein Kampf* will be adequately understood only by men and women able and willing temporarily to become Adolf Hitler's implied readers. Having shed the mental mask and costume required for the proper "performance" of the text, a discerning person will emerge from the ordeal with a keener sense of the despicable part assigned to the book's actual readers; and the impact of such a reading, along with other aspects of a twentieth-century reader's literary and nonliterary experience, will also influence that reader's perception of the worlds evoked and authors implied by, say, *King Lear* and *The Tempest*. The analogy between the virtual system of *langue* and the actual writer and reader becomes clear as we consider that Shakespeare's unrealized or even unconceived projects of further works could have expressed further aspects of his personality by implying other, more or less different authors. Likewise, any text left unread by me has simply not challenged me to test whether the particular constellation of personality traits required to play the part of that work's implied reader might have been produced from the virtual resources of my imagination.

Our chart, or map, suggests a third counterpart to the relationship between *langue* and *parole* in the "northerly" area of information. Here, too, the structure of the potential is altered by its selective actualization. Just as the actual author and reader of *King Lear* or *Mein Kampf* are not exactly the same before and after their respective acts of writing and reading, the world is no longer the same when it is not only capable of containing but actually contains those texts and the information manifested by them. To be sure, the mimetic results of discourse are much harder to systematize than its verbal means; for example, we cannot contrast a tragic to a comic world view with the same degree of precision as we can contrast the comparative forms of adjectives to their superlative forms. Yet the world evoked by a particular work may well be described as a mimetic "message" that is based on the virtual system or "code" of a *Weltanschauung* and actualizes the potential of that world view to disclose aspects of the world.

The speech-act theory of J. L. Austin and his followers has had considerable impact on recent approaches to literature as communication, even though Austin himself was mainly concerned with speaking rather than writing and considered the use that fiction makes of language "parasitic" on nonfictive discourse. Austin analyzed the total speech act into three components: locutionary (what we do when we say something), illocutionary (what we do *in* saying something), and perlocutionary (what we do *by* saying something). For example, the uttering of the words "I will kill you" or "I will marry you" is a locutionary act, the threatening or promising involved is an illocutionary act, and the accomplished frightening or the actual raising of an expectation is a perlocutionary act. Austin's distinction between illocutionary and perlocutionary aspects of communication, as elaborated by John Searle and other philosophers, has attracted particular attention among critics and might be profitably coordinated with the contrast between the implied and actual author, as well as the contrast between the implied and actual reader. A well-known sentence involving speech acts on more than one level of possible analysis will serve as an illustration.

In saying, "Pray you, undo this button," Lear performs the illocutionary act of making a request (*King Lear* V.iii.311). If at least one of the other characters on stage can be assumed to realize that Lear is making a request, the illocutionary force of the utterance has worked, that is (in Austin's terminology), "uptake" has been secured. To be sure, the understanding of Lear's words as a request does not mean that someone will, as seems to happen in the play, decide to comply. Yet only if someone so decides can we say that Lear's perlocutionary intention of making someone "undo this button" has led to its intended perlocutionary impact. *Why* Lear wants a button undone and *whether* someone deciding to oblige him will actually be able to do so are questions related to but not really integrated with the speech act under consideration. To answer those questions we must investigate what might be called the *pre*locutionary input and *post*locutionary outcome of the illocution and perlocution involved.

On a deeper level of analysis, of course, the playwright rather than the character engages in the acts of locution, illocution, and perlocution. The locutionary act of saying (or writing) "Pray you, undo this button" is in fact Shakespeare's, for it was he who assigned to Lear the utterance with its illocutionary force of a request. But *in* doing so, Shakespeare engaged, too, in an illocutionary act—not, of course, in the direct act of making a request but rather in the indirect act of suggesting the former ruler's utter helplessness. If a reader or spectator infers that the words assigned to Lear carry the additional illocutionary force of that authorial suggestion, uptake has been secured once again. Now if we focus on this latter kind of illocutionary force and uptake, we in fact consider what the play's implied reader is meant to perceive the implied author as doing *in* making Lear say, "Pray you, undo this button." Only if we ask ourselves what Shakespeare did or was attempting to do *by* assigning the request to Lear can we infer the actual author's perlocutionary intentions and distinguish between proper and improper kinds of perlocutionary impact of Lear's request on actual readers.

Needless to say, the preceding speech-act analysis takes for granted that the characters on stage understand Lear's words and that we understand Shakespeare's. To be more precise and to employ concepts proposed before the advent of speech-act theory, we understand both what the sentence uttered by Lear *means* in general and what it is *used* by Lear and by Shakespeare *to refer to* in a particular utterance. Elaborating on Gottlob Frege's distinction between sense (*Sinn*) and reference (*Bedeutung*), Peter

Strawson has argued that it is possible to grasp the meaning or sense of a verbal expression but not its reference if one does not know what use is being made of it. For example, the first five words of the sentence "The present king of France is wise" make sense but do not refer to any person if they are uttered in the twentieth century, and the last two words may be seen as making or not making a truthful predication depending on whether the sentence is uttered at the time, say, of Louis XIV or Louis XV. From Strawson's vantage point, the use made of language in a work of fiction results in "spurious" reference. But the literary theorist can invoke Sir Philip Sidney's *Defence of Poesie* (1595) and turn the charge of benign deception into praise: The poet "nothing affirmes, and therefore never lieth," but "lifted up with the vigor of his own invention, doth grow in effect another nature."

On such a view, Lear's utterance "Pray you, undo this button" helps to project a possible world that does not exist prior to and independent of its verbal representation. The sense and the reference of the utterance are, therefore, less clearly distinguishable from one another than they would be if the same sentence were used on a nonliterary occasion. We are not sure, for example, who is supposed to respond to Lear's request. Even stage productions need not specify to whom Lear's "you" refers. They may thus permit the word, whose sense is "the person addressed by the speaker," to refer to "all who have ears to hear," including the spectators. Nor can we be sure whether Lear refers to a button of his own or to one on the dead Cordelia's garment or perhaps to a button of his frenzied imagination. Here again, the muted direct reference can help us to perceive the playwright's indirect reference as his use of Lear's use of the sentence in its context draws attention not to a particular button but to the dying king's fear or experience of suffocation.

In short, the horizontal axis of literary communication requires a great deal of support from the vertical axis of representation: without the understanding of the quoted line's plural sense and polyvalent reference, no "uptake" of its full illocutionary force as a particular kind of request could occur, and Lear's utterance might have no perlocutionary impact and postlocutionary outcome commensurate with the actual author's perlocutionary intentions and prelocutionary motivation. The vertical axis of both literary and nonliterary discourse would in turn collapse if authors and readers (or, more generally, speakers and listeners) did not continually form, use, and modify what are ultimately *their* systems of representation. Just as verbal signs capable of containing information are needed if one person's motivation is to turn into another's action, language needs users if it is to disclose and/or conceal views of the world.

Because of the enhanced interaction between sense and reference in most if not all works generally considered literary, it is tempting to define literature along the vertical axis of the chart. Two twentieth-century attempts to do so have proved particularly illuminating and influential: Roman Ingarden's phenomenological analysis of the role of "quasi-propositions" (*Quasi-Urteile*) in the creative design of "purely intentional" fictive worlds and Roman Jakobson's finding that the "poetic function of language" predominates in elaborately structured verbal sequences that attract attention to themselves for their own sake. Ingarden's full-scale, yet critical, adaptation of Edmund Husserl's early philosophy of thought and language to problems of imaginative literature is far too complex to bear summary in the present context, and Jakobson's pertinent views concerning six ubiquitous linguistic functions—one of which is the poetic—are best summarized by Jakobson himself in a well-known succinct paper. I merely wish to point out that neither criterion—that of quasipropositional fictive discourse or that of conspicuous and therefore self-referential verbal patterning—can help us to establish the value of texts to which it rightfully applies. Such criteria alone do not even permit clear distinctions between lies and fictions on the one hand and versified slogans such as "I like Ike" and poetic lines on the other. At the very least, whoever endorses Ingarden's or Jakobson's concept of literariness will have to agree with T. S. Eliot: "The 'greatness' of literature cannot be determined by solely literary standards, though we must remember that whether it is literature or not can be determined only by literary standards."

Our intuitive need for fusing without confusing criteria of literariness with criteria of value could be satisfied, however, if Ingarden's and Jakobson's observations were correlated with each other and with attempts to define literature from the vantage points of authors and readers along the rhetorical axis of communication. We could, for instance, consider a text or utterance nonliterary to the extent that it invites and rewards the more or less independent study of one or several of its four fundamental relationships to the world: its conscious or unconscious origin in the writer's (or speaker's) private and public motivation, its intended or accomplished impact on the reader's (or listener's) decisions and actions, its traditional or innovative employment of the components and combinatory rules of a language, and its concealment or disclosure of various aspects of what it offers information about. By contrast, a text or utterance should then emerge as literary to the extent that it invites and rewards the integrated study of its fundamental relationships to the world as interacting determinants of its appropriate reception.

In general agreement with a good deal of current critical theory and practice, such a "definition" would allow us to distinguish different kinds and degrees of literariness. Furthermore, it would explain why literary critics tend to value the balanced interplay of as much illocutionary force, perlocutionary impact, verbal elaboration, and imaginative world-making as can mutually enhance each other. But it would not commit us to a particular canon of works or to a timelessly valid critical method of establishing and studying such a canon. It would rather enable us to accept Nelson Goodman's replacement of the question "What is art?" with the question "When is art?" as applicable to individual readings as well as socially endorsed critical procedures. As times change, different texts might be found to invite and reward differently disposed readers to evolve an integrated, that is, literary, response to the constitutive relationships of works with the world. The literary institution could thus endure while some individual authors and works—think of Plato, Revelation, Tacitus, or the Peanuts cartoons, taught and studied "as literature"—are moving into or out of it.

Literature as an institution largely relies, of course, on the activities of that most vocal group of readers—the critics. More often and more systematically than any other segment of a literate population, these men and women turn their reading experience into texts that may serve as occasions for other people's reading experience. The chart correlating the work with the world also suggests how different critical approaches to literature are related to one another. Some critics see literary works mainly as instruments of mimesis: words representing worlds. Others see them mainly as instruments of communication: messages from authors to readers. Because all instances of spoken and written discourse potentially represent and communicate at the same time, it seems unwise, if not self-deceiving, to restrict one's concern completely to what the work is or how the work functions. After all, if a work works, its very being is tied up with its function and vice versa. Yet all critics cannot do all things all the time, and it can be extremely useful occasionally to focus on a selected mimetic or rhetorical aspect of literature's connections with the world.

To give four concrete examples, a critic may well decide to study the prosodic principles of word choice in Shakespeare's sonnets, the characteristic world view of Zola's novels, the implied author's ironic attitude in Book IV of *Gulliver's Travels*, or the effect of *The Sorrows of Young Werther* on the suicide rate among Goethe's eighteenth-century readers. As we move from concrete examples to more generally applicable distinctions, finding the right terminology becomes rather difficult. But four basic approaches to texts emerge as stressing, respectively, a particular work's linguistic features (stylistics), evoked world (poetics), manifested intentions (tactics), and potential impact (dynamics). Likewise, four types of contextual inquiry can be distinguished as principally concerned with the work's system of signification (semiotics), stipulated world view (mythography), historical origin (genetics), and continuing effectiveness (pragmatics). Along the rhetorical axis, interest in a text's private and public genesis or impact thus opens literary criticism toward psychology, sociology, ethics, and politics; and along the mimetic axis, the critic's strictly literary concerns merge with broader ones regarding the role of components and relationships in both the procedures (paradigmatics, syntagmatics) and the products of representation (metaphysics, dialectics). Such a typology of critical orientations, further delineated in the next two paragraphs, locates familiar "schools" of criticism and some of their current or recent representatives on the conceptual map of Chart 2. (It goes without saying that most critics named below do not restrict their attention to just one aspect of literary works and that many important critics not named here are even more resistant to being categorized.)

Authorial intention can be studied in the "tactical" terms of the implied author's attitudes and perspectives (Wayne Booth, Gérard Genette) or in the "genetic" terms of the actual author's private or public motivation (Georges Poulet, Terry Eagleton). A work's impact can in turn be studied in the "dynamic" terms of the moods and insights conveyed to its implied reader (Stanley Fish, Wolfgang Iser) or in the "pragmatic" terms of the work's private or public reception by actual readers (Norman Holland, Hans Robert Jauss). While the stylistic study of verbal occurrences and recurrences investigates language in specific instances of literary representation (Michael Riffaterre, Josephine Miles), semiotics looks beyond the confines of a particular language

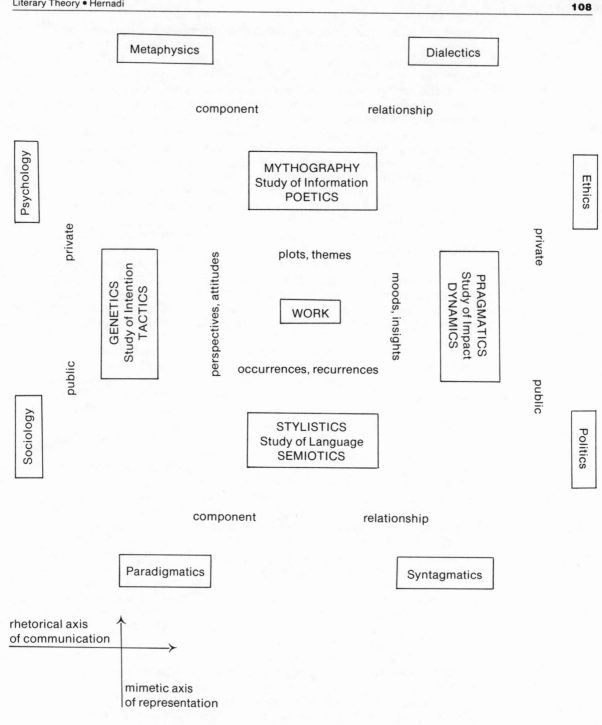

Metaphysics

Dialectics

component   relationship

Psychology

Ethics

private   private

MYTHOGRAPHY
Study of Information
POETICS

plots, themes

perspectives, attitudes

moods, insights

GENETICS
Study of Intention
TACTICS

WORK

PRAGMATICS
Study of Impact
DYNAMICS

public   public

occurrences, recurrences

Sociology

Politics

STYLISTICS
Study of Language
SEMIOTICS

component   relationship

Paradigmatics

Syntagmatics

rhetorical axis
of communication

mimetic axis
of representation

Chart 2

and considers the whole world as a potential reservoir of verbal as well as nonverbal signs (Umberto Eco, Jurij Lotman). In the corresponding "northern hemisphere" of the critical universe, poetics is that branch (or rather direction) of the study of information that looks at verbal mimesis from the point of view of literature; it is chiefly concerned with generic plots and themes or "visions" (Tzvetan Todorov, Murray Krieger) in the complementary sense of the Greek terms for plot (*mythos*) and theme or thought (*dianoia*) adopted by Northrop Frye from Aristotle's *Poetics*: "the *mythos* is the *dianoia* in movement, the *dianoia* is the *mythos* in *stasis*." The reducibility of verbal sequences to firmly, if unconsciously, held views of the world seems to have been assumed by such classifiers of world views as Wilhelm Dilthey and Stephen Pepper or, more recently, Michel Foucault. Indeed, the very word "myth" is frequently used today to refer to the conceptual rationalization of private and collective desires rather than to plots or stories serving as the literary vehicles of such rationalization. "Mythography" (as in Roland Barthes's critical analyses of ideological myth-making) can thus serve to scrutinize our frames of mental reference as man-made systems for encoding and decoding information. Yet one critic's or philosopher's ontology is another's mythology, and the literary theorist may well wish to treat all purported ontologies—including the one implied by Jacques Derrida's categorical denial of the possibility of a valid ontology—as more or less comprehensive, more or less persuasive mythologies.

Corresponding to the private and public dimensions of both the genetics and the pragmatics of literature, two basic orientations may be distinguished within semiotic and mythographic studies as well: one focusing on the respective components of language systems and world views, the other on relationships between the components. Thus the phonetic, lexical, and grammatical principles of every *langue* can be seen either from the paradigmatic point of view of interchangeable components as involving certain procedures of selection or from the syntagmatic point of view of the sequence of components as involving certain procedures of construction. A mythographer's approach to world views will in turn privilege either the metaphysics of being or the dialectics of becoming as it calls for philosophical analysis of either the nature or the functional interplay of represented entities.

To be sure, the "approaches" or "disciplines" characterized here interact much more frequently than their graphic representation in Chart 2 implies. Their interaction in the work of an individual scholar can lead to enhanced penetration. But it can also lead to eclectic dilettantism. Provoked by the latter, some critics feel justified in rejecting all concern with a text's genetic, pragmatic, semiotic, and mythographic contexts. In the heyday of American New Criticism such concerns were pronounced guilty, respectively, of the intentional fallacy, the affective fallacy, linguistic imperialism, and unliterary *Stoffgeschichte*—the literal-minded tracing of the "history" of motifs and other elements of thematic content. Yet the study of why a work was wrought, how it works, what its selective signification conceals, and what the mimetic projection of such concealment discloses can no doubt refine our understanding of the work as it relates to the world including ourselves. Rather than decide in advance about the kinds of approach that alone are "intrinsic" to literature, the important thing for self-respecting critics turning toward or away from a particular text is to know, and let their readers know, in what direction they are heading and why.

By correlating alternative itineraries, literary theory should help critics both to reach specific destinations and to plan further trips within the charted critical landscape. Yet, as Geoffrey Hartman recently observed, "every literary theory is based on the experience of a limited canon, or generalizes strongly from a particular text-milieu." This fact goes a long way toward explaining why any theoretician's view of other theories will display reciprocally conditioned elements of "blindness and insight" (Paul de Man) and why any explicit or implicit "map" of literature and criticism must stay ready to be redrawn in the light of texts, interpretations, and evaluations to which it turns out not to have done justice.

As for the perpetual conflict of evaluations, literary theory may try to correlate but will hardly reconcile the radically different types of standards according to which literature as a whole or individual texts have been judged "good" or "bad." Most such standards no doubt point to the *delectare* and *prodesse* of Horace's advice to the poet: Delight and benefit your reader! But there are many ways to do or to attempt to do that, and the varieties of literary entertainment through thrill and gratification, as well as the various kinds of social and cosmic commitments urged upon us by literary works, continue to be assessed in very different ways indeed. Thus the goal of appraising works seems more appropriate than that of judging them; after all, no one is entitled to the judge's robe in the grand jury investigations of all men's and women's values. Critics may see it as a duty or privilege to cast their individual votes, but they should chiefly act as expert witnesses who combine professional acumen with personal opinion about the case being considered. The more articulate their testimony, the more likely that it will promote the truth-finding endeavor of the readers' courts continually in session.

It is hardly surprising that texts perceived as characterized by the "literary" interplay between various aspects of communication and representation tend to prompt many divergent and even disparate interpretations. As a literary work outlasts the private and public circumstances of its production, its "strategies" (to borrow some key terms but not the conclusion from Kenneth Burke) become operative in the "situations" of later readings, and newly emerging aspects of the work's "design" will supplement or overshadow what it was "designed to do" for the author and the original readers. Critics caught up in interpretive controversies often look to their own or someone else's literary theory for principles of reliable arbitration. And those who look long enough usually find three ultimate principles in apparent opposition to each other. To state them in axiomatic form: authors communicate; texts conceal; readings disclose.

It is true, of course, that more theoretical attention has recently been paid to how and why works work than to how and why they have been wrought. Some critics even attribute a greater degree of reality to the reading than to the text or author whose very existence seems to them to require being hypothesized on the basis of our reading experience. In pure theory, I cannot conclusively refute this or any other form of epistemological skepticism concerning perceived objects and other minds. But as I am drafting this sentence and see my hand moving the pen over a white sheet of paper, I feel inclined to place at least as much faith in the existence of texts and authors as in the existence of readers. And if the self-evidence of the Cartesian *cogito* translates with equal ease into textual decoding and encoding, then the reader's *lego* and the writer's *scribo* are equally plausible antecedents of *ergo sum*, and all three "axioms"—authors communicate, texts conceal, readings disclose—deserve to be retained as hermeneutic principles.

Proponents of the first axiom (E. D. Hirsch, for example) consider texts mainly as communicative signals and plead for "objective interpretation"—the attempted reconstruction of authorial meaning. Proponents of the second axiom consider texts mainly as informative symptoms and plead—usually on the authority of Nietzsche, Marx, or Freud—for the "deconstruction" of the verbal facade in search of the constitutive culture-specific, social, or psychic illusion or repression behind it. Proponents of the third axiom consider texts mainly as occasions for the reader's appropriative experience and plead for enhanced self-understanding through the "depth semantics" of what is being disclosed (Paul Ricoeur) or through the "fusion of horizons" between the text emerging from the past and its present reader (Hans-Georg Gadamer).

The respective targets of the three hermeneutic procedures bring to mind Charles Sanders Peirce's seminal distinctions between symbols, indexes, and icons according to whether a particular sign stands for its object mainly on the basis of conventional association, factual connection, or perceived resemblance. By those criteria, the word "fire" is a symbol, the sight or smell of smoke is an index, and a painted picture is an icon of fire, whereas the weather satellite, aided by cartographical markings for state lines and population centers, projects a very "mixed sign" of a snowstorm on the television screen. Now, in explicating texts as the author's signals we approach literature as a set of (Peircean) symbols: the explication aims at grasping intended meaning by dint of the reader's familiarity with linguistic conventions. In explaining texts as existential, social, or psychic symptoms we approach literature as a set of indexes: the explanation aims at gleaning factual determination by dint of the reader's acquaintance with the historical conditions of human existence. In exploring texts as occasions for appropriative reading we approach literature as the projection of iconic models for experiencing what our world is or might have been or could become: the exploration aims at glimpsing imaginative reference by dint of the reader's own participation in being and becoming. Because signs tend to function in various combinations of the symbolic, indexical, and iconic modes of semiosis, there is no reason why the three axioms of interpretation should not sponsor explication, explanation, and exploration as three interrelated and integratable phases of textual comprehension. Both individually and collectively, critics could shed more light on authors, texts, and readings if they cared to correlate their findings as to what is said, concealed, and disclosed in a literary work.

To be sure, the first reading of a text will yield the reader's meaning rather than the text's or the author's. Only continued or repeated contemplation of text and context can lead to critical distance from the reference entailed by what Strawson might have called one's "first use" of the text. Gaining that distance may in turn bring about, not necessarily in this order and seldom in pure form, (1) the realization that the text makes sense in more than one way; (2) an approximation of the reference entailed by the original use of the text or, in less precise parlance, the author's intended meaning; (3) intellectual penetration of the factual conditions making the production of the text possible; and (4) the reader's "second use" of the text whose enriched reference now incorporates all pertinent implications of the textual sense, authorial reference, and factual context that have so far been appropriated by the reader. After such a "second reading," which may in fact be the fifth or the tenth, the more enlightened and more self-conscious reader will find new sense to construe, new references to approximate, and new conditions to penetrate as he or she engages the text in a "third" (or fifteenth?) reading. And so on and so forth, while the hermeneutic spiral winds its way to higher or deeper levels of understanding.

The textually stated results of even the most comprehensive understanding can, of course, be seen by single-minded proponents of single axioms as mere signals, symptoms, or occasions for appropriative reading. Even a theoretical plea for comprehensive interpretation like the present attempt at conceptual cartography is open to a variety of more or less single-minded interpretations. For example, you may wish to focus on the intellectual attitude of the implied author of this chapter, or psychoanalyze its actual author, or reveal the socioeconomic impact of the proposed theoretical framework. Yes, you may. But your opinion will have to be offered as a piece of language, another "work" in the potential center of attention of other people, who in turn may explicate, explain, or explore the verbal result of your explications, explanations, or explorations in any of those and many other ways. To put it in quite general terms, every politician can be psychoanalyzed; every analyst can be considered as part of a political system; every mythographer can be shown to have employed a special style of rhetoric; every linguist's metalanguage can be viewed as implying a certain type of mythology; and so forth. That even this last string of assertions—so even-handedly pluralistic! so self-critically judicious!—should come not from some infallible oracle of literary theory but from a person with his fair share of hang-ups and ulterior motives may count as one of the many ironies of pluralism.

Bibliographical Note

Along with the items listed in the subsequent Bibliography, the following books and the specialized bibliographies appended to most of them should prove particularly useful. *Critical Theory since Plato*, ed. Hazard Adams (New York: Harcourt, 1971), contains well over a hundred representative statements. *Twentieth-Century Literary Criticism: A Reader*, ed. David Lodge (London: Longman, 1972), includes more than fifty selections, mostly British and American. *European Literary Theory and Practice: From Existential Phenomenology to Structuralism*, ed. Vernon W. Gras (New York: Delta, 1973), offers samples of recent continental developments. Most major representatives of French structuralism and post-structuralism have contributed to *The Structuralist Controversy: The Languages of Criticism and the Sciences of Man*, ed. Richard Macksey and Eugenio Donato (1970; Baltimore: Johns Hopkins Univ. Press, 1972). *Interpretation of Narrative*, ed. Mario J. Valdés and Owen J. Miller (Toronto: Univ. of Toronto Press, 1978) illustrates the possible convergence of formalist and hermeneutic approaches to literature.

Helpful discussions of recent literary theory and its sources will be found in Jonathan Culler, *Structuralist Poetics: Structuralism, Linguistics, and the Study of Literature* (Ithaca, N.Y.: Cornell Univ. Press, 1975); Peter Demetz, *Marx, Engels, and the Poets*, trans. Jeffrey L. Sammons (Chicago: Univ. of Chicago Press, 1967); Victor Erlich, *Russian Formalism: History, Doctrine*, rev. ed. (The Hague: Mouton, 1965); David Couzens Hoy, *The Critical Circle: Literature, History, and Philosophical Hermeneutics* (Berkeley: Univ. of California Press, 1978); Fredric Jameson, *Marxism and Form* (Princeton: Princeton Univ. Press, 1972); and Robert Scholes, *Structuralism in Literature* (New Haven: Yale Univ. Press, 1974). Two collections of essays, *What Is Literature?* (1978) and *What Is Criticism?* (1981), both edited and introduced by Paul Hernadi and published by Indiana University Press, contain a total of forty-three recent attempts to answer the questions expressed in their respective titles.

Selected Bibliography

Austin, J. L. *How to Do Things with Words.* Cambridge, Mass.: Harvard Univ. Press, 1962.

Barthes, Roland. *Mythologies.* Trans. Annette Lavers. New York: Hill and Wang, 1972.

Booth, Wayne. *The Rhetoric of Fiction.* Chicago: Univ. of Chicago Press, 1961.

Burke, Kenneth. *The Philosophy of Literary Form: Studies in Symbolic Action.* 2nd ed. Baton Rouge: Louisiana State Univ., 1967. See esp. pp. 1 and 89.

de Man, Paul. *Blindness and Insight: Essays in the Rhetoric of Contemporary Criticism.* New York: Oxford Univ. Press, 1971.

Derrida, Jacques. "White Mythology: Metaphor in the Text of Philosophy." Trans. F. C. T. Moore. *New Literary History*, 6 (1974), 5–74.

Dilthey, Wilhelm. *Philosophy of Existence: Introduction to Weltanschauungslehre.* Trans. William Kluback and Martin Weinbaum. New York: Bookman, 1957.

Eagleton, Terry. *Criticism and Ideology.* London: New Left Books, 1976.

Eco, Umberto. *A Theory of Semiotics.* Bloomington: Indiana Univ. Press, 1976.

Eliot, T. S. *Essays Ancient and Modern.* 1936; rpt. New York: Haskell House, 1974. See p. 93.

Fish, Stanley E. *Self-Consuming Artifacts: The Experience of Seventeenth-Century Literature.* Berkeley: Univ. of California Press, 1972.

Foucault, Michel. *The Order of Things: An Archaeology of the Human Sciences.* New York: Pantheon, 1970. (Trans. of *Les Mots et les choses.* Paris: Gallimard, 1966.)

Frege, Gottlob. *Translations from the Philosophical Writings*. Ed. Peter
Geach and Max Black. 2nd ed. Oxford: Blackwell, 1960. See pp. 56–78
("On Sense and Reference").

Frye, Northrop. *Anatomy of Criticism*. Princeton: Princeton Univ. Press, 1957.
See esp. p. 83.

Gadamer, Hans-Georg. *Truth and Method*. Translation edited by Garrett
Barden and John Cumming from the second edition (1965). New York:
Seabury, 1975.

Genette, Gérard. *Narrative Discourse: An Essay in Method*. Trans. Jane E.
Lewin. Ithaca, N. Y.: Cornell Univ. Press, 1980.

Goodman, Nelson. *Ways of Worldmaking*. Indianapolis: Hackett, 1978, pp.
57–70 ("When Is Art?").

Hartman, Geoffrey H. "A Short History of Practical Criticism." *New Literary
History*, 10 (1979), 495–509. See esp. p. 507.

Hirsch, E. D. *Validity in Interpretation*. New Haven: Yale Univ. Press, 1967.

Holland, Norman. *Poems in Persons: An Introduction to the Psychoanalysis of
Literature*. New York: Norton, 1973.

Ingarden, Roman. *The Literary Work of Art*. Trans. George G. Grabowicz.
Evanston, Ill.: Northwestern Univ. Press, 1973.

Iser, Wolfgang. *The Act of Reading: A Theory of Aesthetic Response*.
Baltimore: Johns Hopkins Univ. Press, 1978.

Jakobson, Roman. "Linguistics and Poetics." *Style in Language*. Ed. Thomas
A. Sebeok. Cambridge, Mass.: MIT Press, 1960, pp. 350–77.

Jauss, Hans Robert. "Theses on the Transition from the Aesthetics of Literary
Works to a Theory of Aesthetic Experience." In *Interpretation of
Narrative*. Ed. Mario J. Valdés and Owen J. Miller. Toronto: Univ. of
Toronto Press, 1978, pp. 137–47.

Kant, Immanuel. *Critique of Pure Reason*. Trans. Norman Kemp Smith. New
York: St. Martin's, 1965. See pp. 177–78.

Krieger, Murray. *Theory of Criticism*. Baltimore: Johns Hopkins Univ. Press,
1976.

Lotman, Jurij. *The Structure of the Artistic Text*. Trans. Ronald Vroon and Gail
Vroon. Ann Arbor: Univ. of Michigan, Dept. of Slavic Languages and
Literature, 1977.

Miles, Josephine. *Poetry and Change: Donne, Milton, Wordsworth, and the
Equilibrium of the Present*. Berkeley: Univ. of California Press, 1974.

Nietzsche, Friedrich. *The Use and Abuse of History*. Trans. Adrian Collins. 2nd
ed. Indianapolis: Bobbs-Merrill, 1957.

Peirce, Charles Sanders. *The Philosophy of Peirce: Selected Writings*. Ed.
Justus Buchler. 1940; rpt. New York: Dover, 1955, pp. 98–119.

Pepper, Stephen C. *World Hypotheses: A Study in Evidence*. 1942; rpt.
Berkeley: Univ. of California Press, 1966.

Poulet, Georges. *The Interior Distance*. Trans. Elliott Coleman. Baltimore:
Johns Hopkins Univ. Press, 1959.

Ricoeur, Paul. *Interpretation Theory: Discourse and the Surplus of Meaning*.
Fort Worth: Texas Christian Univ. Press, 1976.

Riffaterre, Michael. "Criteria for Style Analysis." *Word*, 15 (1959), 154–174.

Sartre, Jean-Paul. *What Is Literature?* Trans. Bernard Frechtman. New York:
Harper and Row, 1965.

Saussure, Ferdinand de. Course in General Linguistics. Trans. Wade Baskin. 2nd ed. London: Owen, 1974. (Trans. of *Cours de linguistique générale.* Ed. Charles Bally and Albert Sechehaye, with Albert Riedlinger. 2nd ed. Paris: Payot, 1922.)

Schleiermacher, Friedrich. "*The Hermeneutics*: Outline of the 1819 Lectures." Trans. Jan Wojcik and Roland Haas. *New Literary History*, 10 (1978), 1–16.

Searle, John R. *Speech Acts.* Cambridge: Cambridge Univ. Press, 1969.

Skinner, Quentin. "Hermeneutics and the Role of History." *New Literary History*, 7 (1975), 209–32.

Strawson, Peter F. "On Referring." *Mind*, 59 (1950), 320–44.

Todorov, Tzvetan. *The Poetics of Prose.* Trans. Richard Howard. Ithaca, N. Y.: Cornell Univ. Press, 1977.

Wellek, René, and Austin Warren. *Theory of Literature.* 3rd ed. 1962; rpt. New York: Harcourt, 1970. See esp. p. 39.

White, Hayden. *Metahistory: The Historical Imagination in Nineteenth-Century Europe.* Baltimore: Johns Hopkins Univ. Press, 1973. See p. 5.

Wimsatt, W. K., and Monroe C. Beardsley. "The Intentional Fallacy" and "The Affective Fallacy." In W. K. Wimsatt. *The Verbal Icon: Studies in the Meaning of Poetry.* Lexington: Univ. of Kentucky Press, 1954.

Wittgenstein, Ludwig. *Philosophical Investigations.* Trans. G. E. M. Anscombe. 2nd ed. Oxford: Blackwell, 1958. See esp. p. 32.

The Scholar in Society

Wayne C. Booth

> No one can predict what Europe will be like at the dawn of the twenty-first century; yet we know one thing about it. The men [and women] who will be in posts of responsibility then are already university students. The future of the nineteenth-century idea of a university is in their hands.
> —*Eric Ashby*

> It is safer to have a whole people respectably enlightened than a few in a high state of science and the many in ignorance.
> —*Thomas Jefferson*

Not one of your easy assignments, this one. "Say something *useful* to the would-be scholar about how to relate the scholarly role to society." What exactly is a scholar? And what in the world do we mean when we speak of society?

Is the invited essayist himself a scholar? People refer to him as a critic or as a rhetorical theorist. He has done some literary history, in his youth. He lists himself on passports as Teacher. When he reads *The New York Review of Books*, he thinks of himself as an intellectual. Are critics, rhetorical theorists, literary historians, teachers, and intellectuals "scholars"? And—whatever scholars are—what should be their relationship to whatever society is?

I

The scholar. Back in male chauvinist times, someone defined an intellectual as a man who has found something in the world more interesting than sex. Intellectuals have often contrasted scholars and intellectuals, to the detriment of the scholars: a scholar is a professional researcher who is paid to be pedantic, while an intellectual is someone who pursues ideas for their own sake. A scholar once replied that the difference between a scholar and an intellectual is that the intellectual has read an article on a given subject while the scholar has read a book.

Instead of calling names, it should be more useful, as we struggle with an unusually ill-defined subject, to assume that there's nobody here but us scholars—that anyone who will risk being caught reading an essay of this kind in a volume of this kind obviously wants to be not a pedant but a genuine scholar, cares very much about learning for its own sake, and is willing to do what is needed to make sense out of the scholarly enterprise. Part-time intellectuals, part-time teachers, part-time scholars, we here consider what it means to be a scholar, a scholar *in* society.

"A scholar," we might say, "is anyone who sits alone (and often lonely) for as much as three days in a row, reading or thinking or writing about a single problem. She may or may not be paid for it. He may or may not publish.* But what makes a scholar a scholar is the willingness to sit alone, for long periods, trying to learn something that cannot be learned 'in society,' something that cannot be learned except through sustained, private inquiry." It might be objected that the privacy stipulation in this definition rules out team research. No doubt there are some problems that are best pursued in groups, but when such groups are examined they usually reveal the presence of only one or two scholars, who do a great deal of private thinking; the rest are henchmen, who carry out the experiments or data-collecting that the thinking dictates.

The trial definition obviously rules in many people as scholars whom we ordinarily call by other names—certain businessmen, architects, gamblers. It also suggests that many of us who are called scholars are scholars only during brief interludes. Many who sit at their desks regularly, "doing their own work," are not really scholars, because they are trying, not to learn something, but only to find a way of saying again what they already know: they are writers, or publicists, or self-repeating mechanisms, harmless drudges carrying out what amount to clerical tasks assigned by—well, by "society."

Where does the definition place me, asked by my society, the MLA, to sit alone (and increasingly lonely) at a desk increasingly messy with disconnected half-thoughts about the scholar in society? I can see elements of the drudge, elements of the publicist, but where is the scholar? I must get to the library fast and do some scholaring on what other people have said about the scholar in society.

I find a book by Howard Mumford Jones, called *One Great Society: Humane Learning in the United States*, a report on what a whole commission of

---

* Could anything illustrate more clearly my own sense of being an occupied territory—occupied by society—than my discomfort in using *any* of the pronouns, or any alternative stylistic solution, that different readers would elect for this spot? The plural will sometimes work, but usually it weakens the point, as it would do here. In a first draft I tried alternating *his* and *hers* throughout, as I have just done, but two of my three official readers rightly objected that the experiment was immensely distracting. Unfortunately, to make a statement like the following is no real solution: Throughout this essay, all feminine pronouns should be read as referring to females and males alike.

scholars thought about this matter. They all seem to think of the scholar as any serious student who is not a scientist. Scientists do scientific research. Scholars do humanistic research.

Suppose we try out their implied definition: "A scholar is anyone who sits alone for sustained periods trying to solve a problem that cannot be solved by a physical or biological or social scientist."

I must believe that I am making progress or I shall get up from my desk and lose all hope of being a scholar. But there are many difficulties here. I remember that Northrop Frye, who wrote the essay on literary criticism for the precursor of this volume,[1] made a good deal of the claim that criticism is a science; I remember also that much of what my scholarly colleagues do is indistinguishable in method from what scientists do. Come to think of it, for many modern theorists my definition will mean that a scholar works only on problems that cannot be solved at all, since solutions are the domain of the sciences. Maybe I can safely ignore this difficulty, because many other modern thinkers, even more advanced, have given up the notion that even scientists ever solve problems once and for all. But I can't so easily dodge a further difficulty: the definition includes everybody who ever thinks about anything— advertising executives, who wrestle for days on end with the problem of how to sell plastic milk, or those geniuses at playing blackjack who think and think about how to keep the house-man from recognizing that they are calculating the odds.

I must try again. "A scholar is anyone who sits alone for sustained periods trying to solve a problem for the sake of interest in the problem and its solution, not for the sake of some practical achievement in the world like selling plastic milk or winning at blackjack."

This one at least has the virtue of explaining why scholars have always been so concerned about developing clear lines between what they do and what other people do when they sit at desks. As soon as somebody stops trying to solve a problem and starts exhorting people, she is no longer a scholar but someone else, someone who doesn't see sitting at a desk thinking as an end in itself.

I suspect that this definition might have satisfied the founders of the MLA, if we added the simple qualification, "a problem about modern languages and literatures." But it would exclude about ninety percent of what my colleagues and I do in the name of scholarship. It would dictate excluding an essay of this kind from this volume. Or at least it would require that if there were such an essay, its point would be to show scholars how to protect their work from the poisonings of praxis.

My efforts to define seem no more successful than those I find in the stacks. But surely I am accumulating wisdom about my subject as I go. I can now at least list, like a good undergraduate who has done her "analysis" properly, six kinds of people who sit lonely in front of their desks, working over the modern languages and literatures instead of going off to hobnob with the gang at the club or at the national convention of (former) scholars: Intellectuals, who sit at their desks for no more than four hours on any one problem; Drudges, who sit at their desks working at other people's problems; Missionaries, who make *use* of hours at their desks; Publicists, who sit at their desks trying to find some new way of saying what they already knew when they first sat down; Scientists, who are ineffable; and Scholars, who are what we are all presumably trying to become. Some of the time.

Intellectuals we need not worry about; the more of them the better, provided we don't confuse what they do with scholarship. Besides, every good scholar is an intellectual too. Drudges we do not worry about; whenever we drudge—and none of us can avoid it—our relation to society is fixed, so long as we remain Drudges: we *serve* it, often honorably, whether society is a Senatorial committee or only that thesis chairman helping to get the damn thing out of the way. Missionaries we do not worry about for the same reason: when we become evangelical, our relation to society is also fixed, as we try to change it—honorable work, since every free society depends on vast numbers of thinking Missionaries to keep public life from freezing into its naturally wicked paths. Scientists we do worry about; for about three centuries we've spent a fair share of those hours at the desk trying to use or refute or adjust to the latest news from the lab.

The great public that never sits alone at a desk except to balance monthly accounts thinks that all scholars are Drudges, or should be: every scholar's labor should be as visibly useful to the world as the manufacture of safety pins. Drudges think that all scholarship must be drudgery, since they have never known it to be anything else. Missionaries think that all scholars are Irresponsibles. Intellectuals think that all scholars are either trivia experts or obscurantists. Scientists think that the scholars are fakers. And the Scholars—what do they think?

Well, if they *are* scholars, they don't quite know for sure yet. Though they will usually be sure that this unsureness is some sort of blessing, it will look like a curse to everyone else. To the public it is a curse because it means that scholars are always questioning what had seemed established. Intellectuals see it as a curse because it leads people to ask embarrassing questions about evidence and reasons. Drudges see it as a curse because it means that just as the dissertation is about finished that untrustworthy director has changed her mind about the whole problem. Missionaries see it as a special curse because it makes organizing the world for progress so difficult. And to the Scientist, it is *our* special curse: it simply means that *serious* inquiry has not yet been tried.

II

Society. Now, society is . . . well, society is like culture, which means that it is very hard to define. Gerald Holton, introducing *Science and Culture*, another volume that I found when scholaring, says that he can't define it, and he quotes anthropologists A. L. Kroeber and Clyde Kluckhohn, who can't define it either, quoting A. Lawrence Lowell's claim that

> there is nothing in the world more elusive. One cannot analyze it, for its components are infinite. One cannot describe it, for it is a Protean in shape. An attempt to encompass its meaning in words is like trying to seize the air in the hand, when one finds that it is everywhere except in one's grasp.[2]

But of course we've already been defining society. Society, for the scholar, is surely all those other people: the mere intellectuals, the drudges, the missionaries, the scientists, the thesis chairman or tenure committees, the editors of journals and presses, the great public. It is everybody who is not sitting right now at this desk. The only person in the world, right now, who is not society is me, or I, sitting here with society shut out so that I can work at this problem, which is mine, all mine. Society is the telephone, a long-distance call from a student asking why I have not returned his dissertation chapter; it is the daily mail, with a request from NEH; it is the committees, the family, the budget, the daily blasts of horrifying news. It is everything that will do its best to deflect me from solving—whatever this problem turns out to be, once I have thought about it for a few more hours, in private.

Could anything be more misleading than that seemingly inevitable opposition? Like it or not, every scholar is always in a society and could not be a scholar if she were not. It may be a small, clearly defined society, like the monastery that supported and restricted medieval monks and nuns who itched to inquire. More often it is multiple and poorly defined. For every scholar "*in* America," as we say, society is many societies, some of them formally named, like the MLA or NOW or the Democratic party or the board of trustees, but most of them unincorporated, like the growing number of my past students requesting recommendations, the nonacademic friends and relatives who express their wonder about what on earth I am up to, immured in the stacks.

But it is folly to think of society as the enemy, "out there." Society is *in* the scholar. Even when doing the purest scholarship, the scholar works as a member of many groups, belongs to a time and place, asks questions and performs tasks that are in no sense private. Even if we were foolish enough to try to invent our scholarship free of influences, any perceptive observer from any other time or place could easily recognize our origins. We should not need the Marxists to tell us that we can learn only what our time allows us to learn, because we can ask only those questions and use only those methods that are alive in our time.

There is no known instance of an isolated genius raised in an unscholarly society who invented interesting scholarship out of pure native wit. This deeply social truth is only slightly caricatured in the study of Nobel Prize winners showing that most Nobel laureates have associated closely with other Nobel laureates, either as their students or as their colleagues.[3] Every scholar, good or bad, becomes a scholar *by associating*, or, since that word has lost much of its force, we might say *by societing*.

No doubt many of us will continue to derive comfort from the myth that society is simply the enemy; literary portraits of embattled Arrowsmiths are inherently more exciting than sociological reports on how scholars do their actual societing. But even as we do so we will be enacting a role that our society, as playwright, has created for us.

III

If the scholar is someone who tries to learn by sustained private inquiry conducted "for its own sake" and if society is *in* every scholar, we can easily understand why scholarship has always seemed so fragile and why scholars have often seen themselves as in opposition to society. Scholarship as we have defined it is indeed fragile, a late-blooming flower in any civilization (when it blooms at all). It looks hardy in twentieth-century America, or at least it did until recent economic setbacks, only because society had agreed to reward its practitioners with academic positions. Despite current depredations, we still have a larger proportion of paid scholars, I suspect, than any other culture in history.[4]

That the institution of scholarship is fragile we know from history; though it has been often invented, it has almost as often died, or come so near to dying that its preservers—a few crazy monks in Ireland, say, or in Tibet—seem provided only by chance, or by the Great Provider.

That the impulse to scholarship is easily destroyed we know from evidence closer to home: most scholars see its fires flicker and die many times in their lives. Even if we leave aside, reluctantly, the many who, in their forties or fifties or sixties echo those wonderful words of George Eliot's Mr. Brooke—

> I went into science a great deal myself at one time, but I saw it would not do. It leads to everything; you can let nothing alone. . . . I took in all the new ideas at one time—human perfectibility, now. But some say history moves in circles, and that may be very well argued; I have argued it myself. The fact is, human reason may carry you a little too far—over the hedge, in fact. It carried me a good way at one time, but I saw it would not do. I pulled up; I pulled up in time. But not too hard. I have always been in favor of a little theory: we must have Thought, else we shall be landed back in the dark ages. . . .

—even if we leave aside the many who have failed for many years to sit steadily at that desk, whether from anger or contempt or grief or drink, we find that most of us who affect scholarship manage to bring it alive only for brief, blessed periods: a summer here, a year's leave there, a six-week burst of exhilarated inquiry when society, including our teaching, was neglected while we tried to answer some question that had ambushed us. And then, for months, years, decades, not scholarship but something else.

As Yeats says about the poet, all things can tempt us. I see one friend, a "seventeenth-century woman," writing a freshman composition text, and another friend building his own house, nail by nail, and another deciding at last to write his novel. I see but seldom hear from my ABDs out in the tules, accepting a chairmanship, taking up photography, running for political office. I see myself reading *Time* magazine on the plane bound for MLA meetings. . . .

But we are also—young and old—lured away by quite different temptations. Most of us can remember a youthful time when we saw scholarship not only as contemptible but as threatening to what we cared about in literature. How we palpitated to Yeats's "The Scholars":

> Bald heads forgetful of their sins,
> Old, learned, respectable bald heads
> Edit and annotate the lines
> That young men, tossing on their beds,

Rhymed out in love's despair
To flatter beauty's ignorant ear.

All shuffle there; all cough in ink;
All wear the carpet with their shoes;
All think what other people think;
All know the man their neighbor knows.
Lord, what would they say
Did their Catullus walk that way?

Today, along with such youthful and admirable contempt, we see a different attack: after deeply theoretical, perhaps even scholarly, inquiry, humanists young and old are announcing that scholarship is not just absurd but Absurd.

So it is that the scholar, *in* society, inhabited by society, is slave to fate, chance, kings, and desperate men. She doth with poison, war, and sickness dwell. That she survives at all is a wonder. Is it a good thing that scholarly societies should tempt their members further, young and old, to neglect their scholarship in order to think about scholarship?*

Perhaps the answer will depend on the quality of the thinking. It is all very well to circle about the thinker's desk as we have been doing, taking notes, but how are we to *think* about our roles, instead of simply extolling or lamenting them. Thought, presumably, should be in some sense sharable, "objective" at least in the sense of differing from the work of missionaries and publicists. But even to list the issues we face is to violate someone else's list of what the issues should be.

If I ask where the scholar should draw the line in acceding to society's requests, I am already granting society the right to put questions to us. If I ask to what degree a scholar should be held responsible for the ethical consequences of scholarship, I have already ruled into our subject a topic that others would simply rule out from the beginning. And if I ask how the scholar is to reconcile her scholarly life with her role as teacher, I am already granting to teaching the full status as rival that some would deny to it.

IV

In the history of thought about our subject, perhaps the most powerful statements have been those by champions of scholarly autonomy. A free

---

* This is not the first time that the MLA has done so. Though the previous edition of this project contained no essay on this subject—in fact it gave very little hint that such a subject might exist— other publications show that the MLA has almost always seen as one of its tasks support of a social climate in which scholarship could thrive. Anyone reading through those publications will find also, however, that many members thought such matters proper only to organizations like the National Council of Teachers of English, the Conference on College Composition and Communication, or the National Education Association.

scholarship did not come into the world without battle; it had to be earned with argument and, one suspects, with the powerful assistance of the useful results in the world produced by a freed scientific research. In the many past statements defending autonomy, one can detect a short list of persistent fears that always underlay the formulation of issues. Every scholar today has reason still to share those fears, but, for reasons I have already touched on, we cannot allow ourselves to be led by them into a hopeless battle for an isolated and autonomous scholarship.

I must now proceed from fear to fear, attempting to do justice to the reasons for past battles but to move beyond the fears to the issues that every scholar must think about. I cannot hope, in such an inquiry, to suggest what every scholar must think. But I do claim that every responsible scholar should think through each issue in order to be ready at any time, in a sense "on demand," to give to her many societies the grounds for her claim for support. In an absolute monarchy, presumably, a scholar could perform this task by thinking only of the reasons she can give her monarch when the old girl quavers, "What, you need *another* thousand, for *research*?" But in a democracy, the task is immensely complex because our publics are manifold.

The Fear That Scholarly Results Will Be Measured by Unscholarly Standards and Unscholarly People

As soon as a scholar's work is made subject to judgments about its value to someone else, there is clearly a danger that relevance to immediate needs will prevail over scholarly priorities. Researchers in the harder sciences have always had, at least until recently, a fairly good reply to those who sought relevance: engineering made scientific results relevant so quickly after discovery that it was easy to show that pure research was practical. (Now that the practical results threaten to be terrifyingly impractical, scientists have some more thinking to do.) But in the humanities a demand for immediate relevance to social needs would obviously rule out a large share of what we admire most. Is it not safer, then, simply to cut society dead, before it starts asking of us a closer friendship than we care to grant?

The unprepared, the unscholarly, the inexpert are, in a democracy, always ready to believe that one woman's opinion on any subject is as good as another's. America has never lacked a supply of confident critics who, like Senator William Proxmire, know at a glance whether a project is ridiculous enough to deserve his Golden Fleece of the Month Award.

The humanities in America have always been plagued not just by demands for practicality but also by demands that "men of affairs," "men who have met a payroll," dictate what and how the schools should teach. Those who *can*, do; those who *can't*, teach. Let those who *can* dictate to those who *can't*. If I can't understand it, hardheaded down-to-earth type that I am, there can't be much in it. You're filling the heads of the young with insane socialist ideas that make them totally unfit for the real world. You talk of teaching them to "understand literature." Well, what I want to ask is, why subject them to that mad Kafka and that unreadable Faulkner and that gloomy Dreiser and that dirty-minded Joyce and all those corrupt foreigners, when you could uplift them with these fine works that our Board's committee has compiled for you?

A governor of Texas, Jim Ferguson, once vetoed the entire annual appropriation for the University of Texas in the state budget, saying that too many people were going hog-wild about higher education. His veto was finally overridden, but were not the scholars of the state of Texas justified in their fears for the independence of the scholarly domain?

Yet when we try to translate this justified fear into a question to be thought about, it is by no means self-evident that a simple plea for autonomy makes sense. The question might be phrased like this: To what extent should the worth of a given form of inquiry be measured by standards set by someone other than the inquirer?

I suspect that most scholars today would answer, "To no extent at all." Is it not the very nature of genuine inquiry that it must be freed of all restraints except those imposed by the problem and the standards of a given discipline? Yet in recent decades an increasing number of academics have argued either that free inquiry is never attainable and that arguments for it are simply disguises for the status quo, or that it would be undesirable if attained.

Defenders of autonomy can point to innumerable follies committed when the public decides to mock or censor studies in subjects it does not understand; Senator Proxmire amuses us when we know nothing about his subject, outrages us when the subject is our own. Contrary to Jerome Bruner's claim that every subject can be taught in some form to anyone of any age, we all know that a great deal of what we value cannot be explained to anyone but a specialist, at least not within real limits of space, time, and patience.

On the other hand, to every thinking layman—and we are all laymen with respect to most inquiries—it seems obvious that we should not be asked to support many projects that in fact now receive public funding. In every field but my own, I find myself ready to ask a simple and nasty question: "Just how many scholars of that kind does a society *need*?" An intelligent and well-read member of my university's board of trustees once asked me, as we chatted during a banquet, "How many Chaucer scholars does a society need?" He could have made the question even tougher by asking not about Chaucer scholars but about experts in, say, *Piers Plowman*, or the Marquis de Sade, or George Sand. But one need not point only at others. For about two years of my life the United States government supported me (with the GI Bill) while I spent most of my time investigating the history of the self-conscious narrator in comic fiction before *Tristram Shandy*. I have since read many articles and even a book on something like the same subject, and there are hundreds of scholars now working on topics related to that one novel. Just how many scholars devoting their lives to Laurence Sterne does a society need?

Regardless of what subject we think of here, we find that we are driven to acknowledge two seemingly opposing points: no public is qualified to answer the question, yet every public must answer it by the way it allocates its funds and thus rewards (or punishes) scholars who pursue this or that line.

If a Senate Subcommittee on the Worth of Scholarship begins to inquire into the value of my history of the self-conscious narrator, I feel justly indignant as I dig in my heels and tell the senators to go mess with something they know something about. But if you ask whether scholars studying the self-conscious narrator are in general qualified as final judges about how many such scholars I want my society to support, my response is much less clear.

Must we have fifty specialists in *Tristram Shandy*? As Goneril and Regan say, "What need you five-and-twenty, ten, or five . . . ? What need one?" Society long endured without a single scholarly article on *Tristram Shandy*, and if all of the published scholarship on it were wiped out tomorrow, would anyone in the world except us Sterne specialists suffer a sense of loss? As an expert on the self-conscious narrator in comic fiction before 1760, am I the best judge about whether society—let us say through the National Endowment for the Humanities—should provide support for more of my kind of thing? How, then, can we justify a national educational system that rewards and encourages scholarly specialization of this kind, often at the expense of simple essential matters like teaching the young how to read and write?

The scholar is, after all, not always the best judge of what her work is worth. She has put too much labor into it, whether it is good or bad, to be able to judge fairly whether it deserves public support.

My wife asks me to go cut some roses in the garden for the dinner we're giving tonight. For perhaps five minutes I do the best scholarly job I can of selecting the freshest ones, and we make a bouquet together. During the dinner I notice myself noticing the flowers more than I would have if she had cut them. My investment. My product. My roses. I find the bouquet good.

The scholar is like that, after the thinking is done. Anything I have put a great deal of myself into becomes my property, in a good old sense of the word: I have in it a piece of my *amour propre*. If any silly Senator Proxmire comes along and scoffs at it, so much the worse for him, I say; I *know* it is valuable.

It is thus almost certain that I will overvalue the importance of my own work, even when I see its faults. And scholars in general must surely overrate the importance of what they do as a body. We see this happening clearly to our colleagues in other disciplines. All the scientists we know naively overvalue science and undervalue the humanities. Every historian thinks history more important than it really can possibly be. Every social scientist similarly. . . . Why can't they all see that the most important scholarship is what we do—we *humane* inquirers?

But who, then, is to judge the importance of what we do, if we cannot be trusted? Why of course it must be other people—finally it is going to be people not yet born, but right now it is going to be *someone else out there*—some other scholar, if the question is the importance of "my own work" compared with "your own work," and some nonscholarly collectivity when the question is whether what we do is more important than what other scholars or teachers or postmen do.

My various societies thus allocate their resources and boost or hinder me in my scholarly endeavors. They support research about Chaucer or *Tristram Shandy* or Alcanter de Brahm because they have become somehow convinced, as we are convinced, that preservation of our literary culture is a good thing, that somehow literary culture graces or enhances their lives.

It is obvious that they will do this allocating well only if we have managed to teach them how to do it. We scholars have taught, after all, in our role as teachers, every member of society who carries much weight in society's allocations. And we continue to teach and thus to make our society, by the nature and quality of what we do; they learn from us whether or not to take our work seriously.

In comparison with other cultures, America has not done at all badly in producing a public that believes in higher education and the scholarship that feeds it, or should feed it, from the top down. Abuses of scholarship are somehow seen as a necessary cost paid for scholarship's ultimate value. The treatises on trivia and the nonsense that nobody will ever read must be tolerated in order to preserve the treasures that make a culture worth having. Whatever the reasons for past support, future support will depend on our ability to deepen and strengthen that conviction. And that in turn will depend more on what we do in the classroom than on what we publish. What the senator remembers about his teachers of literature will affect his vote much more strongly than any suspect scholarly title he happens to stumble upon in a busy day. We must be able to look him in the eye and say, with pride and assurance, that we deserve even more support because a society simply cannot have too many *teachers* who, because of their scholarly training, can teach Shakespeare, or Chaucer, or Sterne, or Dickens, or Mark Twain, in the illuminating and life-enhancing ways that he experienced in school and college.

There is another form of teaching that might also affect his vote, one that is perhaps even more badly neglected than classroom teaching. Our increasing specialization seems to have led to decreasing interest in addressing our results to nonspecialists. Most of what most scholars were writing in 1900, or 1925, or even 1950, could have been understood by any literate layman. It might have been found boring, but it would not have been unintelligible. Too much of what we publish now is both boring and unintelligible. No doubt many of our new problems deserve to be discussed with specialists in specialists' language. But most of our important work deserves also to be translated into a language that will, by its nature, teach the public that we are serious and that what we do can be important to more than a priestly cult. America has a distinguished tradition of *haute vulgarisation*—of chautauquas and lyceums and college lecture series and literary journalism. The tradition is not dead, but I have the impression that it is pursued these days more vigorously among scientists than among humanists. Where is the Lewis Thomas of literary critics? Where is the *Scientific American* among our journals of literary study?

How many Chaucerians does a society need? An unanswerable question, because we could get along with none. How many good teachers of Chaucer does a society need? Another unanswerable question, because there is simply no limit. Would it not make sense to say that a society in which everyone was able to teach Chaucer—that is, to discuss him with pleasure and profit—would be a better society than one in which only, say, five hundred specialists could do so?

Thinking about our question has not, then, led us to an unequivocal answer giving the scholar the sole right to judge the worth of what she does. The scholar who works as amateur, devoting spare time to scholarship, may let her own curiosity or pleasure dictate whether she studies Pushkin or the game of push-pin. But the scholar who is paid *for* her scholarship must either find ways to teach its value to the world—whether the "world" consists of students or senators—or be prepared for the day in which California's Proposition 13 will be remembered as a mere hint of the drought to come.*

Fear That the Quest for Knowledge Will Be Abandoned for Other Goals, Worthy or Unworthy

We have all known many attacks on the primacy of cognitive aims in education. When Emerson pled, in his great Phi Beta Kappa address, for an *American* scholar, his ultimate appeal was not to something known but to something wished for. When John Dewey and other pragmatists attacked a kind of cognitive education that dealt, as they saw it, in frozen concepts, and substituted a pragmatic appeal to experience, many scholars were horrified. When pragmatism was taken up, often in garbled form, and turned into a "progressive education movement," many scholars felt that the vandals were at the gates; it became widely believed that the many indubitable academic deficiencies in entering college classes in the fifties and sixties were a direct result of the schools' teaching "not the subject but the child," substituting notions like "growth," "personal well-being," and "maturation" for intellectual mastery.[5]

An urbane expression of the fear of a different kind of corruption can be found in the essay on literary criticism in the precursor of this volume. Northrop Frye's *bête noir* is "evaluation" or "judicial criticism." The true end of criticism is "to add to the understanding of a writer" (p. 72), and if what is added is to have any standing as *knowledge*, it cannot be evaluative. "Value judgments may be asserted, intuited, assumed, argued about, explained, attacked, or defended: what they never can be is demonstrated" (p. 74). "Judicial criticism is based on good taste, and good taste is a skill founded by practice on the knowledge the critic has; academic criticism [which is the only proper subject for the academic scholar] is a structure of knowledge" (p. 74).

Frye states again and again that he does not wish to disclaim the usefulness of judicial criticism, *in its proper place*. But that place is not the academy, and it is clear that if it enters the academy the proper order of things will be destroyed. It is only after cognitive criticism has done its work of showing how "the form of literature as a whole becomes the content of criticism as a whole" that we can face—in a final paragraph or two and not as literary scholars but as moralists and social critics—the question of what literature "does for society" (p. 81).

The threat of an unscientific criticism that merely emotes or expresses preferences is only one of many dangers that scholars have discerned from the time when academic departments of modern languages and literatures were first founded—and that time was, we should never forget, only yesterday.

---

* Since such hot issues cool quickly in public memory, it should perhaps be noted that Proposition 13 mandated for California the first nationally publicized tax cut that had drastic statewide consequences for educational budgets.

Modern languages have always been in some sense confused and beleaguered subjects—or rather, loose federations of subjects. The typical English department today is not even a federation, but rather a confederation of specialists in British literature, American literature, world literature, folklore, philology and linguistics (of increasingly varied shapes and shades), bibliography and editing, film studies, literary theory, rhetoric and composition, and sometimes black studies, American studies, women's studies, Indian culture, and so on. Such being the case, what is English?

I can remember the cries of alarm from the French department of a small eastern college when the chairman took off for a couple of years to study the culture of a small village in France. It was not just that he risked becoming a sociologist, which would be bad enough; he clearly risked coming up with results that could in no sense be verified or replicated. He was abandoning both literature and the cognitive study of literature, and it did not assuage the fears very much when, on the basis of the splendid book he wrote, he was called to a prestigious chair in French Civilization and Culture.

The study of literature will lose its scholarly status, the fear tells us, unless it yields knowledge comparable to the knowledge offered in traditional academic disciplines. And it will not do that if we allow ourselves to whore after these false gods of evaluation, or cultural relevance, or public service, or retribution for past social wrongs.

As we begin the 1980s, we have seen enough shoddy programs motivated by social concerns to justify the most extreme fears. Much that is published in the name of various new "scholarly" causes is clearly motivated not by any desire to know or learn, in any sense of the words, but by the desire to make converts. And it is not hard to imagine what some of the more rigorous scholars of previous generations—the great editors, the great literary historians—would have to say about the results of our forgetting their reasons for insisting on what one of the greatest of their time, Max Weber, called "value-free inquiry."

But as a profession we cannot simply revert to earlier cognitive models of inquiry, now that we know what we know about the dangers and errors in the assumptions underlying those models. The knower, we all now know, *is* entailed in what is known, and the bonds are far more intricate than anyone suspected before this century. Even the hardest of the sciences, we are now told on what seems unimpeachable authority (I name only Gödel's proof, that staple reference of all of us half-informed humanists) cannot prove their own first principles or give a scientific or mathematical defense of their methods.[6] And if this is true of the physical sciences, how much more obviously true of the humanities, in which the structure of thought is always visibly entwined in fundamental convictions about what is in fact valuable. If it is still true that one purpose we all should share is to discover knowledge, it is also true that other purposes for many of us seem legitimately to rival or surpass the desire to increase what is known. Even when I try to inquire *qua* scholar, I inevitably serve *these* values rather than *those*, and thus I should, *qua* scholar, bring into my work a conscious and deliberate assertion and defense of the values I serve.

Our fears thus again turn into issues to be thought about:

Will what I am trying to discover in any way contribute to the vitality of literary culture? Can I hope that anyone who reads it in the spirit in which 'tis writ will experience a stronger sense of the value either of the literature I am studying or of this way of studying it?

Is my scholarly project something I would choose to undertake if there were no institutional pressure to do research? If not, how do I justify spending my precious life on it?

Is my scholarly project as important to me or to anyone else as other projects I might spend similar amounts of time on—teaching, for example?

In my project, have I taken hold of the handle that I honestly think is most important? If so, how would I explain that importance to a skeptic? If not, do I have good reasons for not shifting from low into high gear?

But before we make the burden of these questions more than any young scholar should be asked to bear, we should listen to another fear.

Fear of a Novelty That Will Swamp Valued Traditions

Society is always up-to-date. The humanities never can be, try as they will. They are always harking back, reconsidering, trying old tasks once again. I can hear a voice—shall we call it not an elderly but a mature one—saying, "If you insist on encouraging the young to think about how their work serves society, you may find—as indeed we all found in the sixties—that Shakespeare, Milton, Chaucer, Molière, and Goethe are being replaced in the literature classes by Norman Mailer on Vietnam or Erica Jong on how to talk tougher than any man."

The notion of the autonomous scholar was developed in societies with strong traditions that often opposed the novelties of the new science. But it was then found important to humanists whose traditions were no longer taken for granted by a public that had learned to admire the practical results of physical science and its engineering by-products. How do you defend professors who work at Greek philology or Assyrian lexicography to a public caring only about the latest development in airplanes, cars, and kitchen gadgets? Obviously you cannot, so the best choice is not to try: that is, to argue the *general* case for professorial autonomy, leaving particular research tasks in the closet. Knowledge for knowledge, a discovery about a hitherto misunderstood diacritical mark cannot compete, in the public eye or even in the eye of the youthful scholar, with whatever sensation *Time* magazine or the little literary magazines will feature today. So the best line was thought to be simply, "Leave us alone and we'll at least do you no harm, because we preserve the past and we say nothing about the present or future. And we'll teach our young charges to do the same."

But of course a general defense of culture and its preservers will not make the problems go away, and the problem we face here is whether we can defend *to ourselves* the inquiries we undertake. We may be quite right in resisting any demand that we make our scholarship relevant to immediate interests. But we cannot be justified in undertaking research that we ourselves do not believe in, and the fact is that our profession has, for complex reasons, developed a strange capacity to generate a kind of research that is not only irrelevant to the society but irrelevant to the interests of the researcher.

What right have we, then, to place the burden of judging on the young scholar, if "we" provide circumstances that will punish her if she chooses to be honorable. If we have in fact invented a system that encourages what we might call unscholarship—that kind of research not dictated by a desire to learn something—do we have any right to ask young people to combat that system at personal cost?

From the point of view of anyone pursuing our common welfare, it would be hard to say who is more to blame for the flood of unscholarship, young scholars or old. All older scholars know that young scholars publish too much too soon, but we force the young plants by the way we play our roles in tenure and promotion decisions. Young scholars know that old scholars also publish too much, because the academic plums continue to fall to those who publish more and more, throughout a lifetime. And the young, who should ideally be the source of a rigorous criticism that would save the oldsters from providing steady evidence of their decline, are caught instead in such a flood of stuff to be read fast that they soon develop habits of nonattention that make serious criticism impossible. Go to the library stacks, O skeptic, and look at the books and unpublished dissertations in your own specialty; pick out any half-dozen volumes at random, and ask yourself whether the world would be the poorer if half of them had never been loosed on the world.

The issue to be thought about, then, underlying the fear of novel standards and ways, is this: is it possible, without simply embracing every novelty, to invent ways to improve the quality of the scholarship we lead each other to produce? If we are to do so, the inventions will most likely come from young scholars, not from the old. Can we find ways to reward that kind of inventive service to scholarship and to society?

V

The dangers for any young scholar who attends to what I have been saying are obvious; if she does not play the game as it is now designed, if she does not succumb to ambition, mendacity, or cowardice and produce *instanter* that book or article that should in fact have five more years of gestation, the ax will fall, but not on me. It is scarcely fair of me to urge individual victims to go courageously to the slaughterhouse. What must be changed are the rules of the house, and nobody knows quite how to do that without losing more than we gain.

When literal thought fails, let allegory prevail. Let us imagine a visitor who comes to America from a strange land, Eupaideia, a land that has miraculously ordered its scholarship and teaching according to a reasonable ideal. Asked to testify before the new Commission on Rational Promotion and Tenure Procedures, this is what the sibyl says:

> We order all these things better in Eupaideia, and we are able to do so because we know what it is that we want from our educational system. We have agreed that what we most need is for every citizen to be curious about how to make life more humane. Our schools are organized not

around reading, writing, and 'rithmetic but around a sequence of curiosities: Curiosity I, about what nature is up to; Curiosity II, about what is humane; Curiosity III, about what makes an admirable human achievement; Curiosity IV, about why things so often go wrong; Curiosity V, about why they ever go right; and so on. Our colleges are organized similarly, with Curiosity 101, 102, 103. . . .

We impose no norms about what words like "curious," "humane," and "achievement" are to mean, and we have learned that the local curiosity of individual teachers and principals gives a much better guide to curriculum building than any impositions from more distant authorities. But we do impose two absolute rules: no curriculum can be adopted without a free vote of all teachers on the question, "Does this program interest *you*?" and every curriculum must be revised every five years by a committee of teachers elected from the school where it will be taught.

More pertinent to your problems are our ways of relating scholarly inquiry, publication, and reward. Both college and school teachers are judged, for retention and promotion, mainly according to whether they can arouse the elected committee members' curiosity about the subjects they teach. Each teacher whose fate is in the balance can choose any method for interesting the committee: published writing, unpublished essays or lectures, tapes, a prolonged group discussion. If curiosity about where she will go next (that is, about what she might be able to teach them next time around) is roused, she is hired, retained, or promoted. Every five years each teacher undergoes the same test, throughout her life, and those who fail are, regardless of their age, given a one-year sabbatical to allow for preparation for a second try; if after a year of free inquiry she still cannot arouse anyone's curiosity, she is asked to seek employment in some line of work not centered on competence in the Curiosities.

What this has meant for us is of course that nobody writes and publishes unless that route has for her proved the best way to learn. We were a bit surprised to find that the amount of *writing* did not go down markedly, while the amount of *publication* dropped by about seventy-five percent. Obviously most scholars find that trying to write a coherent statement is the best way to learn, yet most find the results of the try not ready for publication.

I should perhaps mention that in carrying out this plan we were immensely aided by our National Tax on Verbal Profits. It was instituted long ago for different motives entirely: to remove the immense rewards, so striking still in your society, for corrupting life by abusing language. . . . [The report then describes this tax in some detail. It is simply a steeply graduated tax on all publications that make money for author or publisher: standard income tax on anything up to one fifth of the basic annual academic salary, rising rapidly to one hundred percent on high income from advertising copy, best sellers (including textbooks), TV and movie scripts. The motive for becoming a deliberate miseducator is thus drastically reduced. The fortunate side effect is to remove all financial incentive for publishing scholarly works and textbooks.]

Thus you see that in Eupaideia no one ever writes anything unless she wants to, and no one is ever in the position of wanting to publish something no matter what. Why write a book unless one cannot *not* write a book?

I cannot overstate the resulting differences in attitude between your young scholars and ours. Our youths naturally postpone publication as long as possible—until they cannot resist the itch to spread their ideas through the world. Insofar as their thoughts are on future professional success at all (and that seems to be about the same as in your society), they are driven to think hard and long about how on earth they are to interest that review committee a few years on. And they soon learn that the best way to prepare for *that* is to learn how to rouse the curiosity of their students. . . .

Our entire professoriat is thus, you see, attending to the task of discovering whatever is truly interesting in the world and to teaching the arts of such discovery. Not the least of the resulting blessings is that everyone who picks up a new scholarly book can be fairly sure that its author wanted to write it and believed in it as the best possible under the circumstances. As bibliographies have shrunk, the quality of writing has improved, and sales figures for individual titles have soared. Scholars have rediscovered the wisdom of ancient Slower Reading Programs: the fewer pages you cover in a given time, the more you learn. You tell me that in your society the slow reader is doomed. I can well believe it, because we were once ourselves in danger of becoming a nation of desperate skimmers. But now. . . .

Needless to say, your problem of the opposition between traditional values and the novel idea or movement simply does not arise. Since the curiosity of well-educated men and women can be on the whole as well aroused by an old problem or old text as by the most recent novelty, people are free to pursue in their own way that great truth enunciated by Aristotle: All men by nature desire to know. . . .

Obviously no one could seriously recommend the Eupaideist's program to America today. It was designed for a less sophisticated society than ours, and for scholars who have not eaten of the tree of knowledge. But the naive stranger does dramatize for us how strange is our practice of leading thousands of citizens, especially the vulnerable young, to publish books and articles against their will, books and articles that nobody will read—except for other reluctant scholars who are led to "cover the literature" in their own unreadable first chapters.

We should remind ourselves that there are other ways of managing things. Less than a century ago there was no university in the country that required the Ph.D. for academic appointment and no university that insisted on publication for those who were retained and promoted. Though in America William James was already by 1903 writing his lament about the "Ph.D. Octopus,"[7] in Germany, where teachers were paid a capitation fee depending on attendance at their lectures, Max Weber could complain that promotion and tenure decisions took no account of scholarship whatever (thus we see how the Eupaideist's scheme would actually work out in a fallen world: as Weber complains, lecturers learn to use the cheapest tricks to "interest" large audiences, instead of keeping their minds on scientific inquiry!).[8]

VI

How could a young scholar hope to answer any of the questions I have raised? How is she to know whether what she does is important enough to justify the time and energy taken from other good things in the world?

There can be no easy way, but a first step is surely to be clear about why attempting good scholarship is in itself a service to society, regardless of the subject. How can anyone claim, as I want now to do, that to be a good scholar is to perform a service that no other "estate," no other establishment, can perform?

Our service, whatever it is, will be performed at the frazzled end of a three-century history that every scholar knows by heart: the struggle for the one supreme value, objective truth. Our world has been shaken by a series of scientific revolutions, from Copernicus through Einstein to more recent forlorn questionings about whether physical scientists may not after all be probing into sheer chaos. Perhaps just beyond the next experimental step into the unknown will be a revelation showing not only that God does play dice with the universe but that there is simply nothing "out there" to be known.[9] Each major revision of our view of the world was initiated by immensely courageous scholars who followed truth where it led—so the history runs—regardless of how badly personal preferences were trampled in the process. It is easy for us now to debunk this myth by showing that none of its heroes really foresaw where the inquiry would lead—they were all, in Arthur Koestler's apt description, "sleepwalkers." But the myth was intellectually and morally powerful, with its implied metaphor of an "edge of objectivity" moving courageously and impersonally into the unknown; its inherent heroic appeal was steadily reinforced by the spectacular practical results that flowed in the wake of the ship of objective intellectual progress.[10]

It is scarcely surprising, then, that most serious students of human nature and its achievements should have emulated the students of physical nature. The ideals of objectivity that accounted, or so it seemed, for scientific triumphs should surely yield similar triumphs in the study of societies. Why not ultimately, then, even in the study of that most mysterious of all our mysteries, the creative achievements of genius? If God's wondrous creation could be demystified with such spectacular results, why should we not demystify the acts of creative genius? But clearly we can do so only if we are willing to cast as cold an eye on the works of mankind as we have cast on the works of God. Our duty will be to exercise as much courage and honesty in our work as the most dispassionate scientific investigator has ever displayed.

But the ideal of a "value-free" objectivity in humanistic studies has been inevitably troublesome to every powerful inquirer embracing it. One of the greatest of these I have already mentioned, Max Weber. He is often now described by new subjectivists as almost villainously given to an irresponsibly impersonal scholar science. But he was in fact always struggling to combine his justified sense of the necessary scholarly virtues with his personal responsibility to fight, as scholar and editor of *Archiv*, for the "values" he considered "higher."[11]

Anyone reading through Weber's immensely influential essays about academic freedom, or his explanations of how the editors of a journal of economics can and must both follow scientific truth wherever it leads, in value-free objectivity, and at the same time express their "ethos" by supporting the causes in which they believe, must be struck by the driving sense of social purpose that informed both sides of the scholar-citizen's effort.

Literary scholars seem not to have grappled quite so profoundly with these issues. But everyone in this century has had to think about them, because every modern scholar encounters a tension between the undeniable scholarly "value," pursuit of the "factual," and the undeniable fact that every step in humanistic inquiry, from the choice of subject and problem to the choice of relevant data and appropriate methods, is value-ridden. And since scholars have inherited, along with their scholarly ideals, the conviction that about values there can be no rational inquiry but only personal assertion ("propositions of value cannot be derived from propositions of fact"), they can be shown to suffer a deep sense of conflict between their desire to honor the scholarly virtues and their awareness that their lives are devoted to discriminations of value and to the service of what is peculiarly excellent.

Now that we no longer need be defensive about a scholarship that carries the taint of value judgments,[12] can we restate the virtues* required *for* scholarship (and thus *taught by* scholarship) in a way that can make clear why the service of a genuine scholarship can never be in opposition to the values that any defensible society would want to promote?

The first is obviously honesty. If all the thousands of exhortations to objectivity were assembled and collated to determine what virtue they shared, we would discover at the core a refusal to lie about something that we know, even if lying will serve something else that we value. In the days when it was generally believed that we could not *know* values, this virtue inevitably led to the notion that to be honest we must suppress our sense of values in the service of what we do know: we must be "objective." But if we do in fact know some values, then this virtue can now be seen not as some separable quality that a scholar might well add to her character but as the very basis for scholarly inquiry. Inquiry begins when one thing that we know seems to conflict with some other thing that we know, generating a problem that we must then—if we are honest—inquire into. All true inquiry is generated in this very practical kind of conflict between at least two valued convictions, neither of which can, in all honesty, be simply ignored.

What is impressive about Weber's continuing discussions of a value-free

---

* For many readers today the word "virtues" is misleading. If it seems moralistic, substitute "powers," or "habits," or even that weasel term from the social sciences, "traits." Or "strengths." Or "characteristics."

inquiry practiced by a value-ridden scholar is precisely his refusal to deny either side of what he knew: on the one hand, if I allow my personal preferences to contaminate my inquiry, what it yields may be worthless as knowledge, and on the other hand, if I do not pursue my highest values (which were, for him, not on rational grounds distinguishable from "mere personal preferences"), I lose all self-respect. That conflict generated thought, and at the same time it set a model of scholarly behavior that all of us might emulate. Reading Weber now in his attack on the "operators," the academic toadies who modulate their conclusions to please the powers, it is the moral fervor of the man that is infectious. And that morality is inseparable from his passion for scholarly truth. It is, in short, an expression of the same honesty—though not of the same drive for "objectivity"—that Weber shows when he tries to study how the world's religions really work without letting his own religious preferences get in the way.

What the scholar in our time must be honest about cannot be dictated by anyone but herself, but of course it will be dictated, in a sense, by every part of the experience she has made her own, including whatever societies she is made of. Some of the academic revolts that began in the late sixties have been precisely an expression of an honesty turned onto experiences that "objective" scholarship had ignored.[13] "Objective scholarship" could, for example, study the history of the novel without mentioning the biases of religion, class, race, and sex that even the greatest of novels reveal and that most of the scholars tacitly shared. An "objective" female scholar thus would not mention, surely, that her own soul was violated by this or that work, and she would not include in her account how she actually felt as she read. It may be that we now face the opposite danger, from polemicists who can too easily give an honest report of their justifiedly angry responses to various biases but without mentioning their inescapable admiration for qualities that accompany the offenses. Honest scholars can be moved to new kinds of honest inquiry only when they place what they know from traditional scholarly pursuits together with all that they find in personal experience. The alternative to a dry (and secretly biased) objectivity is not thus "subjectivity"—whatever that might be—but honest inquiry.[14]

The second untarnished virtue is courage. What the myth of the objective scientist held up for our emulation was a picture not just of honesty but of courageous honesty: the lover of truth willing to risk personal harm for the sake of proclaiming an unpopular or even destructive truth. Though the myth seriously understated the ways in which honest inquiry often will actually buttress social norms and commonplaces, it had this much truth to it: all honest inquiry destroys something, if only the complacent acceptance of two incompatible convictions in the same mind. In all genuine thought I must give up something, discarding one or the other of the clashing commonplaces with which I began or finding a new synthesis that leaves neither of the prior elements unchanged. Such destruction always takes courage. Thought is always to some degree threatening; it is always easier not to think than to think, whether the results of thought finally turn out to be revolutionary or conservative. As Pete Hein's little verse has it,

Problems worthy
Of attack
Prove their worth
By hitting back.

The scholar is the only person charged by society to carry the burden of thought to its extremes, even when thought hits back. All professions require brain work, but only the scholar is charged primarily with exercising critical thought that will stick—will stand up to further criticism. Intellectuals appoint themselves, of course, to this same task, and their barbs are often essential in goading scholars into thought. But the intellectual who would make her barbs *stick* must either depend on scholars to think out their implications or turn themselves into scholars—that is, sit back down at that desk and start looking at the *reasons* on all sides of the question. All scholars know, of course, that even their hardest won conclusions may not survive for long. On the other hand, they may survive indefinitely.*

Courage thus reveals itself as of two kinds, depending on what kind of threat is defied. The scholar must be willing to face conclusions that destroy her own intellectual comfort—conclusions that she "personally" would rather not believe. And she must be willing to profess conclusions that go against her interests in the world: she must be—to use a good old word that is rapidly losing its usefulness—disinterested. She will not follow the advice of one of our most prominent and successful literary critics, whose scholarship grows weaker and weaker as he heeds his own advice telling us to keep our ears to the ground and our noses clean and to pursue whatever is the latest critical fashion to its most colorful extreme.

To resist such advice requires a third virtue, one not shared with the "mere" intellectual: persistence. Whatever future shock the scholar experiences as citizen, as scholar she persists on some one line for as long as is required. If her problem is "What words did Shakespeare, or Calderón, or Goethe actually write?" she may persevere for a lifetime without coming to an end. Living in a world increasingly jumpy, a hopping, a saltatory world where everyone changes neighborhoods, spouses, professions, crises almost as fast as she can flick the dial to a new program, the scholar necessarily digs in deep and long.

It is for this reason that those who accuse scholars of defending the status quo are quite wrong; the scholar often never even catches up to it, so persistent is she on that problem she began with before all these changes occurred. Day after day, year in year out, she goes to that desk and faces that problem until it is either solved or proved pointless. Ask any scholar whose

---

* I don't know why it is that everyone these days seems to stress the first truth much more strongly than the second. But a few hours spent with any great work of scholarship—Thucydides, Gibbon, Johnson's *Dictionary* or *Lives of the Poets*, Bernard Weinberg's *A History of Literary Criticism in the Italian Renaissance*—will show that the proportion of what later scholars reject to what they still accept is always reassuringly small. It does seem true that less survives in my particular line of country—literary criticism and rhetorical studies—than in literary history.

book or article has made a difference for you how long she worked on it. For most books the answer will be "from five to ten years." Often it is "all my life." The scholar persists—or stops being a scholar.

Like all other virtues, persistence can corrupt unless it is tempered by other virtues. Whether the world will view the persisting scholar as pig-headed or plain crazy depends in part on the accident of whether the world has any notion of what she is up to and in part on whether the goal pursued is clearly separate from whatever rewards may accompany success. As I see it, we in America are desperately short of models of honest courageous persistence in the pursuit of anything but money or notoriety. Now that all of the fine arts except musical performance can be mastered—or so we are told—simply by letting one's genius hang out, without persistence, and now that the persistence required for athletic preeminence is increasingly focused on the money and not on victory in grace, scholarly persistence seems about the only source of models of that wonderful weird human quality of steady, concentrated, unrewarded labor for an uncertain and seemingly impractical goal.*

A fourth scholarly virtue we might call consideration, though the word has lost much of its force. Good scholarship requires, contrary to some popular notions of the lone scientist or scholar inventing private truths, a steady habit of sustained attention to other people's reasoning. It is thus largely good listening and reporting. The floods of bad scholarship that we swim against have drowned out what was originally the clearest acknowledgment of this habit: the opening section of the book or dissertation in which the "state of the question," as others have treated it, is "considered." In that opening, so hard to write and often now mere ill-considered summary and thus boring to read, one showed a consideration of the opinions of other scholars in preparation for one's own effort to carry the question further—with the implication that one is carrying one's colleagues along as well.

That opening section has become harder and harder to write as publications have increased. When I did my dissertation it was possible, though arduous, to read just about everything that had ever been written about *Tristram Shandy* (except, of course, in languages beyond me; like Casaubon, I did not know that some of my grappling had been anticipated by "foreigners"— in my case, the "Russian formalists"). Writing *The Rhetoric of Fiction*, again I read "everything" ever said about narrative point of view. It would be absurd to ask any student to attempt either of those tasks now, since both "literatures" have doubled many times. But the student who has discovered a genuine scholarly problem about either of these inexhaustible subjects will, must, attempt something like this considerate survey of what other people have thought, knowing that some of them will have something to teach her. Though the task of winnowing becomes more difficult as the bibliographies lengthen,

---

* Practical skills and crafts survive, of course, and they all require at least one of these three virtues: persistence. More time and energy and skill go into a typical thirty-second spot for a network commercial than went into many a Restoration comedy, say, that we still remember and admire. See *Thirty Seconds*, by Michael J. Arlen (New York: Farrar, 1980).

no publishing *scholar* will ever want to ignore the sometimes glorious, sometimes disillusioning companionship and tutelage of those who have tilled this field before.

We often debase this point to the relatively unimportant matter of not wanting to say what someone else has already said, as if no truth should ever be said more than once. Perhaps from the influence of the hard sciences, where new discoveries seldom require much repeating before they begin to do their work in the world, we forget that most of the knowledge we care about in the humanities is of a kind that cannot be considered and repeated too often, provided that the scholar who does the repeating has found a way of reasoning about it that makes it come alive again for her.

In short, scholarship as we have defined it depends on a "decent respect for the opinions of mankind," past, present, and future. Scholarly problems as we encounter them would not exist at all without our heritage of opinions about literary works and about how to discuss them. Any present effort to solve a given problem and present the results in written form would make no sense whatever if we did not "consider" ourselves bound to a society of scholars who will attempt to follow our arguments.

In this way consideration, in several senses of the word, must affect how we write as well as what and how we read. The scholar will always make her results as intelligible to other scholars as the inherent difficulties of the subject allow, and she will not be embarrassed if this means writing so that any literate person can follow. The inherent drive of scholarship itself is thus toward a considerate style that assists other people as much as possible in a joint endeavor: understanding this problem and this possible solution to it. We may find this claim a bit hard to believe in these days when mystifying opacities fill our books and journals. But we should remember that some subjects *are* in fact difficult, even mystifying, and that no reader can determine simply from a difficult or easy surface whether the author is showing a proper consideration.[15]

Every genuine scholar who ventures into domains other than bibliography and editing knows a sense of failure in this effort to find a style that shares, that considers, that joins a subject to a proper reader. Her problems are always complex, her solutions are usually uncertain and unclear until the last page is completed—at which point she should start over with page one and rewrite the whole thing. But since we do not live in Eupaideia, revision must stop before it should, and the final presentation is not as clear as the inherent complexities would have allowed.

And it is not all a matter of insufficient time. The very respect for the opinions of other people that leads one to try for clarity will lead often into obscurity, because the opinions of the various factions one addresses will inevitably be diverse. It is not simply that each potential audience will expect, even require, a different rhetoric. It is that if one pays a decent and sustained respect to the opinions of one's "societies," one's original hypotheses become challenged, one's theses grow more and more complicated, and finally one's whole project may collapse in confusion or surrender to a project more plausible in the light of the voices one has considered. Dealing as we do with value-laden concepts, we embrace them *as* laden with the values our readers (and those we have read) place upon them. To the degree that the opinions of our various possible readers come to us with the support of scholarly reasoning, they tend to become our own opinions, and they must then somehow be accommodated—not to persuade others, though that is part of our aim, but to achieve some sort of resolution of the problem for "oneself"— that internal society of scholarly selves that every scholar has become as she receives her training.

Implied by these four virtues is a schooling, finally, in a fifth: humility. Attempting to do scholarly work is in my experience a deeper schooling in humility than can be found anywhere except in trying to teach well and trying to be a good husband and parent.

It is true that humility, like all the others, can be destructive if uncorrected by those others, especially by courage. It is also true that arrogant young scholars often achieve—especially in the natural sciences—results that their humbled elders would never dare seek. But the fact remains that as we peer about the world seeking examples of people who have the humility that the best philosophers have taken as the root and fountain of all human excellence,[16] the only examples we find of *intellectual* humility (as distinct from various self-denigrations and inferiority complexes that must not be confused with it) are scholars who have tested their powers for discovering truth and have discovered instead vaster and vaster domains of ignorance. Only the scholar who has honestly, courageously, persistently, and considerately tried to solve one genuine problem can know how little she can do to reduce her own ignorance.

We have no single name for all of these habits of mind taken together. For some philosophers in the past, "reason" and "rationality" were rough synonyms for the collection as a whole. But like all words in the scholarship family, these have been narrowed in modern usage to suggest an insistence on an emotion-free, linear logicality that is at most a small part of what I am suggesting. Still, we do need a name for them, and since they cannot be called simply the "scholarly habits" (after all, we know that they are shared in various combinations with nonscholars, and we hope they will be shared with more), I suggest that we think of them as the "habits of rationality." After all, with a little consideration of what our predecessors (before the last hundred years or so) thought that rationality entailed, we should be able to use the word, and the richnesses it connotes, as an aid in saying to our various publics that we stand for something that they too can respect.

Can we not say that the chief duty of the scholar "in society," as of the scholar at her desk, the duty without which all other services to society will be corrupted, is to practice the rational habits—to show not just a private commitment to them but to show in her public acts, in teaching, in publishing, as in all political and social life, an unswerving desire to honor the honest, courageous, persistent, considerate, and humble pursuit of that special kind of opinion that can be pursued only in the courts of a shared reasoning?

Not everyone should be a scholar. Not everyone can be a scholar. But there is no human being whose life would not be enhanced by earning some share in the rational habits. And it is our task to keep those habits alive. The book-person who sullies the name of scholar by publicly abandoning those habits, by refusing to teach them to others, or even by playing the increasingly popular game of pretending that they don't matter or that they are simply indefensible values like all our other "mere" preferences—such a scholar is no scholar, no matter how long she sits in front of that desk. She is a disgrace to the profession and—if paid by society—a cheat. Whether society quite knows what it wants, as it pays us to be scholar-teachers, what it really seeks, more or less blindly, is to keep the rational habits passionately alive in the world. Only if we do that job well, by the way we think, the way we teach, and the way we write, can we claim that we have honored the society that we are in and the society that is in us.

The days of simple oppositions are past, if indeed there ever were such days. No informed inquirer will ever again believe that her scholarly inquiry is innocent of political bias or social effects. The way she inquires, indeed whether she will be allowed to inquire at all, will depend on the society in which she lives. And what she does—both the subjects she chooses to investigate and the modes she chooses for reporting her findings—will not simply affect her society; it will to a large degree constitute the society in which she lives.

When we choose to become scholars, we join the guild of professional inquirers, the guild of those who profess the rational habits. The rights and privileges of that guild are different from those of any other guild, as are its responsibilities. In our society, no other guild is charged specifically with preserving the rational habits. It sometimes seems that we may soon have no other guilds committed to *any* of the virtues.

Whatever happens to our society, we cannot afford to spend any time proclaiming our helplessness before its forces. As one of the most powerful of society's "estates," we can be sure that whatever conditions we find in the world as we continue our efforts at scholarship have been to a surprising degree of our own making. In what we write, and perhaps even more in what we teach, we make the society in which we shall continue to remake ourselves.

Notes

1 James Thorpe, ed., *The Aims and Methods of Scholarship in Modern Languages and Literatures*, 2nd ed. (New York: MLA, 1970).

2 Gerald Holton, Introduction, *Science and Culture: A Study of Cohesive and Disjunctive Forces* (Boston: Houghton Mifflin, 1965). Most of this volume was originally an issue of *Daedalus* (Winter 1965), based on a conference that in a sense was entirely devoted to our problem here—but with the word "science" substituted for our word "scholarship." To anyone interested in how our social role relates to that of the "scientist," I recommend especially the essays by James S. Ackerman, Don K. Price, Eric Weil, and Robert S. Morison.

3 Harriet Zuckerman, "The Sociology of the Nobel Prizes," *Scientific American* (Nov. 1967), 25–35. See esp. the chart on p. 33.

4 This statement may seem to understate the seriousness of current threats to our profession, but I take those threats to be serious indeed. (See my little cry of alarm, "A New Use for the Dyshumanities," *ADE Bulletin*, 54 [Sept. 1977], 6–11; rpt. in *Profession 77* [New York: MLÁ, 1977], pp. 1–6.) We cannot know, in the midst of the current job crisis, whether the effects will be worse than

those, say, of the Depression, or of World War II. But they *might* be, unless the profession finds ways to combat the loss of nerve that to many seems even more threatening than the loss of jobs. My essay here obviously has only oblique relevance to the latter, but the two losses are obviously close knit. No scholar who ignores the plight of junior humanists without jobs can be said to be a humanistic scholar.

5 My younger readers may not remember the popularity of such books as Rudolf Flesch's *Why Johnny Can't Read—and What You Can Do About It* (New York: Harper and Row, 1955) and Arthur Bestor's *Educational Wastelands: The Retreat from Learning in Our Public Schools* (Urbana: Univ. of Illinois Press, 1953). In the sixties and seventies similar impulses were expressed in the popular slogan, "Back to the basics!"

6 Ernest Nagel and James R. Newman, *Gödel's Proof* (New York: New York Univ. Press, 1958).

7 *Harvard Monthly*, 36 (March 1903), 1–9. Reprinted in *Memories and Studies* (1911; rpt. New York: Greenwood, 1968).

8 Max Weber, *Max Weber on Universities: The Power of the State and the Dignity of the Academic Calling in Imperial Germany*, ed. and trans. Edward Shils (Chicago: Univ. of Chicago Press, 1973). See esp. pp. 23–25.

9 "And now a significant number of our most thoughtful scholars seems to fear . . . the labyrinth with the empty center, where the investigator meets only his own shadow and his blackboard with his own chalk marks on it, his own solutions to his own puzzles" (Holton, *Science and Culture*, p. xxix). Holton was writing before the empty-centered labyrinth and related metaphors—webs, prison-houses, aporias, *mise en abîmes*—had become commonplaces in literary criticism, and it is clear in the context of his statement that he does not himself see the universe quite in this way. It seems obvious that every scientist must disregard, except when theorizing, the fear that there is nothing to be known. If there is nothing to be known, both scientists and scholars should fold up shop and find some honest way to make a living. But of course every scholar, like every scientist, knows that genuine knowledge can be earned, regardless of what a given theory may claim to have shown.

10 The myth, as pursued quite recently by an intelligent believer, can be found in Charles Coulston Gillispie's *The Edge of Objectivity* (Princeton: Princeton Univ. Press, 1960).

11 Weber's most important work on the problem of objectivity in social science is found in *Max Weber on the Methodology of the Social Sciences*, ed. and trans. Edward A. Shils and Henry A. Finch (Glencoe, Ill.: Free Press, 1949).

12 In 1974 I compiled a little bibliography of more than a score of modern refutations or reconsiderations of the fact-value split, many of them purporting to demonstrate that the "ought" can be derived from the "is." See the Appendix to my *Modern Dogma and the Rhetoric of Assent* (Notre Dame, Ind.: Univ. of Notre Dame Press, and Chicago: Univ. of Chicago Press, 1974). Since then there have been many others, the most fully developed being that of Alan Gewirth, *Reason and Morality* (Chicago: Univ. of Chicago Press, 1978).

13 See Chomsky's "Objectivity and Liberal Scholarship" in *American Power and the New Mandarins* (New York: Pantheon Books, 1969), pp. 23–158.

14 It takes very little experience with the terms "subjective" and "objective" to recognize that they are almost useless for serious inquiry. Not only is it true that historically the terms have radically shifted meanings; they are now both used as terms of praise and abuse, and they never mean the same thing for their proponents as for their enemies. A clear instance is David Bleich's *Subjective Criticism* (Baltimore: Johns Hopkins Univ. Press, 1978). The subjectivity that Bleich and other "reader" critics would restore to criticism is not the "opposite of objectivity" that their opponents fear. After all, to ask students to respect and describe their first-hand experience is very close to asking them to exhibit one aspect of the "objectivity" that the myth tells us made the scientific revolution possible.

15 A good account of some of the complexities that underlie our usual insistence on a clear, accessible style is given—in plain style—by Geoffrey Hartman in "Literary Criticism and Its Discontents," *Critical Inquiry*, 3 (Winter 1976), 203–20. See especially Part II. I have recently made several attempts to describe at length the dangers implicit in Hartman's defense of a deliberately "inconsiderate" style (for example in "Do Reasons Matter in Criticism: Or, Many Meanings, Many Modes," *Bulletin of the Midwest Modern Language Association*, 14 [Spring 1981]).

16 The most forceful defense of humility I know is in Iris Murdoch's *The Sovereignty of Good* (London: Routledge and Kegan Paul, 1970).

Bibliography

Any full bibliography of works on "the scholar in society" would of course be immense. I give here a selection of twentieth-century works only, one that ranges over the major issues touched on in the essay. (I especially regret omitting the ancient quarrel between philosophy and the sophists and rhetoricians, and the various modern quarrels between the "ancients" and the "moderns.")

Ashby, Eric. "The Future of the Nineteenth-Century Idea of a University." *Minerva*, 4 (Autumn 1967), 3–17.

Ashworth, Kenneth H. *Scholars and Statesmen: Higher Education and Government Policy.* San Francisco: Jossey-Bass, 1972.

Barnard College Women's Center. *The Scholar and the Feminist IV: Connecting Theory, Practice, and Values.* New York: Barnard College Women's Center, 1977.

Barzun, Jacques. *The House of Intellect.* New York: Harper, 1959.

———. *Teacher in America.* Boston: Little, Brown, 1945.

Bendix, Reinhard, and Guenther Roth, eds. *Scholarship and Partisanship: Essays on Max Weber*, Berkeley: Univ. of California Press, 1971.

Black, Max, ed. *The Morality of Scholarship.* Studies in the Humanities. Ithaca: Cornell Univ. Press, 1967.

Butler, Nicholas Murray. *Scholarship and Service: The Policies and Ideals of a National University in a Modern Democracy.* New York: Scribners, 1921.

Chomsky, Noam. *American Power and the New Mandarins.* New York: Pantheon, 1969. See esp. the essay, "Objectivity and Liberal Scholarship," pp. 23–158.

Cole, Michael, et al. *The Cultural Context of Learning and Thinking: An Exploration in Experimental Anthropology.* New York: Basic Books, 1971.

Committee on Science and Freedom. *Freedom and Responsibility: The Role of the Scholar in Society.* Bulletin of the Committee on Science and Freedom, No. 13, November 1959.

Congress on Freedom and Restriction in Science. *Freedom and Restriction in Science and Its Aspects in Society.* The Hague: Martinus Nijhoff, 1955.

Daiches, David. *Literature and Society.* 1938; rpt. Folcroft, Pa.: Folcroft, 1969.

Dewey, John. *The Public and Its Problems.* New York: Holt, 1927.

———, and Horace M. Kallen, eds. *The Bertrand Russell Case.* New York: Viking, 1941.

Emerson, Ralph Waldo. "The American Scholar." In *The Collected Works of Ralph Waldo Emerson.* Ed. Robert E. Spiller and Alfred R. Ferguson. Cambridge, Mass.: Harvard Univ. Press, 1971, I, 49–70.

Goodman, Paul. *The Community of Scholars.* New York: Random House, 1962.

Holton, Gerald, ed. *Science and Culture: A Study of Cohesive and Disjunctive Forces.* Boston: Houghton Mifflin, 1965.

James, William. "The Social Value of the College-Bred"; "The University and the Individual: [I.] The Ph.D. Octopus." Both in *Memories and Studies*. 1911; rpt. New York: Greenwood, 1968.

Jones, Howard Mumford. *One Great Society: Humane Learning in the United States*. New York: Harcourt, 1959.

———. *The Scholar as American*. Cambridge, Mass.: Harvard Univ. Press, 1960.

Lewis, John. *Max Weber and Value-Free Sociology: A Marxist Critique*. London: Lawrence and Wishart, 1975.

Lippmann, Walter. *The Scholar in a Troubled World*. New York: Press of the Woolly Whale, 1932.

McKeon, Richard. "The Problems of Education in a Democracy." In *The Bertrand Russell Case*. Ed. John Dewey and Horace M. Kallen. New York: Viking, 1941.

Mead, C. David. *"The American Scholar" Today: Emerson's Essay and Some Critical Views*. New York: Dodd, Mead, 1970.

Morison, Samuel Eliot. *The Scholar in America: Past, Present, and Future*. New York: Oxford Univ. Press, 1961.

Shils, Edward. *"The Intellectuals and the Powers" and Other Essays*. Selected Papers of Edward Shils. Vol. I. Chicago: Univ. of Chicago Press, 1972.

Thorpe, James, ed. *The Aims and Methods of Scholarship in Modern Languages and Literatures*. 2nd ed. New York: MLA, 1970.

Weber, Max. *Max Weber on the Methodology of the Social Sciences*. Ed. and trans. Edward A. Shils and Henry A. Finch. Glencoe, Ill.: Free Press, 1949.

———. *Max Weber on Universities: The Power of the State and the Dignity of the Academic Calling in Imperial Germany*. Trans. and ed. Edward A. Shils. Chicago: Univ. of Chicago Press, 1973.

Znaniecki, Florian. *The Social Role of the Man of Knowledge*. 1940; rpt. New York: Octagon, 1965.